Sc
Cooperation

DATE DUE

Scarcity, Conflicts, and Cooperation

Essays in the Political and Institutional Economics of Development

Pranab Bardhan

The MIT Press
Cambridge, Massachusetts
London, England

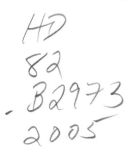
MIT Press books may be purchased at special quantity discounts for business or sales promotional use. For information, please e-mail ⟨special_sales@mitpress.mit.edu⟩ or write to Special Sales Department, The MIT Press, 5 Cambridge Center, Cambridge, MA 02142.

This book was set in Palatino on 3B2 by Asco Typesetters, Hong Kong.
Printed and bound in the United States of America.

Library of Congress Cataloging-in-Publication Data

Bardhan, Pranab K.
Scarcity, conflicts, and cooperation : essays in the political and institutional economics of development / Pranab Bardhan
   p.   cm.
Includes bibliographical references and index.
ISBN 0-262-02573-6 (hc. : alk. paper) — ISBN 0-262-52429-5 (pbk. : alk. paper)
1. Economic development. I. Title.
HD82.B2973   2005
338.9—dc22   2004052440

10 9 8 7 6 5 4 3 2 1

Contents

Preface

In the last few years, several technical books and many journal articles have been written about institutional economics and political economy. The purpose of this book is less to present original research contributions to this literature, more to provide an integrative and somewhat reflective account of where we stand today, particularly on some of the major issues of that literature as they relate to problems in developing countries. The treatment in most of the chapters here is more discursive than in technical journal articles, although I'd like to think that the arguments are not loose, they instead provide a coherent logical structure and an "analytical narrative".

Since my intended readership goes beyond the research community in economics to include most social scientists and policy thinkers in general, I have tried to avoid formal models. In two chapters, however (chapters 7 and 10), I briefly outline new models to formalize some ideas, partly because of a dearth of formalization in areas that are underresearched at present. In some other chapters (for example, chapter 4), I review the existing models without elaborating on their formal details, focusing instead on their essential ideas. In economics the prevailing culture does not take researchers seriously if they come unarmed with (or should I say, unescorted by) a model. I find models particularly useful in helping me to puzzle out the various assumptions that are often needed to derive what seem like intuitively obvious conclusions and to decipher unifying principles that connect seemingly unrelated case studies. But the world of institutional and political economy is full of ambiguities, contextual nuances, and multidimensional complexities, which—given the current state of empirical knowledge—are extremely difficult to capture with necessarily oversimplified quantitative exercises in model building or hypothesis testing. Research, of course, progresses with abstractions, but at these early stages of inquiry into this rather murky territory, undue preoccupation with precision may often mislead us about the larger picture, and we may never find the missing keys if we confine our search only to the lighted area. Some, of course, go to the other extreme of echoing what Ansel Adams once said about photography: "There is nothing worse than a sharp image of a fuzzy concept".

Institutional failures, weak accountability mechanisms, and missed opportunities for cooperative problem solving constitute the running themes of our story of economic underdevelopment. The institutional framework of an economy defines and constrains the opportunities for individuals, determines the business climate, shapes the incentives and organizations for collective action by local communities in resolving their common problems, and encompasses the structures of commitment and accountability that the political authority in society provides. In all these respects the institutional framework is weak in many poor countries, and that is the main concern in most of the chapters in this book. Chapter 1 introduces the recent literature on institutions and development, examining the current emphasis on quantifying the macroeconomic effects of institutional quality (taken largely in the limited sense of secure property rights). Apart from pointing to the usual econometric problems in identifying the impact of property rights institutions on the basis of crude cross-country data, it is arguable that other institutional variables play as important a role as secure property rights. For example, we show the significance of the regime of political rights in determining particularly outcome variables measured in the standard human development indicators. Also, particular social and political institutions that coordinate individual actions are of critical importance in economic performance, but their effects are usually hard to quantify. So here we move on to a comparative-historical analysis of the various imperfect coordination mechanisms of society (state, market, business groups, local community networks, and so on) that attempt to correct the pervasive coordination failures that beset the early stages of industrial transformation.

Chapter 2, after exploring the various processes through which dysfunctional institutions seem to persist in poor countries, emphasizes (contrary to much of the literature) the role of distributive conflicts to show why few self-correcting forces work to change these institutions. It is often claimed that certain cultures (such as Japan or Sweden) seem to find it easy to orchestrate improvements in institutional arrangements through coordination or collective action. I have no doubt that these cultural factors are important in determining a country's institutional history. But one common thread running through some of the chapters here (chapters 2, 3, 5, 6, 9, 10, and 11) is how these institutional differences may be related to underlying social or ethnic heterogeneity and initial inequalities in asset distribution.

Since much of the political economy of institutional change involves distribution of power, we analyze the structural basis of the concept of power in chapter 3, after looking at various social battlefields where power is exercised and linking power to inequalities in resource endowments. As is now widely recognized in the political economy literature, processes to work out better institutions are often blocked by different kinds of commitment problems. In interactions between the state and private economic agents (and among the agents themselves), various commitment devices can play a crucial role, particularly in decisions involving long-term investment, which is discussed in chapter 4, along with the issue of tradeoffs between commitment and accountability. Issues of accountability bring to mind the various democratic rules of ensuring accountability, which are discussed in chapter 5 in the context of examining the complex relationship between democracy and poverty in a large poor democracy, India, and this democratic country's rather slow grappling with its mass poverty. We illustrate with concrete examples how the welcome expansion of democratic rights for the hitherto subordinate groups in a poor country can sometimes overwhelm the usual commitment procedures that are indispensable for both governance and long-term investment. One way to mitigate the conflict between the procedural and participatory aspects of democracy is to bring accountability and responsibility face to face at the local level. A lot of attention has been paid in this context in recent years to the accountability mechanism that works through decentralization and devolution of power, which is the theme of chapters 6 and 7. In spite of the informational and other advantages of decentralization in situations of weak political accountability, it has some special problems not discussed in the standard literature on fiscal federalism. One problem relates to the frequent cases of elite capture of local governments in cases of a high degree of social and economic inequality. One question then arises about how prone government is to capture at its different levels. Chapter 7 works out in a theoretical model the conditions under which the capture of governments by elite interests is stronger or weaker at the local level compared to the central level. Weak accountability is also behind the common institutional failure called *corruption*; its effects, reasons for persistence, and policy issues that it raises are discussed in chapter 8. Institutional failures, rather than cultural antagonism, is also the focus in chapter 9, which looks at the raging ethnic conflicts in different parts of the world, the difficulties of containing them, and the policy lessons that can be drawn from them.

Bringing about institutional changes requires collective action, and chapters 10 and 11 analyze the impediments to attempts at collective action—particularly those posed by distributive conflicts in heterogeneous groups and unequal societies (a problem that links up with the role that is played by distributive conflicts in the persistence of dysfunctional institutions, which is discussed in chapter 2). Chapter 10 investigates theoretical issues, both at the macro and the micro levels, and chapter 11 illustrates with an empirical study of collective management of irrigation water in rural south India, which quantifies the social and economic determinants of conflict or cooperation by local communities of farmers in water management, with a particular emphasis on the role of initial wealth inequalities.

Finally, in chapter 12 the discussion goes beyond national boundaries and explores the effects of global rules, institutions, and market processes from the point of view of the world's poorest people. The focus here is on domestic institutional quality, which often determines how much a poor country can both participate in the opportunities opened up by globalization and at the same time minimize the concomitant hardships.

In chapters 7 and 10 where we have explicitly introduced formal models, we have confined the models in starred sections, so that readers who are not interested in the technical details may skip those sections; there are some pointers and summaries of the main arguments in the other sections of the chapters. Chapter 4 reviews an array of theoretical models, focusing on some of their essential ideas without elaborating on the technical details. But those nonspecialist readers who find the chain of analytical arguments rather heavy going can look for the summaries of the main arguments at the beginning and also in various sections of the chapter.

Some of the chapters draw on and revise materials that have been published in the *American Economic Review*, the *Journal of Economic Literature*, the *Journal of Economic Perspectives*, *Economic Development and Cultural Change*, *World Development*, and *Economics and Politics*. I worked with Dilip Mookherjee in developing the model in chapter 7 and with Tsung-Tao Yang on chapter 10. Tsung-Tao also assisted me in researching the materials in some other chapters. I have also benefited from comments from Samuel Bowles, Maitreesh Ghatak, Karla Hoff, and Gerard Roland on parts of the manuscript and from three anonymous referees who read the complete manuscript. While working on this book I received financial assistance from the Network on Inequality and Economic Performance, which is funded by the MacArthur Foundation. I am grateful to all of these people and organizations.

Scarcity, Conflicts, and Cooperation

1

History, Institutions, and Underdevelopment

1.1

As in much of institutional economics, this book interprets institutions in the very general sense of rules of structured social interaction. In the field of development economics, earlier preoccupations with the forces of capital accumulation or technological progress have been widely replaced by a belief that the institutional framework of an economy is crucial for an understanding of the process of development or lack of it. Institutional explanations, including an analysis of state-society relations, are becoming increasingly common as economists try to understand why South Korea and the Philippines had similar per-capita incomes and human-capital endowments in 1960 but developed so divergently over the next three decades or why the economic transition to capitalism in the 1990s was so different in Poland compared to Russia. Economists are, of course, not fully comfortable with this unless they can somehow quantify the effects of institutional frameworks. In the literature on rural development at the micro level, there have been many attempts to quantify the impact of institutions such as land tenure on productivity or the effect of credit and risk-sharing institutions on consumption and production efficiency. For an overview of some of the major theoretical issues in that literature and empirical references, see Bardhan and Udry (1999). This overview, however, does not consider the macro level, where there has been a flurry of empirical activity in the recent literature, largely on the basis of cross-country regressions, to determine the relative importance of geographical as opposed to institutional factors in explaining differential economic performance in different parts of the world.

I have always been rather skeptical of the value of such cross-national studies in giving good insights into the *mechanisms* of development or underdevelopment. Apart from questions about the quality and comparability of data for a large set of poor countries, there are the usual econometric problems—like endogeneity (the independent variables may themselves be determined by other factors that may simultaneously influence both dependent and independent variables), selection (the data may have systematic bias, in terms of cases left out or excluded-zero values, or may be chosen by some principle that may be indicative of some relevant information), and particularly omitted variable bias (in this context, when one has to take the lowest common denominator of variables that are available for all the countries in the sample, many obviously important variables are left out, sometimes leading to spurious correlations between the reported variables). There is also a tendency to read too much into the results based on the United Nations principle of "one country, one vote" (which is anomalous in a situation where the large majority of countries are tiny and the substantial numbers of the poor in the world get a much lower weight by virtue of living in a handful of large countries). Finally, institutions and the policies as actually implemented at the local level *within* a country are often quite diverse and heterogeneous, except for a few countrywide macroeconomic institutions governing monetary policy, exchange-rate policy, and so on.

Nevertheless, this section briefly assesses some of the general findings of this macro literature. In the appendix to this chapter, a cross-country empirical exercise of our own focuses on a quantification of the impact of institutional and political variables as an extension of the existing literature. This exercise suggests, among other things, that we should go beyond the narrow focus of the current literature on the undoubtedly important *institutions that protect individual property rights* and that other *institutions like those related to democratic political rights* may also be quite significant, particularly in explaining cross-country variations in human-development indicators (including literacy and longevity and not just per-capita income). In the next section of this chapter the importance of social and political *institutions that may correct some of the pervasive coordination failures* that afflict an economy at early stages of industrial transformation (and remain important even if property rights were to be made fully secure) are discussed. These coordination mechanisms are underemphasized in the institutional economics literature but can sometimes be as indispensable as property-rights institutions. So a major purpose of this chapter is to "unbundle" some of the institutions that are supposed to be important in development and draw attention to institutions other than those securing property rights. A point that is not pursued here is that even in the protection of property rights different institutions have different consequences for different social groups (for example, the poor may care more for simple land titles or relief from the usual harassments by local goons or government inspectors, whereas the rich investor may care more for protection of their corporate shareholder rights against insider abuses or for banking regulations), and may therefore have different degrees of political sustainability.

Those who emphasize geography as destiny, more than institutions, point to the disease environment of the tropics, types of crops and soil, transportation costs, handicaps of land-locked countries—that afflict many of today's poor countries. These problems make attempts to climb out of poverty more difficult. But as Acemoglu, Johnson, and Robinson (2002) point out, many such geographically handicapped countries that are now relatively poor in the world were relatively rich in 1500 (the Moghal, Aztec, and Inca empires occupied some of the richest territories of the world in 1500; Haiti, Cuba, and Barbados were richer than the United States in early colonial times). These reversals of fortune have more to do with colonial history, extractive policies, and institutions than with geography. Of course, geographical factors are more conducive to some types of institutions than others. For example, Engerman and Sokoloff (2002) emphasize the effects of geographical (and other factor-endowment) preconditions on the evolution of particular institutions in the colonies established in the Caribbean or Brazil. Climate and soil conditions were extremely well suited for growing crops like sugar that were of high value on the market and were produced at low cost on large slave plantations. These conditions led to systematic institutional differences in these colonies compared to those established (later) in the temperate zones of North America. Acemoglu, Johnson, and Robinson (2001) suggest that the mortality rates among early European settlers in a colony (obviously related to its geography and disease patterns) determined whether the Europeans decided to install resource-extractive or -plundering institutions there or to settle and build European institutions, like those protecting property rights.[1]

---

1. Engerman and Sokoloff (2002) raise a doubt for the early colonial period: European settlers in the New World formed communities even in the high-mortality but the then rich colonies, and the areas with low mortality were often unattractive to settlers. There may also be a reverse causality, with settler mortality being lower in areas of better institutions.

The work of both Engerman-Sokoloff and Acemoglu, Johnson, and Robinson correctly shows the importance of institutional overhang in history, so that institutions once established have long-run effects on economic performance, and these effects linger even after the original institutions decay or disappear. This has been also confirmed in a more disaggregative study within a country across districts: Banerjee and Iyer (2002) have traced the significant effects of different land-revenue systems (that were instituted by the British in India during the early nineteenth century and discontinued after Independence) on present-day economic indicators in agriculture.

The ideas of reversal of fortune in many of the countries colonized by Europe or of the adverse impact of landlord-based revenue institutions in colonial India have been around for decades. Recent work has made the hypothesis testing more rigorous by trying to take particular care of the problem of endogeneity of institutions. For example, Acemoglu, Johnson, and Robinson (2001) use mortality rates of colonial settlers as an instrument for institutional quality. While this may be an acceptable instrument[2] for the immediate statistical purpose of avoiding the problem of endogeneity of institutions compared to income because it accounts for a part (though usually a rather small part) of the exogenous (not income-dependent) variations in institutional quality, it is doubtful that this approach captures the major historical forces that affect the social and economic institutional structures of a former colony. Just consider the markedly different historical forces that have shaped the institutions in former colonies (with quite bad disease environments) like Brazil, India, and the Congo. Then consider countries that mostly escaped colonization,[3] like China, Thailand, and for most of history, Ethiopia. In such cases, it is improper (and much too Eurocentric an approach) to attribute underdevelopment largely to 'bad' colonial institutions imposed by Europeans.

Furthermore, Przeworski (2004) points out that the institutions, as measured by Acemoglu, Johnson, and Robinson (2001), have changed quite a bit over time in many countries. So an instrument for the initial institutions need not be a valid instrument for the current ones. If good institutions are more likely to survive in more affluent countries, then institutional quality today is still endogenous with respect to income.

2. It is not clear if the settler-mortality variable excludes the effect of some other deeper factors. For example, density of population may be one such deeper factor; a direct effect is that it is easier to settle in more sparsely populated areas, and an indirect effect is that density is conducive to the spread of some diseases.

3. As Rodrik, Subramanian, and Trebbi (2002) point out, the noncolonized group of countries includes some very high-income countries (such as Finland and Luxembourg) as well as very poor countries (like Ethiopia, Yemen, and Mongolia), and these income differences cannot obviously be related to any colonial experience.

In particular, countries with a long history of state structure and bureaucratic culture may have substantial institutional residues, even after the colonial interregnum,[4] that may be quite different from countries that did not have that history. Bockstette, Chanda, and Putterman (2002) have computed an index of state antiquity for over one hundred countries; it shows that among developing countries state antiquity is much lower for sub-Saharan Africa and Latin America than for Asia, and even in Asia the index for Korea is several times that for the Philippines (a country that lacked an encompassing state before the sixteenth-century colonization by Spain). The appendix to this chapter discusses some of the cross-country effects of this state-antiquity index. Many African countries had a relative lack of state antiquity (in the sense of a continuous territory-wide state structure above the tribal domains) in precolonial times.[5] They were artificially regrouped (and cartographically carved out in the state rooms of Europe) by the colonial rulers, so that the postcolonial state was often incongruent with precolonial political structures and boundaries. This had a serious adverse effect on the legitimacy[6] of the state and the efficacy of state institutions.[7]

The recent literature has emphasized (and in some cases over-emphasized, in my judgment) the impact of the colonial legacy on postcolonial institutional performance over the last four to five decades and has also sometimes distinguished between the particular European sources of that legacy in terms of legal systems. For example, La Porta et al. (1998) have called attention to the superior effects, across countries, of the Anglo-Saxon common-law system (based on judicial precedents) over the civil-law system (based on formal codes) on corporate business environments in terms of flexibility toward the changing needs of business and in terms of protection for external suppliers of finance to a company (whether shareholders or creditors). Apart from some doubts about the establishment of causality in these cross-national studies, one can also question the historical evidence in the

---

4. Even during the colonial period in India, what is described as a British landlord-based revenue system was shaped largely out of the preexisting land-revenue systems of Moghal India.

5. Herbst (2000) argues that in land-abundant Africa in the precolonial period, land rights were not well defined, and political entitities with vague borders and no well-defined territory to defend did not invest in bureaucracies or fiscal and military institutions.

6. Most African states are low in the legitimacy scores given by Englebert (2000).

7. In some situations the different ethnic groups were never reconciled to unification under one state even at the beginning of its formation, as in the case of the southerners in Sudan or the Eritreans in Ethiopia.

rich countries themselves. Lamoreaux and Rosenthal (2001) have done a comparative study of the constraints imposed by legal systems on organizational choices of business in the United States (with its common-law system) and France (with its civil-law codes) during the middle of the nineteenth century around the time when both countries were beginning to industrialize. They conclude that nothing inherent in the French legal regime created either a lack of flexibility or a lack of attention to the rights of creditors or small stakeholders. Many of the rules in the United States for minority shareholder rights actually came *after* the insider scandals of the 1930s Great Depression period. Rosenthal and Berglöf (2003) also question the primacy of legal origin in explaining institutions of investor protection; drawing on the legislative history of U.S. bankruptcy laws they show how the United States, with English common-law legal origins, ended up with a bankruptcy regime quite different from that in the United Kingdom and how political and ideological forces shaped financial development.

The French-legal-origin developing countries are often in Africa, and a legal system may be standing as a proxy for other (unmeasured) deficiencies in state capacity in many African countries. In any case, the importance of the legacy of the formal legal system is moot where much too frequently in developing countries the enforcement of whatever laws are in the statute books is quite weak, and the courts are hopelessly clogged and corrupt. It should also be recognized that with weak markets for related transactions, the net benefits from the transplanting of a European legal system to replace the indigenous customary system were in many cases rather limited. In a study of the impact of the introduction of civil courts in British India on the agricultural credit markets of the Bombay Deccan, Kranton and Swamy (1999) show that the courts led to increased competition but reduced lenders' incentives to subsidize farmers' investments in times of crisis, leaving them more vulnerable in bad times with insurance markets largely absent.

As suggested above, much of the recent cross-country regressions literature seems preoccupied with finding clever instruments that help avoid the endogeneity of most determinants of income, but finding an instrument that identifies an exogenous source of variation in the income determinants is quite different from unearthing an adequate and satisfactory causal explanation. In the inevitable absence of detailed and relevant data across a number of countries, researchers often resort to general qualitative comparative-historical analyses of the development process to understand the impact of institutional arrangements, and much of the rest of this chapter is in that old-fashioned mode. This is, of course, not to deny that comparative-historical analysis at most gives some general insights into mechanisms and processes, but it does not clinch quantification issues, allow us to control for other factors that may simultaneously impinge on the variable in question, or sort out the endogeneity or reverse-causality issues. For quite a long time to come, both methods will have to be utilized, with their limitations noted, and conflicting issues will not be resolved until much more detailed datasets (particularly datasets involving panels within at least some major countries) become available.

1.2

For Western Europe and North America such a comparative-historical analysis of the institutions that are essential in the development process has been successfully tried by North (1981, 1990) and Greif (1992, 1997). North has pointed to the inevitable tradeoff in the historical growth process between transaction costs and economies of scale and of specialization. In a small, closed, face-to-face peasant community, for example, transaction costs are low, but production costs are high because specialization and division of labor are severely limited by the extent of a market that is defined by the personalized exchange process of a small community. As the network of interdependence widens in a large-scale complex economy, the impersonal exchange process gives considerable scope for all kinds of opportunistic behavior, and the costs of transacting can be high. Greif examined the self-enforcing institutions of collective punishment for malfeasance in long-distance trade in the late medieval period, and in a comparative study of the Maghribi and the Genoese traders explored the institutional foundations of commercial development.

In Western societies complex institutional (legal and corporate) structures have been devised over time to constrain transaction participants, to reduce the uncertainties of social interactions, to prevent transactions from being too costly, and thus to allow the productivity gains of larger-scale and improved technology to be realized. These institutions include elaborately defined and effectively enforced property rights, formal contracts and guarantees, trademarks, limited liability, bankruptcy laws, large corporate organizations with governance structures to limit problems of agency, and what Williamson (1985)

has called "ex post opportunism." Some of these institutional structures are nonexistent, weak, poorly devised, or poorly implemented in
less developed countries. The state in these countries either is too weak
to act as a guarantor of these rights and institutions or is much too
predatory in its own demands and poses a threat to them.

Beyond the face-to-face village community (when transactions are
not self-enforcing), the institutions that a society develops (or fails to
develop) for long-distance trade, credit, and other intertemporal and
interspatial markets provide an important indicator of that society's
capacity for development. In this context the analysis of North (1990),
Milgrom, North, and Weingast (1990), Greif (1992), and Greif, Milgrom, and Weingast (1994) have brought attention to the importance
of several institutions—like the merchant guild (for example, those in
Italian city-states or intercity guilds like the German Hansa), the law-
merchant system (like private judges recording institutionalized public
memory at the Champagne fairs, which provided an important nexus
of trade between northern and southern Europe), and the Community
Responsibility System in Mediterranean and European trade during
the late medieval commercial revolution in the eleventh through four-
teenth centuries. These institutions facilitated economic growth by
reducing opportunism in transactions among people largely unknown
to one another and by providing a multilateral reputation mechanism
supported by frameworks of credible commitment, enforcement, and
coordination.

Greif has suggested that in informal enforcement of mercantile contracts, those who are dependent on bilateral reputation mechanisms
(where the cheater is punished only by the party that is cheated) are
usually more costly than multilateral reputation mechanisms (where
punishment is inflicted by a whole community to which the party that
is cheated belongs) or than a community-responsibility system in
which a whole community is jointly liable if one of its members cheats.
In the case of bilateral reputation mechanisms, simple efficiency-wage
considerations suggest that to keep a long-distance trading agent
honest the merchant (the principal) has to pay the agent a wage that is
higher than the agent's reservation income, whereas in more "collectivist" forms of enforcement this wage need not be as high because the
penalty for cheating is higher or because peer monitoring makes cheating more difficult. But in a world with information asymmetry, slow
communication, and plausibly different interpretations of facts in a
dispute, an uncoordinated multilateral reputation mechanism may not

always work and may need to be supplemented by a more formal organization to coordinate (the expectations and responses of different members of the collectivity) and enforce. In medieval Europe the merchant guild provided such an organization. In governing relations between merchants and their various towns and the foreign towns with which they traded, the guilds had the ability to coordinate merchants' responses to abuses against any merchant and to force them to participate in trade embargoes. This credible threat of collective action from the guilds enabled medieval rulers to commit to respecting the property rights of alien merchants and thus facilitated exchange and market integration.

Many developing countries in the world have a long history of indigenous mercantile institutions of trust and commitment (based on multilateral reputation mechanisms and informal codes of conduct and enforcement). Examples of such institutions of long-distance trade and credit abound among mercantile families and groups in precolonial and colonial India, Chinese traders in Southeast Asia, Arab "trading diasporas" in West Africa, and so on. For precolonial India, for example, Bayly (1983) cites many cases of caste-based (and sometimes even multicaste) mercantile associations and *panchayats* (or local tribunals or arbitration panels), which acted much like the merchant guilds and the law-merchant system respectively of medieval Europe, over a vigorous and far-flung mercantile economy. Credit instruments like the *hundi* (or bills of exchange), even though their negotiability was not always recognized in formal courts of law (in British India), governed trade across thousands of miles. Firms kept lists of creditable merchants whose credit notes—*sahajog hundis*—could expect a rapid discount in the bazaar. While Bayly writes about community institutions that flourished primarily around the so-called burgher cities of Allahabad and Benares in precolonial north India, Rudner (1994) studies the south Indian caste-based mercantile organization of the Nattukottai Chettiars in the colonial period, whose elaborate system of *hundis* over long distances (with the caste elite firms or *adathis* acting as the clearinghouses), collective decisions on standardization of interest rates, and caste *panchayats* with customary sanctions provided the basis of indigenous banking networks spread out in large parts of south India and British Southeast Asia.

The institutional-economics literature, however, suggests that the traditional institutions of exchange in developing countries often did not evolve into more complex (impersonal, open, legal-rational) rules or institutions of enforcement as in early modern Europe and emphasizes the need for such an evolution. But the dramatic success story of rapid industrial progress in Southeast Asia in recent decades often under the leadership of Chinese business families suggests that more "collectivist" organizations can be reshaped in particular social-historical contexts to facilitate industrial progress and that clan-based or other particularistic networks can sometimes provide a viable alternative to contract law and impersonal ownership. In a study of seventy-two Chinese entrepreneurs in Hong Kong, Taiwan, Singapore, and Indonesia, Redding (1990) shows how through specific social networks of direct relationship or clan or regional connection the entrepreneurs built a system dependent on patrimonial control by key individuals, personal-obligation bonds, relational contracting, and interlocking directorships.[8] As Ouchi (1980) noted some years ago, when ambiguity of performance evaluation is high and goal incongruence is low, the clan-based organization may have advantages over market relations or bureaucratic organizations. In clan-based organizations goal congruence (and thus low opportunism) is achieved through various processes of socialization; performance evaluation takes place through the kind of subtle reading of signals that are observable by other clan members but not verifiable by a third-party authority. Punishment for breach of implicit contracts is usually through social sanctions and reputation mechanisms. Another advantage of such clan-based relations is flexibility and ease of renegotiation.[9]

As may be expected, the arrangements in these business families and groups are somewhat constrained by too much reliance on centralized decision making and control, internal finance, a small pool of managerial talent to draw on, a relatively small scale of operations, and in the

8. As Redding (1990, p. 213) points out: "Many transactions which in other countries would require contracts, lawyers, guarantees, investigators, wide opinion-seeking, and delays are among the overseas Chinese dealt with reliably and quickly by telephone, by a handshake, over a cup of tea. Some of the most massive property deals in Hong Kong are concluded with a small note locked in the top drawer of a chief executive's desk, after a two-man meeting." One hears similar stories about the Hasidic diamond traders of New York and about firms in industrial districts in Northern Italy.

9. What Holmstrom and Roberts (1998, p. 81) note for Japanese contracts between automakers and their suppliers is far more generally true in family- and clan-based implicit contracts: "the contracts between the Japanese automakers and their suppliers are short and remarkably imprecise, essentially committing the parties only to work together to resolve difficulties as they emerge. Indeed, they do not even specify prices, which instead are renegotiated on a regular basis.... The key to making this system work is obviously the long-term repeated nature of the interactions."

case of large organizations a tendency to subdivide into more or less separate units, each with its own products and markets. A major problem of such collectivist systems of enforcement is that the boundaries of the collectivity within which rewards and punishment are practiced may not be the most efficient ones and therefore may inhibit potentially profitable transactions with people outside the collectivity. So as the scale of economic activity expands, as the need for external finance and managerial talent becomes imperative, and as large sunk investments increase the temptation of one party to renege, relational implicit contracts and reputational incentives become weaker.[10] As Li (2003) has pointed out, relation-based systems of governance may have low fixed costs (given the preexisting social relationships among the parties and the avoidance of the elaborate legal-juridical costs, public-information costs, and verification costs of more rule-based systems) but may have high and rising marginal costs (particularly of private monitoring) as business expansion involves successively weaker relational links.

In general, in the history of most developing countries, even when the indigenous institutions of a mercantile economy thrived, the development of sequentially more complex organizations suited for industrial investment and innovations (as is familiar from the history of the West) did not take place or was slow to come. Nationalist historiography in these countries has blamed this failure on colonial or neocolonial policies. While not denying the importance of the effects of these policies and the lasting wounds of colonialism, I largely confine myself in this chapter (and the next) to a discussion of indigenous institutional impediments to development, which may be just as valid and significant for those poor countries that do not share a colonial history.

A major institutional deficiency[11] that has blocked the progress of a mercantile economy into an industrial economy in many poor countries relates to the financial markets. Even when caste-based or clan-based mercantile firms thrive in their network of multilateral reputation and enforcement mechanisms, the latter are often not adequate for supporting the much larger risks of longer-gestation, large sunk-cost industrial investment. These firms, by and large, have limited

---

10. Some of the pros and cons of relational contracting are empirically studied in the case of Vietnam's emerging private sector by McMillan and Woodruff (1999).
11. Another equally important institutional deficiency in this context relates to agrarian institutions (which are commented on in the next chapter) that can provide a sustainable rural base for industrialization programs.

capacity (either in finance or specialized skills) to pool risks and mobilize the capital of the society at large in high-risk high-return industrial ventures (their own reinvested profits and trade credit from suppliers are not enough). Diversified business groups, which are ubiquitous in developing countries, are sometimes regarded as active players in risk sharing. With a new dataset on business groups in fifteen emerging markets, Khanna and Yafeh (2000) examine this, and find that while there is some corroborative evidence for this risk sharing in Brazil, Korea, Taiwan, and Thailand, this kind of coinsurance is not generally significant or adequate in the larger set of countries.[12]

The usual imperfections of the credit and equity markets emphasized in the literature on imperfect information are severe in the early stages of industrial development. First of all, the investment in learning by doing is not easily collateralizable and is therefore particularly subject to the high costs of information imperfections. Aoki (2001) points to the importance of close relations between banks and firms,[13] based on tacit, uncodified knowledge, at a stage when firms are not yet ready for the securities market with its demands for codifiable and court-verifiable information.[14] Very often such close relations between banks and firms require some support and underwriting of risks by a more centralized authority in situations of undeveloped capital markets, as well as tight centralized monitoring to prevent collusion and malfeasance.

In addition, the technological and pecuniary externalities in investment between firms (and industries)—emphasized analytically (though difficult to pin down empirically) in early as well as more recent development literature—give rise to "strategic complementarities" and positive feedback effects resulting in multiple equilibria.[15] This is

---

12. With the existing data it is also difficult to distinguish empirically between risk sharing and minority shareholder appropriation or "tunneling."

13. A study in Mexico (see La Porta et al., 2003) associates such related lending with "looting" of banks by related companies. One would like to see more empirical evidence on this question. In Menkhoff and Suwanaporn (2003) an in-depth study of the lending decisions of banks from 1992 to 1996 (the prefinancial-crisis period) from 560 credit files from the majority of Thai commercial banks comes to a conclusion about related lending that is quite different from that in La Porta et al. (2003).

14. Aoki (2001) points out that even in the United States venture-capital financing of start-up firms shares characteristics with relational finance (as opposed to arm's-length finance).

15. This has a long history in the postwar development literature from Rosenstein-Rodan (1943) to Murphy, Shleifer, and Vishny (1989). The recent economic-geography literature has emphasized similar kinds of strategic complementarities and agglomeration economies.

particularly important when externalities of information and the need for a network of proximate suppliers of components, services, and infrastructural facilities with economies of scale make investment decisions highly interdependent. Private financiers who are willing and able to internalize the externalities of complementary projects and raise capital from the market for the whole complex of activities are often absent in the early stage of industrialization. Motivated by some historical examples from nineteenth-century continental Europe, Da Rin and Hellmann (1996) show in a model with complementarities of investments of different firms that private banks can act as catalysts for industrialization, provided that they are sufficiently large to mobilize a critical mass of firms and that they possess sufficient market power to make profits from costly coordination. These necessary conditions were not met, for example, in the case of unsuccessful industrial banks in Spain and Russia in the nineteenth century. This is where government-mediated coordination may be potentially useful (though at the possible cost of dampening private incentives to discover or experiment with superior coordination tactics).

Whereas Da Rin and Hellmann suggest that centralized financing may assist in resolving coordination problems rooted in the borrower's side of the market, Dewatripont and Maskin (1995) focus on the manner in which centralized financing may help to resolve coordination problems rooted in the lender's side of the market. In a model of a decentralized banking system where capital ownership is diffuse, they show that banks tend to underinvest in long-term projects that involve large sunk costs requiring cofinancing by several banks. This is because such cofinancing leads to a free-rider problem in monitoring by each bank.[16]

Historically, in some countries (for example, in postwar East Asia) the state has played an important role in resolving this kind of "coordination failure" by facilitating and complementing private-sector coordination. In this context one may note that Gerschenkron (1962) emphasized the role of state-supported development banks for the late industrializers of Europe in the nineteenth century. Government-supported development banks (like the Crédit Mobilier in nineteenth-century France; after the first World War, Crédit National in France

---

16. There is actually a tradeoff here. Decentralized financing may lead to failure to fund some socially worthwhile projects (what is sometimes called type 1 error); centralized financing, on the other hand, may lead to failure to terminate socially inefficient projects (type 2 error).

and Societé National de Crédit á l'Industrie in Belgium after the second World War, Kredintaltanlt für Weidarufban in Germany, Japan Development Bank, and the Korea Development Bank and recently, the China Development Bank) have played a crucial role in long-term industrial finance and acquisition and dissemination of financial expertise in new industrial sectors in periods of large-scale reconstruction and acute scarcity of capital and skills in both past and recent history.

But the experiences of government-supported development banks in other developing countries (say, in India or Mexico in recent decades) has been mixed at best. Armendáriz de Aghion (1999) points out that unlike government-supported development banks in France, Germany, and Japan, the development banks in other countries have often been controlled by the government in an exclusive and heavy-handed way, without cofinancing (or coownership) arrangements with private financial intermediaries (which help risk diversification and dissemination of expertise) and without sector specialization (which helps with the acquisition of specialized expertise in financing projects in targeted sectors). This is even apart from the usual moral-hazard problem in subsidizing the sometimes necessary losses that the pioneering development banks will have and the ever-present dangers of loan operations getting involved in the political patronage-distribution process.

Thus in the crucial leap between the mercantile economy and the industrial economy, the ability of the state to act as a catalyst and a coordinator in the financial market can sometimes be important. In much of the literature on the new institutional economics, the importance of the state is recognized but only in the narrow contexts of how to use its power to enforce contracts and property rights one the one hand and how to establish its credibility in not making confiscatory demands on the private owners of those rights on the other. This dilemma is implicit in the standard recommendation in this literature for a "strong but limited" government.

It is, however, possible to argue that in the successful cases of East Asian development (including that of Japan) the state has played a much more active role—intervening in the capital market sometimes in subtle but decisive ways, using regulated entry of firms and credit allocation (sometimes threatening withdrawal of credit in not so subtle ways) to promote and channel industrial investment, underwriting risks and guaranteeing loans, establishing public-development banks and other financial institutions, encouraging the development of the

nascent parts of financial markets, and nudging existing firms to up-
grade their technology and to move into sectors that fall in line with
an overall vision of strategic developmental goals.[17] In this process,
as Aoki, Murdock, and Okuno-Fujiwara (1997) have emphasized, the
state has enhanced the market instead of supplanting it; it has induced private coordination by providing various kinds of cooperation-
contingent rents. In the early stages of industrialization, when private
financial and other related institutions were underdeveloped and coordination was not self-enforcing, the East Asian states created opportunities for rents that were conditional on performance or outcome (in
mobilization of savings, commercialization of inventions, export "con-
tests," and so on) and facilitated institutional development by influencing the strategic incentives that were facing private agents through
an alteration of the relative returns to cooperation in comparison with
the adversarial equilibrium. (Such contingent transfers are akin to the
patent system, where the monopoly rent is contingent on successful
innovation.) The performance criteria in East Asia often included export success, which in a world of international competition kept the
subsidized firms on their toes and encouraged cost and quality con-
sciousness. The government commitment to maintain rents for banks,
contingent on performance, also gives banks more of a stake in long-
run relations with firms and a stronger incentive to rescue investment
projects that are suffering from temporary financial distress. This is
particularly important when in the absence of a vigorous and reliable
stock market the risk-averse savers put much of their money in banks,
which lend it to firms, which thereby acquire a high debt-equity ratio,
making them particularly vulnerable to temporary shocks.

One should not, of course, underestimate the administrative difficulties of such aggregate coordination and the issues of micromanage-
ment of capital may be much too intricate for the institutional capacity
and information-processing abilities of many a state in Africa, Latin
America, or South Asia. There is also the problem of how credible the
commitment of the state is (for a more general discussion of the issues
of credible commitment, see chapters 2 and 4) in implementing the
contingent transfer and actually carrying out the threat of withdrawing
the transfer when performance does not measure up. In this the states
in Africa, Latin America, or South Asia have often been rather lax

---

17. For a recent account of the role of the state in facilitating and engendering coordination, networking, and technology upgrading in the electronics and information technology industry in Taiwan, see Lin (2003).

compared to East Asia, and the contingent transfers have soon degenerated into unconditional subsidies or entitlements for favorite interest groups. As the more recent East Asian experience of financial crisis warns us, there are moral-hazard problems in too cozy a relationship between public banks and private business and in the political pressures for bailout that a state-supported financial system inevitably faces.

As economic stagnation has been prolonged in Japan in the last decade or so, the East Asian model has faded from public approbation. As pointed out by Aoki, Murdock, and Okuno-Fujiwara (1997), when technologies become more complex, the exploration of new technological opportunities become highly uncertain in a world of intense global competition, and when demands for more flexibility in decision-making become more insistent in the face of rapid changes, then the state loses some of its efficacy in guiding private-sector coordination, and relation-based systems may delay active restructuring.[18] It should be stressed, however, that this is not the major problem facing poor countries at their early stages of industrial transformation, when they are still struggling to reach the largely known production-possibility frontier (though subject to problems of technology adaptation).[19] I think in general that the lessons of the East Asian model for early stages of industrial transformation in poor countries are being dismissed much too easily (with reference to the recent problems of Japan and South Korea), but given the choice many poor countries would rather be in their shoes now. In fact, one arguable position is that the East Asian financial crisis has been due less to the failure of the devel-

18. It may also be the case that the entry barriers that gave rise to the cooperation-contingent rent for the initial producers made it more difficult over time for new entrepreneurs to challenge incumbents and that this has slowed adoption of new technology. For a theoretical model of this, see Acemoglu (2003).

19. In a widely noted book, Parente and Prescott (2000) identify the main reason for low total factor productivity in developing countries as the barriers imposed by their governments to adopting internationally available technology and the opposition from influential special-interest groups like labor unions. These are, of course, important obstacles. But as Pack (2003) points out in a review of this book, much of the effective use of technology is not codified but is implicit or tacit and cannot be purchased from abroad. Domestic efforts to adapt and assimilate are critical, and government investment in market-supporting infrastructure, research, training, and extension are quite important. He compares the total factor productivity (TFP) in Chile after economic liberalization with that in Korea and Taiwan. Chile's was much more thorough, and Korea and Taiwan in the initial decades of industrial growth had much more protective regimes and gave more monopoly rights to domestic firms, and yet the productivity performance in the latter was better than in Chile.

opmental state and more to its partial and haphazard dismantling—giving up some of its traditional functions of coordinating investments (creating large-scale excess capacity in industries) and the financial regulations, allowing lax monitoring, particularly of the growth of short-term debt denominated in foreign currency. This dismantling *preceded* the onset of the financial crisis (such as the case of South Korea in the mid-1990s, when it was in a hurry to be accepted into the OECD fold). And even through the years of crisis in neighboring countries, the state-owned China Development Bank has been playing a dynamic role in lending to infrastructure projects and basic industries and in catalyzing growth. The standard complaint that East Asian growth has been more in capital accumulation and less in total (multifactor) productivity is also of limited relevance for poor countries. Almost all countries, including the United States throughout much of the nineteenth century (Eichengreen, 2002), show a similar pattern in the early stages of industrialization.

In this section we have emphasized the role of the state in the necessary coordination functions in the early stages of industrial development. This is meant partly to shift the current preoccupation of the institutional economics literature with the institutions for protecting property rights.[20] Economies at early stages of development are beset with coordination failures of various kinds and alternative coordination mechanisms—the state, the market, the community organizations[21]—all play different roles, sometimes conflicting and sometimes complementary, in overcoming these coordination failures, and these roles change in various stages of development in highly context-specific and path-dependent ways. To proclaim the universal superiority of one coordination mechanism over another is naive, futile, and ahistorical.

Markets are superb coordination mechanisms in harmonizing numerous noncooperative interactions, in disciplining inefficiency, and in rewarding high-valued performance. But when residual claimancy and control rights are misaligned (say, on account of initial asset-ownership differences that constrain contractual opportunities) and there are

---

20. As Rodrik, Subramanian, and Trebbi (2002) point out, the primacy of property rights in their institutional-quality variable does not necessarily imply the superiority of a private-property-rights regime over other forms of property rights. Russia, for example, scores considerably lower in its institutional-quality indicator than China, despite having a formal legal regime that is much more in line with European norms than China's.

21. For a good overview of the strengths and weaknesses of these three types of coordination mechanisms, see the last chapter of Bowles (2003).

important strategic complementarities in long-term investment decisions, markets fail to coordinate efficiently. The implications of "imperfections" in (and sometimes the nonexistence of) credit and insurance markets are severe for the poor, sharply reducing a society's potential for productive investment, innovation, and human-resource development. The state can provide leadership in (and offer selective incentives and disincentives to) individuals interacting cooperatively in situations where noncooperative interactions are inefficient. But the state officials may have neither the information nor the motivation to carry out this role. They may be inept or corrupt, and the political accountability mechanisms are often much too weak to discipline them. In the context of these pervasive market and government failures, it is often pointed out that a local community organization that has stable membership and well-developed mechanisms for transmitting private information and enforcing social norms among its members has the potential to provide sometimes more efficient coordination than either the state or the market. But as is pointed out in chapters 2 and 6, community organizations "fail" too when they are "captured" by elite (or sectarian) interests or are hamstrung by the secession of the rich and the talented from local communities, and they may face covariate risks and costs of small scale.

Thus all three types of coordination mechanisms have their strengths and weaknesses, and they sometimes work in mutually conflicting ways (state versus market is, of course, the staple of traditional left-right debates; for the community organizations many will point out how bureaucratic as well as market processes encroach upon traditional community management, say, of environmental resources, and so on). But it is also important to keep in mind that their relationships need not be adversarial, that these three types may have institutional complementarities in many situations. There are many cases of public-private partnerships (for example, joint-venture industrial and trading firms and research in crops, vaccines, and drugs), of community organizations using market processes (for example, business-nongovernment-organization partnerships in Bangladesh that improve access to telecommunications in rural areas), and of community organizations linking up with the government (for example, joint forest management between the Indian forest department and local communities, and the Self-Employed Women's Association, SEWA, which covers the health-related risks of its members through the government-owned insurance companies, utilizing the larger risk-pooling advantages of the state—or increasingly of the market, as the insurance sector in India has been partially denationalized). Institutional economics will be much richer if the horizon of the discussion is widened to admit a variety of institutional arrangements for coping with pressing development problems.

Appendix: Empirical Determinants

This appendix looks into the cross-country determinants of development with a particular focus on the role of institutions, ignoring some of the methodological doubts about such exercises expressed earlier in this chapter and following much of the recent empirical literature, particularly papers by Acemoglu, Johnson, and Robinson (2001) and Rodrik, Subramanian, and Trebbi (2002). The exercise presented here is a small extension of the latter literature in the following ways:

• Two types of institutional variables are considered: one is a proxy for the rule of law in the sense of protection of property rights, and the other is a proxy for democratic political rights and relates to voice and participation;

• The state antiquity variable as measured by Bockstette, Chanda, and Putterman (2002) is considered as a possible instrumental variable; and

• As a dependent variable, apart from per-capita income of countries, other indices of "human development"—like literacy, longevity, and the composite human development index of the UNDP—are considered.

The two-stage regressions reconfirm the results of Acemoglu, Johnson, and Robinson (2001) in terms of the effectiveness of the colonial settler-mortality variable as an instrument and the significance of the rule-of-law variable in influencing per-capita income across countries (and also longevity and the human-development index, in this case). The state antiquity measure (indicating a continuous history of state structure) can also sometimes act as an alternative good instrument, and the proxy for democratic rights is a more significant determinant when literacy is the dependent variable and is significant along with the rule-of-law variable in influencing other elements of or the composite human-development index. This may suggest that some aspects of human development may be advanced both by the progress of democratic institutions and by the establishment of property-rights protection.

Table 1.1
Descriptive Statistics

Variable	Mean	Std. Dev.	Minimum	Maximum
Larger sample (n = 98):				
Log GDP per capita	8.40	1.16	6.27	10.24
Literacy 2000	78.32	21.46	15.90	99.00
Life expectancy at birth 2000	64.88	12.83	39.30	81.00
HDI .10	6.88	1.96	2.77	9.42
Rule of law (RULE)	0.13	0.98	−1.49	1.91
Weak political rights (WPR)	3.10	2.05	1.00	7.00
State antiquity (STATEHIST)	0.41	0.25	0.07	1.00
Ethnolinguistic fragmentation (ELF)	0.35	0.30	0.00	0.86
Land-locked (LLCK)	0.16	0.37	0.00	1.00
Medium sample (n = 69):				
Log GDP per capita	8.04	1.07	6.27	10.24
Literacy 2000	73.53	21.56	15.90	99.00
Life expectancy at birth 2000	61.47	12.68	39.30	81.00
HDI .10	6.31	1.84	2.77	9.40
Rule of law (RULE)	−0.18	0.84	−1.49	1.85
Weak political rights (WPR)	3.59	1.97	1.00	7.00
State antiquity (STATEHIST)	0.34	0.22	0.07	1.00
Ethnolinguistic fragmentation (ELF)	0.39	0.31	0.00	0.86
Population density in 1500 (DENS)	6.08	14.15	0.00	100.46
Smaller sample (n = 57):				
Log GDP per capita	8.09	1.04	6.27	10.24
Literacy 2000	73.22	21.61	15.90	99.00
Life expectancy at birth 2000	63.70	11.59	40.20	79.50
HDI .10	6.40	1.77	2.77	9.40
Rule of law (RULE)	−0.21	0.86	−1.49	1.85
Weak political rights (WPR)	3.67	1.99	1.00	7.00
State antiquity (STATEHIST)	0.32	0.18	0.07	0.93
Ethnolinguistic fragmentation (ELF)	0.39	0.31	0.00	0.86
Population density in 1500 (DENS)	5.36	14.20	0.00	100.46
European settler mortality (ESM)	4.67	1.29	2.15	7.99

Table 1.2
Correlation Matrix ($n = 133$)

	Log GDP per Capita	Literacy 2000	Life Expectancy at Birth 2000	HDI .10	Rule of Law (RULE)	Weak Political Rights (WPR)
Log GDP per capita	1.00					
Literacy 2000	0.75	1.00				
Life expectancy at birth 2000	0.84	0.75	1.00			
HDI .10	0.93	0.89	0.93	1.00		
Rule of law (RULE)	0.82	0.55	0.64	0.73	1.00	
Weak political rights (WPR)	−0.58	−0.44	−0.51	−0.55	−0.65	1.00

Table 1.1 presents the descriptive statistics for different variables for three alternative sample size of countries (since data on some variables are not available for some countries). Tables 1.2 and 1.3 presents the corresponding pair-wise correlation matrix. Table 1.4 provides the results of an ordinary-least-squares (OLS) regression, suggesting that both the institutional variables considered—rule of law (RULE) and weak political rights (WPR)—are highly significant in explaining variations in per capita income across countries. But both of these institutional variables are endogenous and may be simultaneously affected by forces that govern per-capita income. So we have recourse to the standard technique of instrumental-variables (IV) regression.

In table 1.5, for a sample of ninety-eight countries, panel B shows the first-stage regression results where the measure of state antiquity (STATHIST) has a highly significant positive association with the rule-of-law variable (RULE), and ethnolinguistic fragmentation (ELF) has a highly significant negative association with it. This may suggest that continuity over a long period of some kind of supralocal bureaucratic structure over a particular territory may help the preservation of rule of law, whereas the collective-action problems arising from social fragmentation may undermine it. For the corresponding second-stage equation for explaining both per capita GDP in 1995 and the life expectation at birth in 2000 and the composite human-development index, the IV estimate of the coefficient on the institutional variable RULE is positive and significant. But when the literacy level in 2000 is the dependent variable, the IV estimate of the coefficient on RULE

Table 1.3
Correlation Matrix ($n = 57$)

	Log GDP per Capita	Literacy 2000	Life Expectancy at Birth 2000	HDI .10	RULE	WPR	STATE-HIST	ELF	DENS	LLCK	ESM
Log GDP per capita	1										
Literacy 2000	0.74	1									
Life expectancy at birth 2000	0.85	0.75	1								
HDI .10	0.93	0.89	0.94	1							
Rule of law (RULE)	0.77	0.51	0.66	0.72	1						
Weak political rights (WPR)	−0.46	−0.58	−0.59	−0.60	−0.43	1					
State antiquity (STATEHIST)	0.08	−0.16	0.16	0.01	0.09	0.23	1				
Ethnolinguistic fragmentation (ELF)	−0.44	−0.43	−0.65	−0.56	−0.33	0.38	0.04	1			
Population density in 1500 (DENS)	−0.12	−0.26	−0.05	−0.13	−0.01	0.26	0.34	−0.14	1		
Land-locked (LLCK)	−0.35	−0.25	−0.37	−0.37	−0.26	0.12	−0.15	0.24	−0.01	1	
European settler mortality (ESM)	−0.73	−0.56	−0.67	−0.72	−0.63	0.36	−0.27	0.43	−0.02	0.28	1

Table 1.4
Ordinary-Least-Squares Regressions

Dependent Variables

	Larger Sample (n = 98)				Medium Sample (n = 69)				Smaller Sample (n = 57)			
	Log GDP per Capita	Literacy 2000	Life Expectancy at Birth 2000	HDI	Log GDP per Capita	Literacy 2000	Life Expectancy at Birth 2000	HDI	Log GDP per Capita	Literacy 2000	Life Expectancy at Birth 2000	HDI
Rule of law (RULE)	0.91 (0.08)*	10.07 (2.15)*	7.24 (1.16)*	1.30 (0.15)*	0.89 (0.11)*	9.30 (2.78)*	7.05 (1.58)*	1.24 (0.20)*	0.83 (0.11)*	7.93 (2.86)*	6.71 (1.33)*	1.15 (0.19)*
Weak political rights (WPR)	−0.07 (0.04)***	−2.85 (1.03)*	−1.57 (0.56)*	−0.22 (0.07)*	−0.08 (0.05)	−3.96 (1.19)*	−1.85 (0.68)*	−0.27 (0.09)*	−0.09 (0.05)**	−4.81 (1.24)*	−2.21 (0.58)*	−0.32 (0.08)*
F (p-value)	121.43 (.000)	37.61 (.000)	56.16 (.000)	94.91 (.000)	49.28 (.000)	20.25 (.000)	24.17 (.000)	41.44 (.000)	42.42 (.000)	19.46 (.000)	34.28 (.000)	44.54 (.000)
R²	0.72	0.44	0.54	0.67	0.60	0.38	0.42	0.56	0.61	0.42	0.56	0.62

* represents significance at the 1 percent level, ** at the 5 percent level, and *** at the 10 percent level.

Table 1.5
2SLS Regressions

Dependent Variables

Panel A. Two-Stage Least Squares:

	Larger Sample (n = 98)				Medium Sample (n = 69)				Smaller Sample (n = 57)			
	Log GDP per Capita	Literacy 2000	Life Expectancy at Birth 2000	HDI.10	Log GDP per Capita	Literacy 2000	Life Expectancy at Birth 2000	HDI.10	Log GDP per Capita	Literacy 2000	Life Expectancy at Birth 2000	HDI.10
Rule of law (RULE)	1.07 (0.31)*	3.15 (9.48)	10.24 (5.49)***	1.37 (0.71)***	1.50 (0.41)*	13.71 (9.69)	23.09 (7.36)*	2.62 (0.82)*	1.20 (0.27)*	10.04 (7.02)	10.99 (3.16)*	1.68 (0.47)*
Weak political rights (WPR)	−0.21 (0.22)	−12.39 (6.76)**	−5.40 (3.91)	−0.82 (0.50)	−0.14 (0.17)	−9.52 (4.11)**	−1.36 (3.12)	−0.44 (0.35)	−0.14 (0.13)	−9.32 (3.44)*	02.48 (1.55)	−0.50 (0.23)**
R^2	0.70	0.35	0.52	0.62	0.60	0.37	0.39	0.55	0.61	0.41	0.55	0.62

Panel B. First Stage for Endogenous Variables:

	RULE	WPR	RULE	WPR	RULE	WPR
State antiquity (STATEHIST)	1.25 (0.35)*	−0.36 (0.81)	0.89 (0.48)**	0.42 (1.11)	−0.34 (0.60)	2.46 (1.47)***
Ethnolinguisitic fragmentation (ELF)	−1.12 (0.30)*	2.30 (0.70)*	−0.93 (0.32)*	2.35 (0.75)*	−0.18 (0.35)	1.73 (0.86)**
Land-locked country (LLCK)	−0.25 (0.23)	0.48 (0.54)				
European settler mortality (ESM)					−0.42 (0.08)*	0.47 (0.21)**

Population density in 1500			−0.62	3.60	−0.08	3.18
(DENS)			(0.75)	(1.75)**	(0.71)	(1.76)**
F (p-value)	14.51	5.22	4.22	4.31	8.84	6.05
	(.000)	(.002)	(.009)	(.008)	(.000)	(.000)
R^2	0.32	0.14	0.16	0.17	0.40	0.32

Notes: STATEHIST: An index of state antiquity constructed by Bockstette, Chanda, and Putterman (2002). The index awards points to any given country based on the following criteria: the length of time over which there has existed a government above the tribal level, the extent (indexed over time) to which that government has been locally rather than foreign-based, and the percentage of the country's territory ruled by that government (again indexed over time). We use the original authors' preferred data series, which they term STATEHIST5.

ELF: An index of ethnolinguistic fractionalization taken from La Porta et al. (1998). The average of several measures of ethnic diversity.

RULE: Taken from Kaufmann et al. (2002). A composite index measuring the quality of the rule of law, including the following indicators: perceptions of the incidence of both violent and nonviolent crime, the effectiveness and predictability of the judiciary, and the enforceability of contracts.

DENS: Population density in 1500. Computed by dividing population in 1500 (measured in tens of thousands) by arable land area (measured in millions of square kilometers). Data are drawn from McEvedy and Jones (1978).

WPR: Weak political rights on a scale of 1 to 7 (the larger the score, weaker are the political rights) for the year 2000, taken from the UNDP Human Development Report 2002. The political rights include free and fair elections for offices with real power, freedom of political organization, significant opposition, freedom from domination by powerful groups, and autonomy or political inclusion of minority groups.

ESM: Logarithm of estimated European settlers' mortality rate taken from Acemoglu, Johnson, and Robinson (2001).

LLCK: Dummy variable equal to 1 if country does not adjoin the sea, taken from Parker (1997).

GDP per capita in 1995 in PPP U.S. dollars is taken from Penn World Tables. HDI (Human Development Index, multiplied by 10), life expectation at birth, and the literacy rate all relate to year 2000 and are taken from the UNDP Human Development Report 2002.

* represents significance at the 1 percent level, ** at the 5 percent level, and *** at the 10 percent level.

is not significant. Instead, a different institutional variable—an index of weakness of political rights (WPR)—is significant: the weaker the political rights are, the lower the literacy. This may suggest that democratic voice and participation are conducive to mass literacy campaigns. In the first-stage regression WPR is significantly related to ELF but not to STATEHIST.

Table 1.5 also presents a smaller sample of sixty-nine countries that allows a historical (relating to the year 1500) population-density variable (DENS) to be utilized. The results are similar to those described in the preceding paragraph, with the difference that at the first stage the significance of STATEHIST diminishes somewhat in influencing RULE, and DENS has a positive and significant association with weak political rights. At the second stage, literacy is again significantly and negatively associated with weakness of political rights. My speculation about why in countries with historically high population-density political rights are weaker in general is that in these countries with labor abundance and low market power of workers, equality of political power may have been more difficult to establish. This is consistent with a claim by Engerman and Sokoloff (2002) that areas of labor scarcity in the New World in the early colonial period saw more political equality (particularly in terms of voting rights and independence from large landlords).

In table 1.5, for the smallest sample of fifty-seven countries, the European settler-mortality variable of Acemoglu, Johnson, and Robinson (2001) is introduced, in addition to the other variables. As before, in the second stage the IV estimate of the coefficient on RULE is significant except when the dependent variable is literacy. For the latter, WPR is significant, as before. For the composite human-development index in 2000, the IV estimates of the coefficient on RULE as well as on WPR are significant.

In the first-stage regression, as before, ethnolinguistic fragmentation and population density in 1500 are associated with weak political rights. The European settler-mortality variable is significantly related to both of institutional variables. The state-antiquity variable is now (weakly) associated with weak political rights; this may suggest that countries with a long history of an entrenched bureaucratic-military setup need not be hospitable to democratic rights, even when those countries maintain some rule of law regarding property rights.

All the equations in table 1.5 pass the OID test (from regressing second-stage residual on the instrument set) at the 5 percent level.

2

Distributive Conflicts and the Persistence of Inefficient Institutions

2.1

One of the as yet inadequately resolved issues in institutional economics in the context of underdevelopment is why dysfunctional institutions often persist for a long time. Some sections of the property-rights school display a naive presumption of the survival of the "fittest" institution: more efficient institutions and governance structures evolve as the parties involved come to appreciate the new benefit-cost possibilities. There is a certain ahistorical functionalism and even vulgar Darwinism at display here. An institution's mere function of serving the interests of potential beneficiaries is clearly inadequate in *explaining* that institution, just as it is an incompetent detective who tries to explain a murder mystery only by looking for the beneficiary and, on that basis alone, proceeds to arrest the heir of the murdered rich man. The mechanism through which new institutions and property rights emerge or fail to emerge needs to be examined, and the history of underdevelopment is littered with cases of formidable institutional impediments appearing as strategic outcomes of distributive conflicts, which is the focus of this chapter.

Fortunately, the more recent strands of institutional economics are clear in not ascribing optimality properties to institutions, often modeled as Nash equilibrium outcomes. North (1990), Bardhan (1989b), Stiglitz (1989), and others have pointed to the self-reinforcing mechanisms for the persistence of socially suboptimal institutions when path-dependent processes are at work. According to an idea borrowed from the literature on the history of technological change, there are increasing returns to the adoption of a particular institutional form: the more it is adopted, the more it is attractive or convenient for others to conform to because of infrastructural and network externalities, learning and coordination effects, and adaptive expectations. A path chosen by some initial adopters to suit their interests may "lock in" the whole system for a long time to come, denying a footing to later, maybe potentially more appropriate, institutions.

In this path-dependent process North (1990), more than others, has emphasized how interactions between the "mental models" that the members of a society possess and the incentive structure provided by the institutions shape incremental changes.[1] The path-dependent process is also made more complicated by the frequent cases of unintended consequences in history. More than a century ago, Menger (1963/1883) made a distinction between "pragmatic" and "organic" institutions. The former are the direct outcomes of conscious contractual design (as shown in some institutional models in the recent literature on the theory of imperfect information or transaction cost), while the latter (as shown in Menger's theory of the origin of money) are comparatively undesigned, and they evolve gradually as the unintended and unforeseeable results of the pursuit of individual interests. Elster (1989) has referred to intermediate cases where an institution may have originally come about unintended, but agents eventually become aware of the function that an institution serves for them and consciously try to preserve it from then on. In general, certain regularities appear in the evolution of social institutions as social agents repeatedly face the same types of social problems and adapt their behavior, but there are no necessary social-welfare-maximizing mechanisms in the evolutionary process. In the more recent literature on applications of evolutionary game theory to institutional change (see, for example, Bowles, 2003), it is recognized that while efficiency generally contributes to a differential advantage in replication, it is highly unlikely that efficiency and success in replication will always go together given the positive and negative interactions of one institution with other institutions (involving their complementarity and crowding-out) and the payoffs to adherence to particular institutions being dependent on adherence by others.

---

1. One related example may be cited from the comparative study in Guinnane (1994) of credit cooperatives in German and Irish history. The Raiffeisen agricultural credit cooperatives that were successful in nineteenth-century rural Germany provided a model for the introduction of similar organizations in Ireland in 1894. But they did not succeed in Ireland, partly because the social and cultural norms of mutual monitoring and collective punishment among members of a cooperative worked in rural Germany but did not work in the Irish countryside.

Before proceeding any further, a question about "efficient" or "inefficient" institutions that some economists are prone to ask needs to be clarified. We want to be upfront about *not* necessarily referring to Pareto efficiency. We'll more often regard a movement toward a productivity-enhancing institution to be a change in the right direction. The Pareto criterion (of at least one person gaining and nobody losing) and insistence on unanimity are much too stringent (and politically a nonstarter) for most discussions of institutional change. In any case, when one is in search of Pareto efficiency, to make the compensating transfers from gainers to losers incentive-compatible in a situation where the valuation of gainers and losers is private information, it may be difficult to change institutions even with no frictions at all in bargaining (beyond this information problem).[2]

2.2

In the new institutional economics literature, the major stumbling block to realizing potential gains from trade is political (particularly in the sense that those in power find it difficult to commit to not using that power). This is the inherent commitment problem, particularly for rulers who control the state, with its "monopoly of violence." Looking over the last few hundred years of history, North and Weingast (1989)[3] and others have focused on a particular political mechanism of credible commitment that made much of the difference between the success story of western Europe and North America and the stagnation in large parts of the rest of the world over this period. This mechanism essentially involved self-binding by the rulers (like the king giving up royal prerogatives, increasing the powers of the Parliament over the monarchy) who credibly commit themselves to be nonpredatory, secure private property rights, and allow private enterprise and capital markets to flourish.

While not denying that such self-binding mechanisms may have played an important role in history, I think it is possible to argue that they are neither necessary nor sufficient for economic development. They are not sufficient because there are other (technological,

---

2. See Mailath and Postlewaite (1990) for a demonstration of this in the case of collective action on a public project.
3. For some empirical criticisms of the argument for English history, see Carruthers (1990) and Clark (1995).

demographic, ecological, and cultural) constraints on the development process, not all of which will be relaxed when rulers disable themselves. They are not necessary because (as a few non-Western success stories—Japan since the Meiji Restoration, Korea and Taiwan since 1960, and coastal China since 1980—suggest) in most of these cases the rulers often adopted prudent policies (and sometimes even acquired reputation[4] to this effect) but were far from self-disabling their discretion. (The theoretical issues of credible commitment are discussed in greater detail in chapter 4.) Major economic transactions in the successful East Asian cases have often been relation-based rather than rule-based. While charges of cronyism have been bandied about in the diagnosis of the recent Asian financial crisis, the more long-term success stories in East Asia at *early* stages of industrial transformation even with relation-based systems cannot be denied, as is argued in the preceding chapter.

The political stumbling blocks to beneficial institutional change in many poor countries may have more to do with distributive conflicts and asymmetries in bargaining power. The old institutional economists (including Marxists) used to point out how a given institutional arrangement serving the interests of some powerful group or class acts as a long-lasting barrier (or fetter, to quote a favorite word of Marx) to economic progress. As has been suggested in Bardhan (1989b) and Knight (1992), the new institutional economists[5] sometimes understate the tenacity of vested interests, the enormity of the collective-action problem in bringing about institutional change, and the differential ca-

---

4. As Acemoglu (2002) points out in a model of repeated games where reputation may act as a substitute for a commitment contract, the efficacy of self-binding depends on the patience and time horizon of the rulers. This is related to the point made by Evans (1995) on the importance of meritocratic career bureaucrats ("Weberian"), with a longer time horizon in South Korea compared to the bureaucrats in Latin America, who were more dependent on short-term political patronage.

5. North (1990) is an exception in this tradition. He points to the contrasting and path-dependent processes of change in the bargaining power of the ruler versus the ruled in different countries, particularly in the context of the fiscal crisis of the state. In earlier historical literature on the transition from feudalism in Europe, Brenner (1976) provides a major departure from the usual analysis of transition in terms of demography or market conditions: he provides a detailed analysis of the contrasting experiences of transition in different parts of Europe (those between western and eastern Europe and those between the English and the French cases even within western Europe) in terms of changes in bargaining power of different social groups or in the outcomes of social conflicts. Brenner shows that much depends, for example, on the cohesiveness of the landlords and peasants as contending groups and on their ability to resist encroachments on each other's rights and to form coalitions with other groups in society.

pacity of different social groups in mobilization and coordination. The collective-action problem can be serious even when the change would be Pareto-superior for all groups. There are two kinds of collective-action problems involved: one is the well-known free-rider problem about sharing the costs of bringing about change; the other is a bargaining problem where disputes about sharing the potential benefits from the change may lead to a breakdown of the necessary coordination. There are cases where an institution that nobody individually likes persists as a result of a mutually sustaining network of social sanctions that cause each individual to conform out of fear of loss of reputation from disobedience.[6] Potential members of a breakaway coalition in such situations may have grounds to fear that it is doomed to failure, and failure to challenge the system can become a self-fulfilling prophecy.

The problem may be more acute when there are winners and losers from a productivity-enhancing institutional change, which is the usual situation. The costs of collective action of such a change may be too high. This is particularly the case, as we know from Olson (1965), when the losses of the potential losers are concentrated and transparent, while gains of the potential gainers are diffuse[7] (or uncertain for a given individual, even though not for the group, as suggested by Fernandez and Rodrik, 1992). There is also the inherent difficulty (emphasized by Dixit and Londregan, 1995) that the potential gainers cannot credibly commit to compensate the losers ex post.[8] Ideally, the state could issue long-term bonds to buy off the losers and tax the gainers to repay. But many developing countries have serious limitations on the government's ability to tax and on its credibility in keeping inflation under control, and the bond market is thin. Losers also fear that once they give up an existing institution, they may lose the *locus standi* in lobbying with a future government when the promises are not kept (exit from a current institutional arrangement damaging their voice in the new regime in future), and so they resist a change today that is

---

6. For a well-known static analysis of such a case, see Akerlof (1984). For a more complex model in terms of stochastic dynamic games that explain the evolution of local customs or conventions, see Young (1998).

7. As Machiavelli reminds us in *The Prince* (1513, ch. 6, p. 51), "the reformer has enemies in all those who profit by the old order and has only lukewarm defenders in all those who would profit by the new."

8. Some societies may be able to develop in repeated situations appropriate norms of compensation to losers, but the preservation of such a norm itself may require collective action.

potentially Pareto-improving (in the sense that the gainers could compensate the losers).

The obstruction by vested interests can also be formalized in terms of a simple Nash bargaining model, where the institutional innovation may shift the bargaining frontier outward (thus creating the potential for all parties to gain). In the process, however, the disagreement payoff of the weaker party may also go up (often due to better options of both exit and voice that institutional changes may bring in their wake), and the erstwhile stronger party might end up losing in the new bargaining equilibrium. How likely this will be depends on the nature of shift in the bargaining frontier and the extent of change in the disagreement payoffs.[9] As Robinson (1998) has emphasized in his theory of predatory states, institutional changes that safeguard property rights, law enforcement, and other economically beneficial structures may fatten the cow that a dictator has the power to milk, but it may not be rational for the dictator to carry out these changes if in the process his preexisting rent-extraction machinery has a chance of being damaged or weakened. He may choose not to risk upsetting the current arrangement for the uncertain prospect of a share in a larger pie. Acemoglu and Robinson (2002) develop a theory (discussed further in chapter 4) that has incumbent elites block the introduction of new and efficient technologies because these improvements will reduce their future political power. In their example from nineteenth-century history, the monarchy and aristocracy in Russia and Austria-Hungary controlled the political system and feared replacement, so they blocked the establishment of institutions that would have facilitated industrialization. These replacement threats are often driven by extreme economic inequalities in society.

In explaining the divergent development paths in North and South America since early colonial times, Engerman and Sokoloff (2002) have provided a great deal of evidence of how societies with high economic inequality at the outset of colonization establish institutions that evolved in ways that restricted access to political power and opportunities for economic advancement to a narrow elite. Initial unequal conditions had long lingering effects, and through their influence on public policies (in distribution of public land and other natural

---

9. This is the case even if we abstract from the usual case of deadlocks that arise in bargaining with incomplete information, with possible misrepresentation of the type of the bargaining players.

resources, the right to vote and to vote in secret, primary education, patent law, corporate and banking law, and so on) they tended to perpetuate those institutions and policies that atrophied development. Even in countries where initially some oligarchic entrepreneurs are successful in creating conditions (including securing their own property rights) for their own economic performance, as long as that oligarchy remains powerful, it usually gets away with raising entry barriers for new or future entrepreneurs, and this blocks challenges to their incumbency and thus sometimes new technological breakthroughs. See Acemoglu (2003) for a theoretical analysis of this kind of dynamic distortion in oligarchic societies even when property rights are protected for the initial producers.

The classic example of inefficient institutions that persist as the lopsided outcome of distributive struggles relates to the historical evolution of land rights in developing countries. In most of these countries, the empirical evidence suggests that economies of scale in farm production are insignificant (except in some plantation crops) and that the small family farm is often the most efficient unit of production. Yet the violent and tortuous history of land reform in many countries suggests that numerous road blocks on the way to a more efficient reallocation of land rights are put up by vested interests for generations. Why don't the large landlords voluntarily lease out or sell their land to small family farmers and grab much of the surplus arising from this efficient reallocation? There clearly has been some leasing out of land, but problems of monitoring, insecurity of tenure, and the landlord's fear that the tenant will acquire occupancy rights on the land have limited efficiency gains and the extent of tenancy. The land-sales market has been particularly thin (and in many poor countries the sales go the opposite way—from distressed small farmers to landlords and moneylenders). With low household savings and severely imperfect credit markets, the potentially more efficient small farmer is often incapable of affording the going market price of land. As Binswanger, Deininger, and Feder (1995) explain it, land is a preferred collateral (and also carries all kinds of tax advantages and speculation opportunities for the wealthy) and often has a price above the capitalized value of the agricultural income stream for even the more productive small farmer, rendering mortgaged sales uncommon (since mortgaged land cannot be used as collateral to raise working capital for the buyer). Under these circumstances and if the public finances (and the state of the bond market) are such that landlords cannot be fully or credibly compensated,[10] land redistribution will not be voluntary.

Landlords resist land reforms also because the leveling effects reduce their social and political power and their ability to control and dominate even nonland transactions.[11] Large land holdings may give their owner special social status or political power[12] in a lumpy way (so that the status or political effect from owning 100 hectares is larger than the combined status or political effect accruing to fifty new buyers owning 2 hectares each). Thus the social or political rent of land ownership for the large landowner will not be compensated by the offer price of the numerous small buyers. Under the circumstances the former will not sell, and inefficient (in a productivity sense, not in terms of the Pareto criterion) land concentration persists.

Even in the context of increasing returns to land ownership in terms of political rent, land concentration is not always the unique or stable political equilibrium. Much depends on the nature of political competition and the context-specific and path-dependent formations of political coalitions. An interesting example of this in terms of comparative institutional-historical analysis is provided by Nugent and Robinson (1998). Holding constant both colonial background and crop technology, they compare the divergent institutional (particularly in terms of small-holder property rights) and growth trajectories of two pairs of former Spanish colonies that are in the same region (Costa Rica and Colombia, on the one hand, and El Salvador and Guatemala, on the other) and that produce the same principal crop (coffee). The political fragmentation of elites often helps in overcoming obstacles to institutional development. In Costa Rica, for example, the elites of different towns were induced to compete with each other for popular support, which they did by offering private property rights to small holders.

---

10. This is particularly the case if the government has limited ability to tax and low credibility in promising not to inflate away the value of bonds with which landlords are compensated.

11. Busch and Muthoo (2002) develop a model where land redistribution may adversely affect a landlord's bargaining power in *other* markets (labor or credit). The inability to make binding commitments prevents the poor from committing not to exploit their increased bargaining power following land redistribution, and being wealth-constrained they cannot compensate the landlords up front either. The greater the degree of inequality in the players' bargaining powers, the more likely it is that inefficient institutions will persist.

12. Baland and Robinson (2003) have shown from a study of Chile in the late 1950s how in the absence of a secret ballot landowners controlled the voting behavior of farm workers.

In El Salvador and Guatemala, on the other hand, the national elite remained unified in opposition to such an institutional change. Institutional economics will be richer with more such comparative historical studies (instead of more cross-country regressions).

An important aspect of political rent that is overlooked in the usual calculations of the surplus generated by a given institutional change is that all sides are really interested in *relative*, rather than absolute, gains or losses. In a power game, as in a winner-take-all contest or tournament, it is not enough for an institutional change to increase the surplus for all parties concerned to be acceptable. One side may gain absolutely and yet may lose relative to the other side and thus may resist change. If, in a repeated framework, both sides have to continue to spend resources in seeking (or preserving) power or in improving their bargaining position in future, and if the marginal return from spending such resources for one party is an increasing function of such spending by the other party (that is, power-seeking efforts by the two parties are "strategic complements"), it is easy to see why the relative gain from an institutional change may be the determining factor in its acceptability.[13]

2.3

Much of the discussion in this chapter has been about the problem of compensating the losers of an institutional change. In the absence of feasible side payments, many kinds of collective action problems arise in orchestrating institutional change from a low-level to a higher-level equilibrium *even* when all parties would benefit from such a change. These problems are rendered particularly difficult by distributive conflicts.

Let us examine examples first from macroeconomic institutional arrangements and then from microeconomic cases. In macroeconomic comparisons of East Asia and Latin America in the last quarter of the twentieth century, the point has often been made that when wealth distribution is relatively egalitarian, as in large parts of East Asia (particularly through land reforms and widespread expansion of education and basic health services), it has been somewhat easier to enlist the

---

13. For a model of power seeking on these lines to explain why two parties may not agree to obviously mutually advantageous transactions, even when there are simple enforceable contracts and side transfers of fungible resources to implement them, see Rajan and Zingales (1999).

support of most social groups (and isolate the extreme political wings of the labor movement) in making short-run sacrifices at times of macroeconomic crises and coordinating on stabilization and growth-promoting institutions and policies. For example, Campos and Root (1996, p. 71) write: "In contrast with Latin America and Africa, East Asian regimes established their legitimacy by promising shared growth so that demands of narrowly conceived groups for regulations that would have long-term deleterious consequences for growth were resisted. In particular, broad-based social support allowed their governments to avoid having to make concessions to radical demands of organized labor."

This result is not unique to East Asia. In fact, a major institutional lesson that Morris and Adelman (1989, p. 1417) draw from their historical research on the nineteenth-century development experience of twenty-three countries is similar: "Favorable impacts of government policies on the *structure* of economic growth can be expected only where political institutions limit elite control of assets, land institutions spread a surplus over subsistence widely, and domestic education and skills are well diffused."

There is some cross-country evidence (see Keefer and Knack, 1995) that inequality and other forms of polarization make it more difficult to build a consensus about policy changes in response to crises and result in instability of policy outcomes and insecurity of property and contractual rights. Rodrik (1998) cites cross-country evidence for his hypothesis that the economic costs of external shocks are magnified by distributional conflicts that are triggered, and this diminishes the productivity with which a society's resources are utilized. This is also related to the literature on inequality and delayed stabilization in Latin America (see, for example, Alesina and Drazen, 1991). For whatever it is worth, anecdotal evidence suggests that calls for belt-tightening by political leaders in Latin America in the face of macroeconomic crisis are met by derisive comments from members of the working class about the elite salting their money away to Miami but that South Korean women lined up to donate their jewelry to help their government through its financial crisis in the late 1990s. Djankov et al. (2003) refer to the differences between countries in what they call "civic capital," determining the differential location of their Institutional Possibility Frontier that traces the tradeoff between social losses due to disorder and the associated private expropriation and losses due to state expropriation in different countries. The point here (as well as throughout this book) is that distributive conflicts have a decisive influence in determining the availability of "civic capital" in a country.

Below the aggregative or macro level there are many local self-governing institutions—either elected local government bodies (in charge of delivering local public goods like roads, extension service, and public health and sanitation), rural community organizations (in charge of management of environmental resources like forests, fishery, irrigation, and grazing lands), or urban neighborhood associations (in charge of crime-watch, cultural, and social-solidarity-promoting activities)—where distributive conflicts may sometimes lead to institutional failures. As is discussed in chapter 6, in areas of high social and economic inequality the problem of "capture" of even elected local government bodies by the local elite can be severe, and the poor and the weaker sections of the population may be left grievously exposed to their mercies and their malfeasance. Thus one beneficial by-product of land reform, underemphasized in the usual economic analysis, is that such reform, by changing the local political structure in the village, gives more voice to the poor and induces them to get involved in local self-governing institutions. In other cases, the problem of elite capture may be less important but that of elite "exit" may be serious in causing the erosion of political support from the provision of local public goods. When, for example, the rich do not send their children to local public schools and do not use the local health services, the public provision structure often crumbles, as is familiar in both rich and poor countries.

Similar problems, arising from inequality, may afflict local non-government, often informal, community organizations in developing countries. The relationship between inequality and collective action (both in the sense of participating in a regulatory group organization and in the sense of contributing to provision or conservation of some common resource) is an underresearched area in economics. In chapter 10 a simple model structures some of the effects of inequality on cooperation, and chapter 11 provides the results of an empirical study on this question. For a brief account of the theoretical and empirical literature on this question, see Baland and Platteau (forthcoming). Generally, while the effect of inequality is in general ambiguous, there are many cases where the net benefits of coordination for each individual may be structured in such a way that in situations of marked inequality some individuals may not participate or contribute to the cost of collective action. The resulting outcome may be more inefficient than outcomes in situations with greater equality. Inequality may also lead to bargaining disputes that arise from the distribution of benefits of collective action, as is mentioned above. Moreover, the negotiation and enforcement costs for some cooperative arrangements may go up with inequality. In such situations, collective institutional structures and opportunities for cooperative problem solving may be forgone by societies that are sharply divided along social and economic lines.

3 Power: Some Conceptual Issues

3.1

Political economy critically involves the distribution of power, and in this chapter we discuss some of the basic conceptual issues that arise in any analysis of power. Most economists implicitly subscribe to the behaviorist view of power attributed to Simon (1957) and Dahl (1957): A has power over B to the extent that the former can get the latter to do something that he or she would not otherwise do. I shall comment later in the final section of this chapter on the narrowness of the behaviorist interpretation, but it can also be too broad a definition of power. If I draw your attention to the undone lace on your shoe, I shall probably get you to do something you would not otherwise do, yet it is hardly an exercise of my power. This shortcoming is avoided in a definition proposed by Taylor (1982): A has power over B if A can affect the incentives facing B in such a way that it is rational for B to do something he would not otherwise have chosen to do. The incentives facing B are affected by A mainly through the offer of a reward, the threat of a penalty, or some combination of a threat and an offer, which Taylor calls a "throffer" (a chilling example of the latter in the film *The Godfather*: "I'm gonna make him an offer he can't refuse"). Since most economic transactions are of this kind, Barry (1989) calls this—the possession of the means of securing compliance by the manipulation of rewards or punishments—the "economic" variety of power. Mann (1986) distinguishes between different kinds of social power not by what the power is used for but by what means are used to exercise power: for example, the power to tax is political, not economic, power, even though the tax revenues may be used for economic purposes. Economics is, of course, not confined to the exercise of economic power in this sense and is often concerned with the consequences of other forms of power, particularly political and ideological.

In mainstream economics the standard presumption is that there is no exercise of power if both parties voluntarily enter a transaction. But gains from power are conceptually different from gains from trade. As Barry (1989) points out, A can exercise power over B even if B actually gains in comparison with his or her previous situation. A's power consists simply in the ability to obtain low-cost compliance from B; this draws attention to the realities of dependence even in cases of gainful exchange.[1] There are also cases, particularly in poor countries, of what Genicot (2002) calls the "paradox of voluntary choice": while a poor agent may maximize her utility by selecting some option X (say, a bonded labor contract) out of her given choice set, she could in fact gain access to a number of more desirable opportunities if X was removed from her choice set. Genicot constructs a case where the strategic interaction between the landlord and the local credit institutions can constrain the poor peasant to "choose" a bonded labor contract, whereas if bonded labor were banned, it would have resulted in welfare-enhancing credit opportunities for the peasant.[2]

The concept of power also goes beyond the outcome of a given exchange and points to the fact that power may be centrally involved in causing the existing pattern (and in defining the existing parameters) of trade in the first place. Trading within a given system of property rights and institutions may be mutually beneficial, but in the historical process of defining those rights and institutions, the exercise of power (often with violence) by interested actors who would later participate in the trading has been quite common. Bartlett (1989) cites in this context the examples of the violent emergence of the rights of enclosure in

---

1. To quote from Barry's (1989, p. 62) telling example, "It occurred to me, while reading an omnibus edition of the Jeeves short stories by P. G. Wodehouse, how often the plot turns around the dependence of one of Bertie Wooster's fellow Drones on an allowance from some aged relative, and on the need to meet (or appear to meet) the more or less cranky demands of this relative in order to keep the allowance.... It may be noted that this constitutes a case where A (the aunt or uncle) operates on B (the Drone) by rewards rather than sanctions.... We can see that the relationship may not be one of power in the sense of an unequal exchange. It may be that the relative receives less benefit from the Drone's compliance than the Drone does from the allowance. But the point is that the Drone *is* dependent—his behavior is open to control by the aunt or uncle—and the truth of this is not affected by the fact that he prefers dependence to independence on the only terms on which independence is available."

2. Basu (2000) models a somewhat similar case of a woman choosing a "sexual harassment contract" where she would have otherwise been better off if such contracts were disallowed.

England (eliminating the traditional land-use rights of serfs) and that of the supersession of the communal tribal rights in land traditionally enjoyed by the Native Americans in nineteenth-century United States. Even when the new property rights lead to Pareto-superior trade, the very process of their creation involved a brutal exercise of power.

In sections 3.2 and 3.3 of this chapter we discuss in the context of recent advances in economic theory some of the battlefields, so to speak, for the exercise of power: bargaining games in section 3.2 and economic organizations and capitalist authority relations in section 3.3. In all of this we focus on the underlying structural factors. In the last section some problems of both the behavioral and structural concepts of power are discussed.

3.2

In Dahl's (1957) view the "amount" of power can be quantified as the net increase in the probability of B's actually performing some specific action X, due to A's using his power over B. To this Harsanyi (1976) added two other quantitative aspects of a power relation: (1) the opportunity costs to A of exerting power over B and (2) the opportunity costs of B in refusing to do what A wants him to do. Other things being equal, A's power over B is greater as (1) is smaller and (2) is larger. From these two opportunity costs it is a small step to the idea of threat points or disagreement payoffs in a bargaining game. Harsanyi uses the Zeuthen-Nash solution to cooperative bargaining games to characterize the equilibrium in such reciprocal power situations. An alternative but related (to Nash bargaining) approach to defining each player's value in a game is involved in the idea of the Shapley value in n-person games (see Shapley and Shubik, 1954), where a person's power is measured by the probability that he is the pivotal member of a winning coalition, a pivot being one who can convert a losing coalition into a winning one. The Shapley value as a measure of an individual's economic power in market games is denoted by the individual's average of marginal contributions over all possible coalitions that he can join.[3]

---

3. For a discussion of some of the inadequacies of the Shapley-Shubik index of power, see Barry (1989). In particular, giving credit to the pivot for the whole value of the winning coalition is inappropriate in cases where decision making on a public policy is involved, since public policy is a public good and the decision maker cannot fully appropriate the benefits of the policy. In view of this free-riding problem, Barry insists on a distinction between power and luck as alternative ways of getting outcomes that one wants.

In the more recent game-theoretic literature the Nash bargaining solution is usually motivated by the construction of a noncooperative game in which the details of the negotiation procedure are spelled out. In Rubinstein's (1987) model of a multistage noncooperative bargaining process under complete information using the notion of "perfect" equilibrium (where only credible threats have an effect on outcomes), time plays a significant role: bargaining power depends on time discount rates. The more impatient a player, the smaller is his or her share of the pie. Power here is associated with the ability for delay; this also opens the possibility for strategic delay, which clearly the asset-poor can afford (or credibly make) less often.

In this sequential noncooperative bargaining model, the disagreement payoff plays a somewhat different role than it does in the standard cooperative bargaining model. Consider the example of wage bargaining between management and a trade union. If the parties fail to reach an agreement and the firm is shut down indefinitely, the disagreement payoffs of the two parties are given by what are called their outside options: alternative income or reservation wage for the workers and returns from alternative deployment of capital for the owners. If, however, in the bargaining process the production on the firm is only temporarily[4] disrupted by a lockout or a strike, the relevant fall-back alternatives until an agreement is reached are given by inside options: for workers strike funds of the union or, more often in poor countries, income of relatives and for owners inventories, credit, and internal finance. Both inside and outside options are relevant for the outcome of bargaining but in different ways. Noncooperative bargaining theorists point out that outside options constrain the outcome by providing floors to what the parties will get but have no role beyond that. Inside options, on the other hand, influence bargaining power (the distance from the floor) and, in particular, determine whether threats are credible. If the reservation wage (outside option for the workers) goes up, for example, the noncooperative theory predicts no change in the bargaining outcome (as long as it still satisfies the constraints), but a larger strike fund may raise the equilibrium wage.

This argument about what Elster (1989) calls "the irrelevance of outside options" is related in spirit to the condition of independence of irrelevant alternatives used in Nash bargaining models: changes in options or alternatives that would not be realized anyway should

---

4. There are problems in assuming that it is temporary to start with.

not matter for the outcome. This is, however, not very plausible in real-world bargaining situations where "irrelevant" alternatives and outside options often do make a difference, largely on account of the operation of some social norms. In this connection one may note that Kalai and Smorodinsky (1975) have replaced the Nash condition of independence of irrelevant alternatives with that of monotonicity (which implies that if, for a given level of utility obtained by one player, the maximum feasible level attainable by the other is increased, then the solution should be such that the second player's utility will also be greater). Under this condition wage bargaining is sensitive to the maximal feasible gain: a rise, for example, in the worker's reservation wage (reducing the maximal feasible profit of the employer) always strengthens the bargaining power of the worker in the Kalai-Smorodinsky solution.

Apart from time, the other aspects of the bargaining process that have clear implications for power have to do with commitment and information. As is now standard in game-theoretic oligopoly models of market power, the ability to credibly precommit is the essential ingredient of power. If such arrangements involve burning one's bridges to make the commitment look credible, this is one of the costs of power.[5] Examples abound in the literature in terms of strategic overinvestment by an incumbent firm to preempt or deter entry by competitors or predatory below-cost pricing to eliminate or deter rivals. If the necessary temporariness of price cutting by the predator is known to the prey, the latter's inability to wait it out ultimately turns on the differential access to capital of the predator and the prey. The extent of power flowing from precommitment or of its success in inducing timid behavior by rivals will depend on the slope of the reaction curves of the latter.

One of the main ways in which commitments in strategic environments are achieved is through reputation effects.[6] In recent models of dynamic games with incomplete information, reputation for "toughness" plays an important role, and a party's need to maintain its

---

5. Commitment through "bridge-burning" affects outside options, but what Muthoo (1999) calls "partial commitment" (public announcement of the set of bargaining outcomes that a player is willing to accept in the next stage of the game) affects the bargainer's inside options. It is clear that the more costly it is for a player to renege on a partial commitment (by deviating from the earlier announcement), the more favorable is that player's bargaining position.

6. As Thomas Hobbes (1904/1651, ch. 10, p. 54) points out in *Leviathan*, "Reputation of power, is power; because it draweth with it the adherence of those who need protection."

reputation for the future enforces precommitment. Aggressive pricing is often a part of reputation-building predation, and the imperfectly informed potential entrant makes inferences about the incumbent's type from the observed history of his predatory behavior. Power in this context ultimately flows from asymmetric access to information and capital. In the literature on sequential bargaining games with imperfect information, for example, a party can identify himself as a "stronger" player only by making offers and responses that he could not pay a "weaker" player to mimic. Attempts to establish "strength" in this way usually necessitate the "stronger" player's holding out for some time to achieve a settlement superior to an early agreement that his "weaker" counterpart would have reached.

In traditional cultures, sometimes a person's reputation for some kind of "irrationality" or blind adherence to social norms of retribution (following, say, the code of *onore* in Sicily or of *izzat* in Punjab) may enhance the power of a strongman by lending credibility to threats that would not be believable on the part of a "rational" agent. On the other hand, it may be noted that in small face-to-face village communities what anthropologists (like Bailey, 1971) call the "politics of reputation" may provide some modest measure of protection for the weak against the strong: as long as all parties belong to what is perceived to be the same "moral community" in terms of which the reputation is defined, there are some accepted limits and symbolic sanctions against the kind of ruthless exercises of power that are sometimes observed in the cut-throat aggressiveness of impersonal marketplaces. Such sanctions in the village context ultimately act toward what Pierre Bordieu (1971) has called the "euphemization of power" and the legitimization of compliance by the weak.

Uncertainties in the commitment process sometimes lead to what are called "wars of attrition." In a war of attrition, the two players engage in a waiting game, each delaying the transaction until one player gives in and agrees to transact according to her opponent's wishes. Each player prefers that her opponent be the first to concede, but both players suffer increasing losses by delaying the transaction. Thus we may associate the capacity to win a war of attrition with the willingness or capacity to suffer longer for the sake of victory, where victory connotes the implementation of one's own wishes instead of one's opponent's wishes. The central assumption is that each player in a war of attrition is uncertain of how long her opponent is willing or able to hold out for the sake of victory; this uncertainty rationalizes the use of delay tactics, as in its absence a weaker player would always find it rational to concede immediately to her tougher opponent.

Suppose that two players are to bargain over the partition of a pie.[7] Also, suppose that each player's utility is increasing in her share of the pie, and decreasing in the amount of time she must wait to receive any given share of the pie. The game begins when, at time 0, each player makes a partial commitment by announcing the minimum amount of pie that she will agree to accept. In the event that the pie is not large enough to accommodate both players' demands, the players enter into a war of attrition; this war of attrition continues until one player gives in by agreeing to accept less pie than what she had initially specified as her minimum demand (thus reneging on her partial commitment) to accommodate her opponent's initial demand. Since each player chooses her initial demand from a continuum of possible choices, there exists an infinite number of potential winner-loser payoff pairs in this model.

A player who concedes in this war of attrition suffers not only the indirect cost of reduced pie consumption (by agreeing to accept less pie than she had initially demanded) but also a direct cost from reneging on her partial commitment. What threatens to fuel a war of attrition is each player's uncertainty about both her opponent's and her own reneging costs. In this model, power flows to players who face a higher (realized) reneging cost. Intuitively, since these players receive a lower net benefit from concession (which requires reneging), they face a lower opportunity cost from remaining in the war of attrition.

---

7. Here we follow the exposition in Muthoo (1999). Drazen (2000) has an alternative exposition of the war of attrition that he applies to the problem of delay in fiscal stabilization. In Drazen's model the players do not have the option of sharing the responsibility of providing this public good (bearing the cost of fiscal stabilization), so either one or the other must incur the full responsibility. The two models differ in two important respects. First, while Drazen treats what is at stake in the war of attrition as exogenous (meaning that the static payoffs to winning or losing are prespecified), Muthoo treats this as endogenous. In particular, Muthoo assumes that each player forms her initial wishes regarding the details of the transaction after having learned some information about her opponent. This means that the players' initial wishes are endogenous in Muthoo's model; and since what is at stake in any war of attrition is defined by its participants' initial wishes, this too is endogenous in Muthoo's model. This first distinction between Muthoo's model and Drazen's model underlies the second major distinction between the two models: in Muthoo's model, *a war of attrition is averted in equilibrium*, as players are able to anticipate the outcome of a war of attrition accurately enough to make their initial wishes compatible with one another; in Drazen's model, a war of attrition is an unavoidable phenomenon.

In this model each player enters the game knowing the probability distribution for her opponent's reneging cost and the probability distribution for her own reneging cost, and these two probability distributions need not coincide. This implies that while the players are not fully informed at the partial-commitment stage, their information sets are symmetric. Consequently, we may interpret the partial-commitment stage as an opportunity for the two players to adjust the stakes of the game to reflect pertinent and shared beliefs about their particular economic environment. Muthoo (1999) shows that this added degree of freedom is enough to allow the players to avert the war of attrition in equilibrium: in equilibrium, each player makes a demand (through her partial commitment) that is commensurate with her ex ante expected likelihood of winning a war of attrition, and that is compatible with her opponent's demand; as a result, the pie is partitioned at time 0.

3.3

In a world of bounded rationality and asymmetric information, contracts that are necessarily incomplete and cannot possibly take into account all contingencies may transform even large-number competitive cases into power relations of bilateral trading. This is particularly the case when, as Williamson (1985) has emphasized, relation-specific investments (where investments have a much greater use inside the parties' relationship than outside) are large, and postcontractual opportunistic behavior is common. Once such relation-specific investments have been made, one party may "hold up" the other, and the ex post division of surplus may be out of alignment with ex ante decisions. In this division of surplus an agent's bargaining power will be sensitive, as Hart and Moore (1990) show, to who owns and controls the assets that the agent requires to be productive.[8]

---

8. There is a growing literature on corporate governance that deals with power (or authority) in the internal organization of a firm. The model of Aghion and Tirole (1997), for example, examines the relationship between the structure of information and the allocation of authority over a decision process in an organization. A distinction should be made between what this literature means by authority (in general, a type of economic power that is differentially *bestowed on* individuals, so that their interactions may better serve some exogenous and well-defined goal of organizational efficiency) and the type of economic power that exists for its own sake (in the sense that it need not be predicated by any outside objectives). Care needs to be exercised when speaking of "power" relations in the context of (optimized) "authority" relations.

In nonmarket transactions such hold-up problems may even take the form of extortion or blackmail. At this point it may be useful to distinguish between (a) monopoly power, (b) power of extortion or blackmail, and (c) power of robbing someone with threat of violence. The difference between extortion and robbery, following Liebermann and Syrquin (1983), is that in robbery there is an invasion of well-defined property rights, whereas in extortion no violence is involved but there is an abuse of rights implied in the threat to perform an otherwise legitimate act unless paid not to. The extortionist demands compensation (beyond his forgone income) for abstaining from doing something that he may be legally entitled to do—for example, making some information public or imposing some other unpleasant externality on a second party. If this eventuality was anticipated by the latter, contracts could have been designed ex ante to take this into account. But it is the incomplete nature of contracts that gives rise to the possibility of ex post extortion. As for the difference between monopoly and extortion, Demsetz (1972) claims that from the point of view of economic analysis extortion not involving violence does not differ from monopoly. But this is not quite correct. In a standard bilateral transaction with a monopolist (even a perfectly discriminating or "all-or-nothing" monopolist), one can refuse at no cost to take part in the proposed transaction, whereas in the case of extortion the victim's choice set actually shrinks: he would be better off if the extortionist were to disappear.[9]

Williamson (1985) rationalizes vertical integration of firms as an institutional device to reduce the scope of postcontractual opportunistic behavior by altering the claim structure from an arm's-length transaction to an internal one. But integration itself acts as a barrier to entry (more capital, for example, is required to enter the arena than at one production stage alone) and adds to market power of the firm (particularly when economies of scale are substantial). In the recent development literature, the institution of interlocking of transactions (in labor, credit, and land relations) has been similarly rationalized as a device to save transaction costs and to substitute for incomplete or nonexistent credit and insurance markets (see Bardhan, 1984, 1989). Again, such interlocking itself may act as a barrier to entry for third parties and be a source of additional monopoly power for the dominant partner (usually the employer, creditor, or landlord) in such transactions.

---

9. A proper formulation of this point should involve at least a two-period model. If the grounds for blackmail arose from the victim's own choices on an earlier occasion, there should be some discussion of why the chance of blackmail was not anticipated.

Interlinked contracts may also substitute for open nonlinear pricing (which may create socially unacceptable invidious distinctions) or as in the "commodity-bundling" literature, the landlord may "bundle" credit and labor transactions, for example, to discriminate between (and squeeze the surplus from) workers with differential credit needs. Personalized interlocking of labor commitments and credit transactions (involving selective exclusion of others) also divide the workers and emasculate their collective bargaining strength against employers, who use this as an instrument of control over the labor process.

Information asymmetry and agency costs, particularly the cost of surveillance over workers, are invoked by Bowles and Gintis in several papers (see, e.g., 1992) and also by Shapiro and Stiglitz (1984) to explain involuntary unemployment in competitive equilibrium whereby capitalists keep control over the labor process (thus providing microfoundations to Kalecki's view of unemployment as a worker discipline device). Because of the conflict of interest between employer and worker over work effort (the extraction of "labor power" from laborers), the wage rate offered by the competitive profit-maximizing employer has to exceed the market-clearing wage so that the threat of dismissal is a real one. As a result, some workers are rationed out of the job market (partly analogous to the case of credit-rationed borrowers in the credit market). The employer's or the lender's power (Bowles and Gintis call it "short-side power") is related to his favorable position in a nonclearing market. The location of agents to the short and long sides of markets and hence the locus of economic power in this case is not independent of access to resources; ultimately it is connected with the worker's lack of sufficient assets to provide bonds as a condition of employment—collaterals in the case of taking loans—and thus to reduce the costs of contract enforcement. In this model some workers are rationed out because all workers individually have *some* power (in the Simon-Dahl sense)—that of denying the capitalist their full work effort. To neutralize this power the capitalist resorts to the selective exclusion of some workers and the payment of wages at more than their opportunity cost to a coopted group of workers, who derive a strategic rent in the process. The unemployed are powerless to compete away this rent. This enforcement rent is what Harsanyi (1976) would call the "cost of power" for the capitalist.

The power of the worker to shirk is only one of a whole array of strategies of indirect power that the weak often have. Scott (1985), for example, has referred to numerous "everyday forms of peasant resistance"—footdragging, dissimulation, desertion, false compliance, pilfering, sabotage, and many other forms of Schweikian protest without confrontation.

In recent Marxist theoretical models in economics, two distinct forms of power relations have emerged: Roemer (1982) traces the primary locus of capitalist power in unequal distribution of property, whereas Bowles and Gintis trace it to the political structures of control and surveillance at the point of production, both referring to a competitive economy. Roemer reiterates the well-known Samuelsonian proposition that in a competitive model it does not matter whether capital hires labor or labor hires capital, with the important modification that in either case the wealthy "exploit" (take advantage of) the poor. To Bowles and Gintis, on the other hand, the locus of command in the production process is central to the functioning of the system. I find this distinction between domination in production and asset-based power somewhat overdrawn: who hires whom essentially depends on the capacity to bear risks, the wealthy having obviously a larger risk-bearing capacity.

A somewhat related discussion has taken place in the literature on the nature of the firm that followed Coase's classic (1937) paper. Coase argued that the key difference between an employer-employee relationship and a relationship between independent contractors is that an employer can tell an employee what to do but that one independent contractor must persuade another independent contractor to do what he wants through the use of prices. Alchian and Demsetz (1972) criticize this view, arguing that an employer typically cannot force an employee to do what he wants but can only ask him and fire the employee if he refuses, which is no different from one independent contractor "firing" another (quitting their relationship) if he is unhappy with the latter's performance. On this Hart and Moore (1990) have taken the more sensible position that B will put more weight on A's objectives if B is an employee of A working with assets owned by A than if B is an independent contractor working with his own assets. Authority over physical assets provided by ownership thus translates into authority over people.

Capitalist authority relations in the internal organization of the firm and the labor process are usually described by radical economists as organizational devices for exercising power. Transaction-cost theorists like Williamson vigorously contest this. They point to functions of authority as a governance structure that is useful in restraining "worker opportunism" and in facilitating adaptability to changing

circumstances (particularly in cases of assets that are not easily rede-
ployable) by vesting in the asset-owners the residual rights of discretionary control. But at the same time we should not ignore, as Dow
(1987) points out, that such discretionary control (along with hierarchy
and division of labor) generates the structural preconditions for "employer opportunism" by giving the employers strategic advantages of
information over their employees, the ability to use fiat to resolve conflicts in self-serving ways, the opportunity for unilateral introduction
of technical innovations that undercut the bargaining position of
workers, and so on. In any case, since transaction costs can be as difficult to define and quantify as power, in actual empirical or historical
analysis it may sometimes be hard to unscramble the effects of one
from the other. One can also look on some of the transaction costs as
Harsanyi's costs of power, as we have noted before.

In much of the discussion above, power has been traced to differential access to resources and information. In a recent literature on
conflicts and predatory behavior, Hirshleifer (1991), Skaperdas (1992),
Grossman and Kim (2000), and others have pointed to a paradoxical
aspect of the relationship between the ex ante distribution of productive resources and the ex post distribution of power in a world of
insecure property rights. If acquisition of power requires the use of
resources that could be otherwise used in production, resource-poor
individuals have more to gain from predation on the resource-rich
individuals (the opportunity costs of predatory activities on the part of
the latter are higher), and thus the equilibrium distribution of wealth
after the power struggle may be more equal than the ex ante distribution of wealth. But this "paradox of power," as Hirshleifer calls it,
depends on assumptions about the production process and the "technology" of transforming productive resources into effective weapons
of conflict. Grossman and Kim explicitly assume that resources make
one a better producer than a more effective predator. History, however, is replete with instances of resource-rich landlords and local oligarchs who use their comparative advantage in predatory activities,
such as extracting from small farmers (who are often more productive
than large farmers). Even apart from standard comparative-advantage
considerations, sheer increasing returns to scale in predation technology can explain why the resource-rich usually win power struggles.
As we discuss in chapter 2, in a poor village one landlord who owns
100 acres can be more powerful than fifty small farmers who own 2
acres each.

The discussion so far has also largely been confined to the framework of bilateral power relations. There are some interesting extra dimensions of power in triangular (or multiple) relations. In three-way relations it may be possible for the strong party (say, the landlord) to extract more surplus from the peasant than if they were involved in only a dyadic relation. Basu (1986) has constructed a model where the landlord can press the peasant even below the latter's reservation utility in the dyadic case by credibly threatening that, if the peasant does not accept his terms, he will refuse to employ him and also will influence the village merchant not to trade with him.[10] Similarly, the recent industrial-organization literature includes models of strategic contracts made with a third party by an incumbent firm to deter entry by a potential rival. In the model of Aghion and Bolton (1987), the third party is a customer with whom the firm signs long-term contracts to discourage entry by another seller. In the model of Dewatripont (1988), an incumbent firm facing potential entry signs labor contracts that commit it to excessive postentry output. In the context of international relations, Powell (1999) formulates triadic power relations where state 1 is able to leverage state 3's (perhaps begrudging) allegiance to coerce state 2 into positions it would not be willing to accept in a dyadic

---

10. In Basu's original (1986) model of triadic power relations, the Nash equilibrium with triadic coercion—in which the laborer, out of fear of being ostracized, chooses to work for a wage below his conventional (dyadic) reservation wage—is not a subgame perfect equilibrium. Such an equilibrium refers to the credibility of Nash equilibria, where all strategies are best responses to other strategies not only for the original game but also starting from any subgame that emanates from each of the nodes of the game tree in a sequential game situation. The landlord's threat to punish the merchant for transacting with the laborer is not credible, and as a result, his threat to ostracize the laborer (which rests on the credibility of the first threat) is also not credible. Basu (2000) corrects this problem in his updated version of the model by modeling the trade relationship between the landlord and the merchant as a simultaneous coordination game. This adjustment allows the landlord to make a credible threat *not* to cooperate with the merchant and thus lends subgame perfection to the triadic coercion equilibrium.

Naqvi and Wemhoner (1995) demonstrates that subgame perfection of the triadic coercion equilibrium can also be achieved by interpreting Basu's original model as the stage game of an infinitely repeated game. Building on the work of Naqvi and Wemhoner and also working within the context of an infinitely repeated game, Hatlebakk (2002) derives a modified version of the triadic coercion equilibrium. In his model, there exists a subgame perfect equilibrium in which the merchant receives a portion of the rents generated by the coercion-induced labor contract between the landlord and the laborer. Hatlebakk achieves this result by introducing an additional dimension of choice into the landlord-merchant relationship: the landlord and the merchant may choose not only whether to trade but also, if they choose to trade, whether to trade on "normal" terms or on terms that are more favorable *to the merchant*.

setting. These triadic relations can generate situations of "voluntary" transactions that still embody an exercise of power.

Akerlof (1984) has built models to show how the power of social custom (or that of the ruler over the ruled) may persist as a result of a mutually sustaining network of social sanctions when each (rational) individual conforms out of fear of loss of reputation (with third parties) from disobedience. In such a system potential members of a breakaway coalition fear that it is doomed to failure, and thus failure to challenge the power becomes a self-fulfilling prophecy. Kuran (1987) has a related model of collective conservatism (securing the power of an established ruler or custom) that is reinforced by the influence on an individual's private preference formation of the justifications others give for their public preferences for the status quo. In these models the presumption is that someone who does not sanction the nonconformist will himself be sanctioned by others. Elster (1989) has questioned the plausibility of this presumption when it is carried through the chain of interpersonal reactions: do people really frown on others when they fail to sanction people who fail to sanction people who fail to sanction people who fail to sanction a nonconformist?

3.4

Finally, the critique in the recent sociological literature of the behaviorist concept of power is quite applicable to its similar use in much of economics. Simon (1957) wrote: "For the assertion 'A has power over B,' we can substitute the assertion, 'A's behavior causes B's behavior.'" Dahl (1957) has also made an identical statement. This concept of power as an empirical regularity whereby the behavior of one agent causes the behavior of another is clearly limited. It does not distinguish between possession and exercise of power. It usually excludes, as Lukes (1977) has emphasized, agenda-setting power (where the powerful define the feasibility set in terms of which the agent's decisions are made and exclude potential options from the decision process). It misses pervasive instances of power taking the form of self-repression in anticipation of threats and of manipulation of perceptions and preferences of the powerless by the powerful. As Sen (1984, p. 30) has emphasized, "many of the inequities of the world survive by making allies out of the deprived and the abused." Since preferences themselves can be the effect of the exercise of power, Lukes suggests that "what B would otherwise do" can be properly gauged not by B's preferences but rather by B's interest. He then gives this definition of power: A exercises power over B when A affects B contrary to B's interest. But, even without going into the question of how to assess one's interest, one can say that a relation of power can also exist in the absence of a conflict of objective interests. The parent's power over children may be in the latter's best interest, but the relationship is not for that reason any less one of domination and subordination. The same situation arises in some patron-client relationships in development economics.

In game-theoretic terms an inclusive way of defining power may be to say that A has power over B if A has the capacity to alter the game (preferences, strategy sets, or information sets) in such a way that B's equilibrium outcome changes. But power is clearly what Morriss (1987) calls a "dispositional concept"—a capacity[11] that conceptually can stand by itself independently of any investigation of its structure (and should not, therefore, be identified with the latter as some structuralists and "realist" philosophers do) or of the empirical event of its exercise (which the behaviorists including most economists focus on). On the latter Morriss (1987, p. 16) says quite persuasively:

It is, of course, true that one cannot tell whether an actor is powerful unless some set of observations "attests to" his power. But there is no reason whatsoever why these observations should be of the actualization of that power. When I go to a zoo, I can see that a lion is powerful enough to eat me up by observing its jaws, teeth and muscles, and combining these observations with my general knowledge of animals' masticatory performances. If I am still in doubt, I can observe what the lion does to a hunk of meat, and induce. Not even the most dogmatic positivist would declare that he couldn't know if the lion could eat him up until it had actually done so.

Behaviorists want to be careful in not defining power as identical with the resources that give rise to it (wealth or knowledge is not power because the possessor may not use it fully or properly), but for the usual purposes for which we are interested in understanding power, defining power may not be as interesting as finding the source of power. Morriss talks about three such basic purposes of studying power: one is from the practical policy point of view (we want to know who has power because we want to get something done or prevent something from happening); the second is for attributing responsibility

---

11. Barry (1989) adds the qualification that while all power is ability, not all ability is power: the ability to get something if there is nobody stopping you from getting it is not a form of (social) power.

to actors for some outcome (here the definition of power as a capacity implies, as Morriss notes, that we are to be blamed for our acts of commission and omission, but not for having power); the third context is evaluative (when we judge the distribution of power in a social system). For all these purposes, there is no doubt that in reaching assessments of power, particularly economic power, the crucial evidence lies in socially structured relations rooted in differential access to assets and information (as suggested by many of the examples throughout this chapter), and also in skills and organizational capabilities (to effectively use those assets and information).

In this context radical economists and sociologists point their fingers in the right direction but are often methodologically careless. The concept of power is sometimes used by them in a question-begging way: differences in outcome are explained by blanket references to differences in the power of the dominant class or group without an independent quantification of the latter. What is more difficult than this quantification, however, is to provide a fine-tuned discriminating analysis of the diversity of detailed outcomes, selectivity of response, and transition from one mode of control to another, even in cases of similar access to assets and other resources. This failure of structural theories of power has led some scholars to a more careful specification of the context within which power is exercised and of the processes through which resources are converted into capabilities. But the danger in this focus on context is that it lifts the lid on a Pandora's box of intangible factors and makes measurement and generalization problematic. To avoid having descriptions take the place of explanations, the institutional conditions and the range of tactics that are most likely to result in a successful conversion of resources into power need to be specified in advance, and then predictions of systematic outcomes need to be empirically tested.

4

Political Economy and Credible Commitment: A Review

Economic costs often arise from an agent's inability to make credible commitments to future actions. These costs may arise either in the form of missed opportunities or in the form of costs to gain insurance against broken promises. For example, the inability of potential partners to bind themselves from filing future lawsuits against one another may lead them to forgo the partnership altogether (a missed opportunity) or to incur legal fees to draft a prior agreement (an insurance cost). Our focus in this chapter is on problems of credible commitment in political-economic interactions.

Let us have a general preview of the different issues and models that we go over in this chapter. We begin by reviewing a number of issues pertaining to the problem of credible commitment from the state to the public. In this context, the problem of credible commitment surrounds the state's commitment to refrain from various types of future intervention that can damage incentives today. We first describe two well-known instances of the problem in practice: the state's commitment to exercise restraint in monetary policy, and the state's commitment to refrain from either bailing out failed enterprises or expropriating the returns of successful ones. We then turn to some potential mechanisms that can lend credibility to the state. These fall into two inter-related categories: reputational mechanisms and institutional mechanisms. Our focus falls on the often overlooked tradeoffs of costs and benefits that these mechanisms introduce.

We then turn to the problem of credible commitment surrounding adoption of economic reforms. First, we consider barriers to reform arising from a lack of credible commitment from the public to the state. In this context, the problem of credible commitment arises from the tendency of economic reforms to generate political instability. Because the public cannot credibly commit to retain incumbent rulers, these incumbent rulers may attempt to block reforms that threaten their hold on power. Next, we turn to barriers to reform arising from a lack of credible commitment between different segments of the public at large. In this context, the problem of credible commitment arises from the tendency of economic reforms to yield unequal benefits. A reform may generate net gains, but those who stand to lose from the reform may choose to block it unless they receive credible promises of compensation from those who stand to gain from the reform. We begin with the simple case in which incentives to block reform arise from fear of pure economic losses. We then consider the more interesting case in which incentives to block reform are driven by political considerations, and can arise even among agents who stand to gain economically from reform.

Let us start with a general formulation of the credible commitment problem. At time 1, an agent A has the opportunity to perform an action, X_A, and will perform that action if and only if he expects another agent, B, to perform an action X_B at time 2. Agent B would like agent A to perform X_A, and therefore agent B would like to commit at time 1 to perform X_B at time 2. However, once agent A has performed X_A at time 1, agent B can secure a windfall at time 2 by choosing to perform an action other than X_B. Agent A anticipates this and therefore chooses rationally not to perform X_A.

A variety of commitment problems fit this general form. It is possible, for example, that agents A and B are the same individual, albeit with time-inconsistent preferences: in this case, the problem of credible commitment may take the form of a problem of self-control. Alternatively, agents A and B may be two different agents with conflicting preferences, where agent B has something to gain at agent A's expense: a predatory state (agent B) would like to promise to honor the property rights of an entrepreneur (agent A) who faces an investment opportunity at time 1; however, the entrepreneur anticipates that the state will prefer to confiscate his wealth once the investment has matured and therefore chooses rationally not to invest. In this case, the problem of credible commitment is strategic in nature: the party bearing the burden of commitment is hampered by the fact that he is known to have a strategic incentive to mislead the other agent. However, the party bearing the burden of commitment in a strategic setting need not be out to fleece the other agent and may in fact be motivated by what he perceives to be the best interests of the other agent. Finally, let us note that in many instances, problems of credible commitment in a strategic context may be reduced to problems of credible commitment in a self-control context. Specifically, in instances where agent B is worse off in the time-consistent equilibrium than he would be if he could credibly commit to agent A, agent B may be interpreted to face a self-control problem.

The first two parts of this chapter examine "vertical" problems of credible commitment between the state and agents at large. The first part examines vertical problems of credible commitment in which the burden of commitment lies with the state. We shall outline two particular contexts in which problems of credible commitment by the state can play a role, and then proceed to discuss a number of possible solutions, with a focus on solutions of an institutional nature. The second part of this chapter examines a particular example of vertical commitment problem in which the burden of commitment lies with agents at large rather than with the state. In particular, we shall consider some problems that arise from the inability of agents at large to commit to reward a predatory state for adopting socially desirable reforms. The third part of this chapter examines "horizontal" problems of credible commitment among agents at large, and in particular, credible commitment as a barrier to reform in a democratic decision-making context. Reflecting the literature we have reviewed with respect to this third topic, our focus will be on describing variations of the problem rather than on investigating possible solutions.

The distinction between "vertical" (between the state and agents at large) and "horizontal" (among agents at large) commitment problems is made for the sake of giving a simple structure to the exposition. In practice, these two forms of commitment problems might often overlap. In fact, credible commitments among agents at large might often be unnecessary if the state was able to make credible commitments; we need to look no further than the use of money in private transactions for an example. This is a general point worth bearing in mind throughout this discussion of horizontal commitment problems that threaten reform.

4.1 Credible Commitment by the State to the Public

One context for credible commitment by the state that has been studied extensively in the literature involves the problem of time consistency in monetary policy. The standard formulation of the problem begins with the premise that a positive causal relationship exists between unexpected inflation and aggregate output in the macroeconomy. Wage setters from among the public at large negotiate labor contracts that set the growth rate of nominal wages equal to the expected rate of inflation. A socially minded policy maker knows that a relationship holds between unexpected inflation and output and sets monetary policy to strike an optimal tradeoff between his dual goals of controlling inflation and stimulating output. But wage setters anticipate the policy maker's decision rule and therefore raise their inflationary expectations to the point that expected inflation equals the actual inflation rate set by the optimizing policy maker. In equilibrium, the policy maker is unable to stimulate output, while inflation is needlessly high. Since the policy maker cannot fulfill his output goal, he would be better off if he could simply commit to a low inflation target. But in the absence of the appropriate commitment devices, the policy maker's promise to pursue low inflation is not credible: once wage setters have informed their inflationary expectations based on a commitment by the policy maker, the policy maker will have an incentive to renege on his promise to stimulate output.

A second context for credible commitment by the state that has received attention in the literature is broader in scope and involves the state's role in fostering efficient markets. Existing arguments pertaining to this topic generally begin with the observation that efficient markets can emerge only out of a setting in which market participants (agents at large) expect their economic rewards to reflect accurately enough their productive contributions. In this vein, Qian and Weingast (1997) distinguish between the "positive" and "negative" incentives that the state must promote through credible commitments. "Positive" incentives emerge out of agents' expectations that economic success will be rewarded, requiring the state to make credible commitments to enforce agents' property rights (for example, by credibly committing to resist the temptation to tax away gains achieved through entrepreneurship). "Negative" incentives emerge out of agents' expectations that economic failure will be punished, requiring the state to make credible commitments to refrain from offering assistance to unproductive agents in certain instances (for example, by credibly committing to refuse refinancing to unproductive state firms).

Commitments by the state to reward success may be problematic for a number of reasons, including the existence of predatory incentives for the state. Dixit and Londregan (1995) provide an example in which the credible-commitment problem arises not from predatory intent per se but from electoral incentives to redistribute wealth. In their model, certain agents at large have the opportunity to relocate out of their current stagnating industries and into more highly productive industries. Agents who choose to relocate must incur an upfront moving cost but achieve subsequent productivity gains that generate comparatively larger payoffs over the long run. As a result, agents will make the efficient choice to relocate so long as they expect to command a sufficiently large share of the ensuing stream of returns. Agents must decide whether to relocate at time 1. At time 2, two political parties compete in an election. Each party cares only about maximizing its own popularity among all agents at large, and each campaigns on the basis of a proposed policy of redistribution that it designs for this purpose. While each party would like to encourage efficient relocation at time 1, political promises made at this stage are not credible. Once any given agent has incurred the cost to relocate, each party's vote-maximizing strategy is to redistribute his newly created wealth to other voters. Agents contemplating relocation anticipate this and therefore choose rationally not to relocate. The no-relocation equilibrium in this model is conceptually similar to the low-investment equilibrium arising out of models in which a predatory state creates a threat of expropriation. The only difference is that the expropriation threat in this model derives from the seemingly more benign incentive of competing political parties to please the majority interest.

Solutions to Problems of Credible Commitment by the State

In the context of an infinitely repeated game setting, a *reputational solution* may exist to many problems of credible commitment by the state. With respect to the time-consistency problem in monetary policy, Barro and Gordon (1983) have shown that a low-inflation equilibrium can potentially be sustained if the wage setters adopt the following trigger-punishment strategy. If the policy maker has never reneged on a commitment to implement a low-inflation policy, then the wage setters set the growth rate of nominal wages over the ensuing period to match the rate of inflation announced by the policy maker. If the policy maker defects at any point in time, then the wage setters disregard all future announcements by the policy maker, and the economy reverts to its high-inflation, time-consistent equilibrium. Whether a low-inflation equilibrium may be enforced through reputational considerations is therefore determined by the policy maker's discount factor. If his discount factor is sufficiently low, he will always succumb to the temptation to defect, rendering commitment infeasible; conversely, if his discount factor is sufficiently high, the benefit from defection is small relative to cost of the punishment, and his policy commitments will be credible.

Alternatively, problems of credible commitment by the state may be resolved with the aid of *institutional solutions*. In this vein, Buchanan (1987) has argued for the usefulness of a conceptual distinction between two stages of the policy-making process: a first stage involves the design of constitutions or the setting up of the basic institutions of policy making (the stage that sees the "design of the game"), and a second stage involves the strategic actions of individuals and policy makers operating within the constraints of these institutions (the stage that sees the "play of the game"). In the context of this view, an institutional mechanism directed toward any desired policy outcome may be interpreted as a set of constraints that is initially the object of political choice at the "design stage" but that must be subsequently respected by all agents who are making choices over the course of the "game stage."

Institutional solutions to problems of credible commitment by the state might involve direct controls over the behavior of policy makers through constitutional writ or rules and regulations imposed through legislation. With regard to the credible-commitment problem in monetary policy, examples of such direct controls include k-percent monetary-growth rules, which place a hard ceiling on the policy maker's use of expansionary monetary policy, and fixed exchange-rate regimes, which force the policy maker to trade off her output goals against the need to maintain the exchange rate. Institutional solutions might also impose indirect controls over the behavior of policy makers by setting up systems of delegation or separation of powers. Again with regard to the credible-commitment problem in monetary policy, the most commonly proposed institutional solution of this sort involves delegation of monetary authority to an independent central banker whose distaste for inflation is more intense than that of the government (Rogoff, 1985).

With regard to the dual credible-commitment problems that underscore the state's ability to foster efficient markets—committing to reward success and committing to punish failure—it has been argued that federalism provides an effective institutional solution. In chapter 6 a critique of the models of fiscal federalism in the context of developing countries is discussed. But here let us briefly note the main argument for federalism in the matter of credible commitment. The essence of the argument is that federalism helps to discipline the government as a whole by fostering various forms of intragovernmental competition among subunits. This is most clearly illustrated by arguments about the efficiency effects that arise out of interjurisdictional competition among local governments to attract mobile capital. The basic claim is that to attract and retain resources that may be relocated at their owners' discretion, local governments must establish reputations as relative safe havens for those resources. As Qian and Roland (1998) demonstrate, interjurisdictional competition for mobile resources may lend credibility to commitments by the state to punish failure, insofar as that responsibility lies with local governments. They examine the soft budget-constraint problem in a setting where capital is mobile and fiscal policy is fully decentralized.

Setting aside local governments, federalism might also help to discipline the central government's behavior. Two of the main arguments in this context involve the effects of decentralized control over economic regulation. A first argument interprets regulatory decentralization as a means of tying the central government's hands from engaging in various commitment-undermining acts of ex post intervention. Qian and Weingast (1997) articulate the issue in terms of access to information. They argue that when local governments are charged with the responsibility to oversee and police the economic activities of agents and firms within their respective jurisdictions, the central government loses its access to crucial information about the outcomes or various other details of those activities. This works to raise the transaction costs associated with intervention by the central government and therefore has a hands-tying effect that lends itself to credible commitment. A second argument for decentralized control of economic regulation is that a decentralized system may prevent established interests from using their political clout to bring about national controls designed to thwart entry. In this vein, Weingast (1995) cites Root's (1994) argument that a significant part of the difference in growth rates between England and France during the Industrial Revolution may be traced to the countries' contrasting legal responses to the locational decisions of newly emerging enterprises. Whereas French royal courts upheld the claims of French guilds that rural production ought to be regulated, members of the English Parliament and many English justices of the peace refused to extend guild restrictions to the countryside, a decision that opened the door to new industrial activities and anticipated

England's impressive economic growth over that period. Root explains England's resistance to centralized regulation by citing a number of historical circumstances, among them the Glorious Revolution of 1688 to 1689, which tended to relieve English representatives from the burden of demonstrating allegiance to the crown and therefore freed them to pursue policies aimed at local prosperity rather than alternatives that may have been more popular at large.

Complications

Going back to the Buchanan dichotomy between political choices at the "design stage" and the "game stage," securing desired policy outcomes in general and overcoming problems of credible commitment by the state in particular might be seen as purely a matter of getting the institutions right at the design stage. The following five issues highlight the incompleteness of this view.

Credible Commitment to Institutions   So long as it is at least *feasible* to change the rules of the game after they have been set in place, institutional solutions to problems of credible commitment are themselves subject to problems of credible commitment. After all, the introduction of institutional constraints to limit the behavior of policy makers acts, in essence, to shift the burden of commitment away from the policy maker (who must keep his word) and to the institution (which must uphold its own rules). As Dixit (2001, p. 4) observes, "Constitutions themselves can be amended, albeit at a high cost of political effort; legislation that implements the intent of the constitution in specific policy institutions is more easily changeable. For example, the U.S. Federal Reserve is widely regarded as an independent central bank, but it is the creation of an act of Congress, and can be forced to modify its behavior or even dissolved by a future Congress."

   To the extent that the costs associated with their undoing are strictly finite, institutional solutions to problems of credible commitment would appear to be rather tenuous in a stochastic world. And even if the world was not stochastic, it would be difficult at first blush to understand what lends any fortitude to certain types of institutional arrangements based on delegation, such as the one described in the Dixit passage, in which the policy maker whose authority has been taken away (Congress) retains the right to either fire and replace the agent to whom authority has been delegated (the Fed) or simply reclaim authority for himself. By definition, delegation affects credible commitment if and only if the preferences of the two parties differ. But if their preferences differ, the policy maker will at some point desire to reclaim authority or, alternatively, to dismiss the agent and then "fish" for replacements until it finds one more to his liking. Yet another option for the policy maker is to retain the agent but use the threat of dismissal to bend the agent to its will.

Given the tenuous nature of solutions to credible commitment based solely on institutional norms, Lohmann (1998) and others have argued that effective institutional solutions must have reputational under-pinnings: if the rules of the game are to be respected, then there needs to be some reputational cost to changing the rules at one's discretion. But as Lohmann observes, this presents an apparent paradox. For if reputation-based credibility is feasible, then institutional solutions to credible commitment would seem to be unnecessary. She writes (1998, p. 12), in the context of the credible-commitment problem in monetary policy, that "institutional solutions are based on the implicit assumption that the policymaker cannot credibly commit herself to a future path of monetary policy, whereas credible commitments to respect institutional constraints are feasible." And later,

If the political discount factor is low, then credible commitments are infeasible. In this case there is no obvious credibility differential between policy and institutional promises: the temptation to renege on the promise to adhere to a pre-specified future path of monetary policy is, after all, equal to the temptation of defecting, *ex post*, from a central banking institution that implements that same monetary policy rule.

Nevertheless, in Lohmann's view, institutions may still matter insofar as they are reinforced by (rather than seek to replace) reputational con-siderations, in the sense outlined above: *provided that certain institu-tional constraints have already been laid down at the design stage*, there exists a reputational cost to policy makers who are operating at the game stage to violate those constraints, and therefore institutional con-straints can have some bite.

The literature on federalism has also taken up the question of what lends credibility to federalism as an institutional solution or what makes federalism "self-sustaining," in the terminology of that litera-ture. The general objective of this literature is to understand what sus-tains the necessarily delicate balance of power between the central and local levels of government, each of which must be at once sufficiently strong to carry out its own duties and yet also not strong enough to overwhelm the authority of the other. De Figueiredo and Weingast (1997) describe the problem as the two fundamental dilemmas of federalism. First, what prevents the national government from destroying federalism by overwhelming its constituent units? And second, what prevents the constituent units from undermining federalism by free-riding and otherwise failing to cooperate? As they observe, resolving these dual dilemmas is problematic due to the fact that efforts to solve either one tend to exacerbate the other: placing stronger constraints on the national government in an effort to mitigate the first dilemma usually weakens the constraints on the constituent units, exacerbating the second dilemma; on the other hand, stronger constraints on the constituent units, usually imposed by the national government, risks exacerbating the first dilemma.

According to de Figueiredo and Weingast, federalism may be sustained as the equilibrium outcome of a conflict of interests between the central and local governments. But the existence of this equilibrium depends, first, on the central government having access to sufficient resources to police shirking by local governments, and second, on the ability of local governments to police abuses by the central government and retaliate in concert against abuses. With respect to the second condition, Weingast (1998) points to the importance of institutions that lent themselves to a self-enforcing balance between state and national authority in the antebellum United States. How far these institutions are reproducible in developing countries is debatable.

The Myth of the Pristine Design Stage   Dixit (1996, 2001) has argued that while the Buchanan dichotomy is useful for conceptually distinguishing between the design of rules and the play of the game, reality is likely to span a continuum between the two categories. In particular, he argues that it is unrealistic to suppose that institutional reforms are ever conducted in a pristine setting that is uncluttered by special interests and unhindered by problems of information asymmetry. Dixit likens Buchanan's conception of the design stage to a sort of big-bang moment with respect to the evolution of information, at which time there is a great amount of uncertainty but also perfect symmetry of information. In such a setting, it is conceivable that optimal reforms could be agreed on by all players. But Dixit argues that most institutional reforms are attempted at a later, "interim" stage of information evolution, by which time information has begun to disseminate in an asymmetric fashion: players know something about themselves and what they stand to gain or lose from any given reform, but they hold this information privately. In the presence of these information asymmetries, feasible reforms must satisfy an array of incentive compatibility and participation constraints that would not yet have emerged at Buchanan's pristine design stage. Moreover, satisfying these constraints becomes an increasingly tall order as information asymmetries grow more pronounced.

Credibility versus Flexibility   In a stochastic world featuring uncertainty at the commitment stage, efforts to achieve credibility may come at the cost of a loss of flexibility in the face of emerging information. This is true not only for institutional solutions to credible commitment but for reputational solutions as well. As Manin, Przeworski, and Stokes (1999a) point out, politicians have a stake in their future credibility. Even when voters believe that a politician has reneged on a promise in a way that was beneficial for them, they will discount future promises from that politician. As a result, politicians may have an incentive to continue to champion policies to which they have committed themselves even when comparatively more desirable policy choices reveal themselves ex post. Thus while reputation may constitute a means to an end (credibility), in some instances reputational considerations take on a life of their own—when reputation becomes an end in itself.

The tradeoff between credibility and flexibility has also been taken up in the literature on the time-consistency problem in monetary policy: delegating authority to a conservative central banker may help to lower inflation but also ties the government's hands in the face of extreme negative shocks to output (Rogoff, 1985; Lohmann, 1992, 1998). Lohmann argues that under most realistic conditions, the credibility-flexibility tradeoff implies that a rational government will always want to maintain some discretion in the event of certain unforeseen contingencies and will therefore never choose to tie its hands completely. In light of this, she takes issue with the dichotomous view of political commitments as being either strictly credible or strictly not credible and argues that many commitments are partial, where the degree of institutional commitment varies continuously with the cost incurred by the political principal in the event of a defection. With regard to monetary policy, Lohmann (1992) models partial commitment through the existence of costly escape options for the government. In normal times, monetary policy is set at the discretion of a central banker appointed by the government. But when (and only when) large output shocks hit, the government takes advantage of an escape clause that allows it to override the central banker's authority if he fails to respond strongly enough. Lohmann works out the conditions under which this institutional arrangement leads to an optimal tradeoff between inflation stabilization and policy responsiveness. She argues, therefore, that the observation that the central bank occasionally accommodates inflationary political pressures does not necessarily imply that the political commitment to the central banking institution is an empty promise.

Other Limits to Reputation This discussion of reputation-based solutions to credible commitment has so far implicitly assumed that, in the absence of external shocks or other sources of uncertainty, the reputational mechanism should be either able to sustain the first-best outcome or not. That is, the set of possible outcomes is assumed to contain just two elements: the efficient outcome and the time-consistent outcome. The model of Acemoglu (2002), however, allows for a continuum of outcomes to be sustained by reputational considerations. The primary message is that promises that are underpinned by reputational considerations may be able to sustain outcomes that are superior to the time-consistent outcome but generally fall short of achieving the efficient outcome.

The model is fairly technical, but the intuition behind its central result pertaining to our current purpose is simple. Consider an infinitely repeated game between two players—the state and a representative agent. In every period, the agent can choose to participate in either a market sector or a nonmarket sector and selects how much effort to invest in production activity in its chosen sector. Production in the market sector is more efficient than in the nonmarket sector but is subject to discretionary taxation by the state at the end of the period (after all the agent's costs are sunk). Conditional on the agent choosing to participate in the market sector, the state's dominant strategy in the stage game is to grab everything. As a result, the only time-consistent equilibrium involves the agent choosing to produce in the inefficient nonmarket sector.

Outcomes superior to the time-consistent one can generally be sustained with the aid of trigger strategies in the infinitely repeated version of the stage game. In particular, the state can promise to limit its taxation to some specified level conditional on the agent engaging in market production at some specified effort level, with the mutual understanding that any attempt by the state to extract additional taxes will trigger a reversion to the stage-game equilibrium. Under this arrangement, an equilibrium featuring production in the efficient market sector can be sustained so long as the distribution of payoffs satisfies both the individual-rationality constraint of the agent (meaning that the agent is at least as well off as it is under nonmarket production) and the incentive-compatibility constraint of the state (meaning that the state prefers the discounted incremental benefits of cooperation relative to the status quo over the one-time payoff from grabbing everything today).

Intuitively, for any given level of agent effort in the market sector, the individual-rationality constraint of the agent is satisfied for all tax rates up to some T_{max}, while the incentive-compatibility constraint of the state is satisfied for all tax rates greater than some T_{min}. And so long as $T_{max} > T_{min}$, there exists a tax level to sustain market production. However, the spread between T_{max} and T_{min} depends on the specified effort level of the agent: as agent effort rises, T_{max} and T_{min} rise at different rates. The reason for this is that the state's incentive-compatibility constraint (T_{min}) depends only on output, while the agent's individual-rationality constraint (T_{max}) depends on the difference between output and the cost of effort. Acemoglu shows that, as a result, in instances where the first-best effort level cannot be sustained through trigger strategies (because the maximum tax rate that makes that effort level individually rational for the agent is too low to prevent the state from succumbing to the temptation to grab everything today), market production can generally be sustained by adopting a less-than-efficient effort level.

While the particular results of the Acemoglu model are sensitive to model specification, they provide a broader message about the limits of reputation-based mechanisms in overcoming problems of credible commitment. Because reality is likely to span a continuum of possible outcomes rather than a simple (first-best, time-consistent) dichotomy, reputational (as well as other) solutions to credible commitments might be more usefully evaluated on the basis of "how well" they are able to overcome inherent problems of time consistency rather than "whether or not" they are able to do so. In this vein, the Acemoglu model demonstrates that the incentive-compatibility constraints of agents facing the burden of commitment may place limits on the extent of cooperation that can be sustained by informal, reputation-based norms. The first-best outcome (optimal agent effort in the market sector) might be easily sustained in the Acemoglu model with the introduction of additional enforcement mechanisms to complement reputation—for example, a fine or other punishment that can be levied by the public against the state when infractions occur. We might therefore think of the suboptimality of equilibrium-effort choices in the Acemoglu model as a necessary enforcement cost that sometimes emerges due to the absence of those other enforcement mechanisms.

Accountability of the State   A final concern addressed here regarding institutional solutions to credible commitment by the state is the issue of the state's accountability. The literature does not have much of a discussion on formal mechanisms for explaining the potential trade-off between commitment and accountability. The term *accountability* is used here in a particular and fairly straightforward sense, defined below. But what exactly is meant by accountability is an issue in itself. As Manin, Przeworski, and Stokes (1999b) observe, the terms *responsiveness*, *responsibility*, *representation*, and *accountability* have been used by different scholars to describe the same or similar concepts.

Elster (1999) proposes a concept of accountability based on a formal triadic structure: "an agent A is accountable *to* a principal B *for* an action X." Accountability of A to B for X, however it is precisely defined, is generally perceived to be a desirable feature from the perspective of the principal whose agent is accountable; this perception is implicitly adopted here. However, even this is open to theoretical debate. For while it is clear that there are costs to the agent and benefits to the principal associated with the agent becoming "more accountable," costs to the principal and benefits to the agent may also arise (Elster gives some examples). An agent may also in theory benefit from the fact that he will be held accountable if he deviates from the preferred policy of the principal. As Ferejohn (1999) demonstrates, increasing the degree of accountability in an agency contract can increase the power of the agent if it induces the principal to trust him with more resources. While the concept of accountability can thus be complex, let us agree to adopt the following definition, proposed by Manin, Przeworski, and Stokes (1999b): *governments are "accountable" if citizens can discern representative from unrepresentative governments and can sanction them appropriately, retaining in office those who perform well and ousting from office those who do not.*[1]

Persson, Roland, and Tabellini (1997) argue that the separation of powers and the checks and balances that characterize many liberal democracies combine to provide an effective institutional solution to problems of accountability. In this view elected officials may have access to two types of rents at the expense of the public. The first type arises from power between elections. Since elections occur at discrete intervals, the public is in general constrained to delay in disciplining transgressions. Moreover, when politicians value reelection for the sole purpose of retaining access to political rents, the public may be forced to tolerate (rationally) some positive amount of rent extraction by elected officials between elections. The reason is that, if intertemporally optimizing elected officials expect to be dismissed for extracting even a small amount of rent, then they will willingly forgo access to future rents to extract everything that they possibly can today. In other words, the promise of future rents from office may be needed to discipline the behavior of elected officials today. Based on our definition above, the state may therefore fail to be accountable because citizens are constrained in their ability to sanction. The second type of rent available to elected officials arises from the fact that they are often better informed than the public about the merits and precise consequences of alternative policy choices. Based on the definition of *accountability* given above, the state may therefore fail to be accountable because citizens cannot accurately discern whether the state is acting in its interests. In the model of Persson and his coauthors, a separation of budgetary powers between an executive and a legislative branch of

---

1. What exactly constitutes a government that is "representative" rather than "unrepresentative" is in itself an open question. Manin, Przeworski, and Stokes (1999b, p. 2) summarize some of the complexities involved:

Defining representation as acting in the interest of the represented provides a minimal core conception, one on which a number of more specific theories converge. It is compatible with a wide variety of views about what representing implies, depending on how the notion of the interests of the represented is interpreted. People holding the view that a government is representative if it acts on the wishes of voters may agree with our minimal definition on the grounds that the interests of the represented can be taken to mean what the represented themselves see as their interests. But the minimal conception stated here is also compatible with the view that a government is representative if it does what according to its own judgment is in the best interest of citizens. Similarly, our definition of representation does not entail a position on whether the representative should do what voters want him to do at the time a policy is adopted or should adopt the policy that voters would approve in retrospect.

government creates a conflict of interests that serves to limit the state's ability to extract both of these types of rents. The following discussion is based closely on their model.

Suppose that at the end of every period t of an infinitely repeated game, the public at large obtains a level of consumption equal to

$$c_t = \theta_t(1 - x_t),$$

where θ_t is a stochastic and nonnegative productivity parameter, and x_t describes the *aggregate* amount of public resources that has been appropriated by the government as a whole (both the executive and the legislature combined) in that period. The public's only governance mechanism is an election held at the end of each period, at which time it may either remove or reelect members of either of the two branches of government. This means that the public has no direct control over x_t ex ante. Political candidates are homogeneous, so the public realizes that removal of any given official will lead to his or her being replaced by another official with identical characteristics and incentives. Finally, the public cares only about maximizing the present discounted value of its consumption, while government officials care only about maximizing the present discounted value of their appropriated income.

In the event that x_t was controlled by a single governmental decision maker, the government would enjoy rents stemming from power between elections for the reason outlined before: if the public does not tolerate a high-enough value of x_t through its decision rule concerning reelection, the incumbent will always find it in his or her best interests to appropriate everything today ($x_t = 1$). Moreover, in the event that the public cannot observe θ_t, it will be unable to discern whether low observed levels of consumption c_t are attributable to low realizations of θ_t or to high levels of appropriation x_t—creating an opportunity for the government to extract informational rents as well.

An alternative budgetary process features a separation of powers between an executive and a legislature. Suppose that in each period, the two branches of government collectively determine the government's aggregate level of appropriation x_t through the following three-stage process. At the start of the period, the executive proposes to the legislature a level of x_t. Next, the legislature responds with a take-it-or-leave-it offer to the executive outlining how that total budget will be allocated between the two branches. In the final stage, the executive may choose to either approve or reject the legislature's proposal. If the two branches fail to reach an agreement (that is, if the executive exercises its veto power), then total governmental appropriation is limited to some status-quo amount x^{SQ}, of which each branch receives a pre-specified share.

The model has two primary results. To see the first result, assume that the public is able to observe the productivity parameter θ_t—meaning that it may deduce x_t by observing c_t—but that it cannot discern how x_t has been allocated between the executive and the legislature. In the second stage of the budget process, the legislature has received the executive's budget proposal and must form its own proposal concerning the allocation of spending. Because the executive will receive a status-quo payoff if he or she chooses to veto the legislature's proposed allocation of spending, the legislature has no reason to offer the executive anything in excess of the status-quo payoff in a take-it-or-leave-it offer. The executive anticipates this at the first stage of the process and therefore finds no reason to propose a budget greater than the sum of the two branches' status-quo payoffs—for if the budget exceeds this level, the legislature will act as the residual claimant while the executive will have to share in the political costs. All of this assumes that the public chooses to reelect the existing regime when it appropriates at the status-quo level. However, there may also exist equilibria in which the equilibrium level of appropriation is kept at some level strictly less than the status quo: so long as their reservation utilities are sufficiently low, politicians may, if facing the appropriate reelection criteria, prefer to collect an infinite stream of less than status-quo payoffs by remaining in office rather than grab their one-period status-quo payoffs and lose office.

To see the model's second result, assume that only members of the government are able to observe θ_t, so that informational rents are available for the taking. Under the following scenario, the equilibrium of the political game described above may nevertheless continue to obtain. Suppose that at the beginning of each period, each branch of government is required to make an independent announcement to the public concerning the value of θ_t. As Persson and his coauthors argue, this announcement stage may be interpreted as a required public report—such as a State of the Union address or a Senate hearing—or, alternatively, as a preliminary public debate, during which the legislature and the executive make some assessment of exogenous circumstances or of the policy consequences. Given the budgetary process, the public may exploit this announcement stage to gain information.

Specifically, suppose that the public adopts a voting rule that conditions reelection of both the legislature and the executive on the executive's announcement. For example, suppose that the public reelects both incumbents if and only if

$$c_t \geq \theta_t^{\mathrm{E}}(1 - x^{\mathrm{SQ}}),$$

where θ_t^{E} denotes the executive's claim concerning the value of θ_t. It is easy to see why this voting rule eliminates any incentives of the executive to mislead the public by reporting some $\theta_t^{\mathrm{E}} < \theta_t$. Since the executive will be offered his status-quo payoff by the legislature in any event, a report of $\theta_t^{\mathrm{E}} < \theta_t$ serves only to line the pockets of the legislature, which is again the residual claimant with respect to any rents generated by duping the public. Therefore, the executive is indifferent between lying and truth telling, and there exists an equilibrium identical to the one described before. By the same logic discussed above, equilibria featuring less than status-quo appropriation may also be sustainable under the right conditions.

The results of the Persson, Roland, and Tabellini model rest on three important assumptions. The first is that the two branches of government behave uncooperatively. If collusion was possible, or equivalently, if the legislature could credibly commit to reward the executive for setting large budgets, then the two branches could conceivably achieve significantly higher levels of appropriation in equilibrium. It seems important to keep the possibility of collusion in mind, especially since the potential gains to collusion are the highest precisely in those instances where separation of powers is, in theory, most likely to curtail predation and since, at the same time, there is no obvious reason to suspect that the costs of collusion would be higher in those instances than in others. A second important assumption is that there is no common pool problem in the budgetary process. Persson and his coauthors acknowledge this and demonstrate that their results unravel when each of the two governmental branches is assumed to have some discretion to access public funds without the other's approval. In chapter 10 some issues related to the common-pool problem in fiscal policy are discussed. Let us simply note here that collusion between governmental entities has the promise to be welfare-enhancing in the context of the common-pool problem, unlike in the context of separation of powers without common pool. A third assumption of the model, which is actually a series of assumptions, involves the nature of the budgetary process. For example, there is no direct bargaining between the governmental branches at any stage. Perhaps more important, the public is well informed about how the policy process works, including its timing, the capabilities and responsibilities of each branch of government at every stage, and the precise functional form of an equation mapping government transgressions onto observed outcomes (even if one parameter may be unobservable). All of this lends itself to a situation in which the public is well prepared to discern representative from unrepresentative governments, as stated in my definition of governmental accountability.

Whether the public is more informationally advantaged in the Persson, Roland, and Tabellini model than it is in reality dictates is a matter of interpretation. However, to get a flavor of some potential misgivings, consider the following two passages cited by Manin, Przeworski, and Stokes (1999a). First, Alexander Hamilton (1961/1788, p. 455) writes in *Federalist* no. 70:

But one of the weightiest objections to a plurality in the executive ... is that it tends to conceal faults and destroy responsibility.... The circumstances which may have led to any national miscarriage or misfortune are sometimes so complicated that there are a number of actors who have different degrees and kinds of agency, though we may clearly see upon the whole that there has been mismanagement, yet it may be impractible to pronounce whose account the evil which may have been incurred is truly chargeable.

And Bagehot (1992, p. 67) writes:

Two clever men never exactly agree about a budget.... They are sure to quarrel, and the result is sure to satisfy neither. And when the taxes do not yield as they were expected to yield, who is responsible? Very likely the secretary of the treasury could not persuade the chairman—very likely the chairman could not persuade his committee—very likely the committee could not persuade the assembly. Whom, then, can you punish—whom can you abolish—when your taxes run short?

Thus separation of powers creates a multiplicity of suspects for any observed governmental transgression, given that the policy process is somewhat opaque. Moreover, as Bagehot suggests, when politicians have a stake in preserving that opaqueness or even in muddying the process further, separation of powers may grant them with certain woeful means toward that end. Taking the logic one step further, suppose that when a transgression has occurred and the public is unable to make out the identity of the specific offender in a decentralized government, the public assigns blame uniformly across all units. In this event, a portion of the political cost to bad behavior is externalized and is increasingly so as the number of potential suspects rises. The implications for the resulting equilibrium outcome would seem rather bleak.

Hamilton's description of "a number of actors who have different degrees and kinds of agency" within the state leads us to a final point with respect to accountability of the state. Manin, Przeworski, and Stokes (1999b) argue that any account of modern government must consider not only roles played by the traditional branches of government as outlined by Montesquieu 250 years ago but also the role of the nonelected bureaucracy employed by government. Are nonelected officials agents of the people or of the government? And if they are agents of the government, are they responsible to the executive that employs them or to the legislature that funds them? As Manin, Przeworski, and Stokes observe, it is not even clear how we should think of the bureaucracy in the context of the principal-agent relationship of the public and the state.

4.2   The State as a Barrier to Economic Reform

The discussion thus far has considered problems of credible commitment between the state and agents at large in which the burden of commitment lies with the state. The following two models examine a particular context in which the burden of commitment might instead lie with agents at large: state-controlled reform. In both models, reform is economically beneficial but politically destabilizing. A central theme is the tradeoff that incumbent rulers face between economic incentives that favor reform and political incentives that favor protection of the status quo: economic reform promises to increase the intertemporal stream of rents to be divided between the state and agents at large but also threatens to loosen the grip of political incumbents over future rents. As a result, political incumbents with the power to block economic reform may choose to do so if agents at large cannot commit to reward them with a sufficient share of the fruits from reform.

In Acemoglu and Robinson (2000), political control is initially in the hands of a powerful monopolist that is able to tax agents at large according to its discretion. A potential rival has access to a superior industrial technology, and it is up to the monopolist to permit or block the rival's entry. The monopolist is enticed to permit entry, as it will increase aggregate economic productivity and therefore provide the monopolist with a larger tax base. However, the monopolist faces a risk that its political power will be eroded by the rival's entry. Loosely, the monopolist faces a tradeoff between allowing the economic pie to grow in size and securing its grasp over a large enough share of the given pie. When the second consideration dominates the first, the monopolist finds it optimal to block entry. Acemoglu and Robinson describe an interesting application for their model, suggesting that it may help to explain the wide cross-country variance in the attitudes of landed aristocracy in response to the rise of capitalism in nineteenth-century Europe. Their hypothesis is that landed interests opposed the rise of manufacturing in countries where their political power was seriously threatened by the prospect of an emerging industrial sector, as in Russia and Austria-Hungary, but welcomed it in countries where their political interests were relatively more safeguarded, as in Britain and Germany.

Acemoglu and Robinson (2002) incorporate this intuition into a more fully developed model that places the option of ruler replacement in the hands of agents at large. They consider an infinitely repeated game, with the timing of the stage game as follows:

1. The period starts with agents at large capable of producing an amount A_t.

2. An incumbent ruler decides whether to (costlessly) adopt an economic reform. If he chooses yes, then agents at large can produce αA_t instead of A_t, where $\alpha > 1$.

3. The stochastic cost of replacing the existing ruler with an identical counterpart is revealed. If the incumbent ruler has not adopted reform, the cost of replacing him is zA_t. If the ruler has adopted reform, the cost of replacement is $z'A_t$. Observing either z or z', agents at large decide whether to replace the incumbent ruler.

4. If a new ruler is chosen, he or she chooses whether to adopt reform.

5. The ruler in power decides on a tax rate and consumes those tax revenues.

Without going into too much technical detail, let us attempt to sketch out the model's logic. The incumbent ruler contemplating reform at time 2 bases his decision on the options he expects to be available to agents at time 3. A critical assumption is that if the incumbent ruler chooses at time 2 to adopt economic reform, he lowers the expected cost to agents at time 3 of replacing him with a new ruler—that is, the expected value of z' is less than the expected value of z.

Thus the economic benefits of reform (for both agents at large and the ruler that is in power at time 5) are paired with a political cost to the ruler that is in power at time 2. A ruler who adopts reform at time 2 increases the likelihood that he will be replaced before the end of the stage game and therefore be stripped of his access to rents from future periods.

Note that if agents choose to replace the incumbent ruler with a new ruler, the new ruler will always choose to adopt reform at time 4. The new ruler has nothing to lose politically and something to gain economically from adopting reform in the current stage game. Therefore, at time 3, agents at large will choose to replace an incumbent who *has not* adopted reform if and only if $z < \alpha - 1$ and will choose to replace an incumbent ruler who *has* adopted reform if and only if $z' < 0$. As a result, and moving back to time 2, the incumbent will choose to adopt reform if and only if his continuation value under the status quo multiplied by the probability that $z < \alpha - 1$ exceeds his continuation value under reform multiplied by the probability that $z' < 0$.

Acemoglu and Robinson assume that z', the political replacement cost after reform, is distributed uniformly over $[\mu - 0.5, \mu + 0.5]$, while z, the political replacement cost under the status quo, is distributed uniformly over $[\gamma\mu - 0.5, \gamma\mu + 0.5]$, where $\gamma > 1$ (note that z or z' may take negative values, in which case the incumbent is always replaced). The model's key result revolves around the parameters γ and μ. First, reform is always discouraged when γ is higher. This is intuitive, since a higher γ increases the security of the ruler in the absence of reform or, equivalently, implies a greater erosion of the ruler's entrenchment conditional on reform. Next consider the parameter μ. Because μ affects the extent of the incumbent ruler's political entrenchment (the cost of replacing him) regardless of whether reform is adopted, Acemoglu and Robinson interpret μ as a measure of the degree of political competition.

For illustrative purposes, suppose first that $\mu = 0$ (the case of "fierce political competition"). In this case, the expected values of both z and z' are equal to zero, implying that the incumbent can gain no political advantage over a potential replacement by blocking reform. At the same time, the incumbent ruler recognizes that he will very likely be replaced if he does not adopt reform (since $z < \alpha - 1$ with high likelihood). Acemoglu and Robinson show that these two considerations combine to ensure that the incumbent ruler will always adopt reform for sufficiently low values of μ. Next, suppose that $\mu > 0.5$ (the case of "minimal political competition"). In this case, the incumbent ruler recognizes that his position will be secure even if he chooses to adopt reform (since $z' < 0$ with zero likelihood) and therefore has nothing to lose politically, and something to gain economically, by adopting reform. Acemoglu and Robinson show that this consideration ensures that the incumbent ruler will always adopt reform for sufficiently high values of μ. Loosely, in the first case (fierce political competition) the incumbent adopts reform for mainly political purposes, and in the second case (minimal political competition) the incumbent adopts reform for mainly economic purposes. Put differently, the state will choose to adopt reform when the political costs of *not adopting* reform are extremely high and when the political costs of *adopting* reform are extremely low.

The situation is different for intermediate values of μ: provided that γ is sufficiently large in value, it is in this parameter range that the offsetting political and economic considerations of the incumbent ruler may lead him to block reform. Acemoglu and Robinson therefore suggest that whenever the choice to adopt or not adopt reform is in the hands of the state, political incentives to block reform are most likely to dominate economic considerations in settings of moderate political competition. In these settings, the state is neither disciplined to adopt reform by the severe political consequences of not doing so nor free to embrace the economic benefits of reform without political consequence. Clearly, in instances where the incumbent finds it optimal to block reform in the Acemoglu and Robinson model, Pareto improvements could be achieved if agents at large could somehow commit at time 2 to refrain from exercising their right to replace the incumbent at time 3.

4.3 Credible Commitment among Agents at Large: Reform and Redistributive Politics

In this part, we review some issues that arise out of a setting in which the distribution of returns accruing to certain actions that must be undertaken by agents at large today depends on the outcome of a democratic voting process to be conducted at some point in the future. Because the timing of the political game prevents agents today from securing their preferred policy choices pertaining to distributional outcomes in the future, many types of decisions that are rational in the context of political economic considerations may diverge from those that are efficient in a purely economic sense. The problem is described succinctly by Besley and Coate (1998, p. 153): "preferences over policy extend to the future, but political control does not."

Our focus will be on a particular example of the general problem described above, in which agents at large have the opportunity to adopt a prospective reform. The prospective reform exhibits the following three properties. First, every agent knows that the reform will generate positive returns on aggregate, second, every agent knows that the reform will generate a distribution of private returns which favors some agents more than others, and third (an assumption that will be relaxed later) every agent knows the identities of who stands to gain, who stands to lose, as well as by how much each agent stands to gain or lose. In this type of setting, implementation of the reform may require patterns of ex post redistribution that are anticipated ex ante to be difficult or impossible to implement politically. As a result, "non-investment" in the reform may emerge as a political economic equilibrium despite the fact that a Pareto improvement would be obtained through investment and the appropriate subsequent transfers. In the simplest case, the reform generates absolute winners and losers and is impeded by a dyadic conflict of interests between the two groups: the prospective losers will support the reform only if they expect to be suitably compensated after the fact by the winners, but the winners cannot credibly commit ex ante to support such postreform redistributive policies ex post. A more interesting case involves a situation in which the reform generates only relative winners and losers and all agents stand to gain economically from it. Working within this latter framework, even agents who stand to benefit economically from a reform may find political incentives to oppose it. This result illustrates a more general incongruence between the purely economic and political-economic definitions of winners and losers of reform.

Let us begin with the model of Besley and Coate (1998), the economy lasts for two periods and is composed of many heterogeneous agents that differ according to their productivity levels. The median voter at the beginning of each period determines that period's redistributive policy, which specifies a tax rate and a minimum consumption guarantee for all agents in the economy. In addition, voting in the first period determines whether the economy undertakes a public investment. There is no intertemporal borrowing, so fiscal spending in each period must be fully financed by that period's tax receipts. It is understood that public investment in the first period will increase the economy's aggregate productivity in the second period to the extent that the social return to public investment is unambiguously positive. However, public investment yields individual-specific benefits in the second period and is expected to raise the productivity of some agents more than that of others.

Two mechanisms in the Besley and Coate model threaten to deter public investment. To highlight the first mechanism, suppose that absent redistribution in the second period, public investment generates absolute winners and losers. It is easy to see why the prospective losers in this type of setting may be dissuaded from supporting public investment: prospective winners have no way to credibly commit to support any redistributive policies in the second period other than those that best suit their own interests at that point in time. As a result, the prospective losers recognize that they will secure the future compensation that is necessary to make public investment worthwhile for them privately if and only if the second-period policy is to be controlled by an agent who shares their preferences. To take a simple example, suppose that the economy is composed of n agents who are divided into equal numbers of low- and high-productivity types and that each group has a 50 percent chance in each period of having one of its own elected to direct redistributive policy. Suppose, in addition, that public investment costs an amount C and will increase the second-period productivity of high types only—say, by an amount g per high type agent. In the second period, if a high type is elected to direct second-period redistributive policy, then she will choose zero taxation (and the zero redistribution that it implies) irrespective of the first-period public-investment decision. On the other hand, a low type who is elected in the second period will always choose 100 percent taxation (and a resulting uniform distribution of wealth). Moving backward to the first period, it is clear that a low type, if elected, will again always choose 100 percent taxation. The only question is whether he will undertake the public investment. We know that he will do so if and only if the expected gain in second-period consumption, which is equal to $g/4$ (the likelihood of a low type being elected in the second period, 0.5, multiplied by the gain in per-capita consumption generated by the high type's increased productivity, $g/2$), exceeds the cost in first-period consumption, C/N. This constitutes a more stringent standard than the socially efficient one, which dictates public investment conditional on $g/2 \geq C/N$. The emphasis here is on the manner in which the risk of losing political control to agents with opposing preferences may

dissuade agents who are in power today from undertaking investments to improve the economy's long-term aggregate welfare.

To highlight the second mechanism that threatens to deter public investment in the Besley and Coate model, consider the more interesting
case in which, absent redistribution in the second period, public investment yields private benefits for all agents in the economy. In other
words, suppose that the distinction between winners and losers is now
merely a relative one. The central result will be that certain types of
agents may nevertheless find it optimal to oppose public investment
in this type of setting because of how public investment threatens to
change the existing distribution of *preferences over policy*. First, suppose
that the economy again contains high and low types but that it now
also contains a third group of middle types *where no single group of
agents composes a winning majority on its own*. Next, suppose that public investment promises to raise the second-period productivity of all
three types of agents but that it will benefit the middle types to such an
extent that they will find it optimal to shift their political allegiance
from the low types to the high types. Finally, to keep matters simple,
assume that the middle types prefer zero taxation in the second period
conditional on public investment having taken place in the first period
and that they prefer 100 percent taxation otherwise. Given this setup,
the low types will oppose public investment so long as their consumption under the status-quo full-redistribution equilibrium exceeds their
own-produced consumption in a zero-redistribution equilibrium that
does feature public investment. The intuition is quite simple. All else
equal, the low types would prefer to see public investment take place
in the first period due to its promise of private gains in the second
period. But all else is not equal in a political-economic context, and the
low types must contend with how their first-period choices will help
to determine the future balance of political power, in general, and the
majority preference for redistribution, in particular. In certain instances, to access their private gains from public investment will require that the low types incur a comparatively larger cost stemming
from their loss of future control over redistributive policy. Simply put,
agents must contend with both the direct economic effects as well as
the indirect political economic effects of any proposed reform in this
type of setting.

In general, it is not clear a priori whether opposition to a reform of
the type considered here is to come from the relative losers or winners
from the action. Even in this simple example, with a few minor adjust-

ments, opposition to the public investment could very well come from a group that stands to gain the most in both relative and absolute terms economically. For example, suppose that the middle types initially align with the high types politically so that zero redistribution obtains in the status-quo political equilibrium. Now suppose that the middle types stand to benefit to such a large extent from the public investment that they will become the new high types and that the old high types will respond by shifting their political allegiance to the low types. In this case, public investment will lead to a new full redistribution political equilibrium in the second period. For a range of parameter values, the middle types will be able to secure a higher level of second-period consumption by preserving the status quo, even though they stand to "win" in both relative and absolute economic terms from the public investment. To take this analysis one last step further, support for a prospective reform may come from agents who actually stand to lose in absolute economic terms from the reform. Again employing a simple example, suppose that the middle types now align with the high types conditional on public investment having taken place but that the high types now stand to lose in absolute economic terms from public investment. The high types may nevertheless support public investment if they expect these losses to be more than offset by gains associated with a move from full to zero redistribution. A general lesson to take away from all of this is that patterns of support for a given proposed action may be predicated as much on who gains and loses politically as on who gains and loses in a purely economic sense. As a result, any discussion of the conflict of interests between the "winners" and "losers" of a proposed action needs to specify what is meant by those two terms.

That incentives to either gain or retain political influence can motivate agents at large to oppose policies from which they themselves apparently stand to benefit is a theme echoed in Acemoglu and Robinson (2001), who examine the persistence of inefficient *methods* of redistribution in the context of a voting model. More specifically, they are interested in explaining why agents who are in a position to receive subsidies in any case are often observed to support particular methods of redistribution that appear to make everybody (including themselves) worse off. In their model, agents who are incumbent to a flagging sector of the economy may lobby for compensation in the form of either lump-sum transfers or price subsidies. While lump-sum transfers are nondistortionary, price subsidies reduce the economy's aggregate productivity by distorting the occupational choices of new entrants to the labor market. In addition, because price subsidies induce new entrants to the flagging sector, they force the incumbents to share a fixed amount of compensation with a larger pool of claimants. But precisely this labor-market-distorting feature of price subsidies makes them an attractive instrument of redistribution from the perspective of agents in the flagging sector: because price subsidies induce entry by new labor-market participants into the flagging sector *instead of* into alternative sectors of the economy, they help prevent the flagging sector from losing ground politically to other sectors and therefore help to maintain or build the flagging sector's political influence over redistributive policies to be determined in the future.

Let us consider the model is slightly more detail. The economy consists of a low-productivity sector (farming) and a high-productivity sector (manufacturing). As in the model of Besley and Coate (1983), the economy lasts for two periods, and a vote conducted at the beginning of each period determines redistributive policy for that period. Redistribution takes the form of a simple head tax on manufacturers that is used to finance compensation for farmers. Acemoglu and Robinson (2001) assume a reduced-form voting process, in which the head tax levied on manufacturers is simply an increasing function of the fraction of farmers in the population. But the important, more general assumption here is that political influence is an increasing function of group size. Each of the two sectors starts off (at time zero) with an exogenously determined number of incumbent agents, and these incumbents are assumed to be locked into their respective industries for the duration of the model. However, over the course of the first period, new agents join the economy and may choose to enter either sector.

The head tax placed on manufacturers may be used to finance one of two types of compensation for farmers, according to the farmers' wishes: either lump-sum transfers to *existing* farmers (that is, agents who are farmers at the time of each vote) or price subsidies for the farming sector in general. So in the first period, lump-sum transfers accrue only to incumbent farmers, while price subsidies extend also to agents who enter the farming sector in the interim (before the end of the first period). Given this setup, incumbents to the farming sector face a critical tradeoff when deciding whether to request transfers or price subsidies in the first period. Requesting transfers rather than price subsidies will lead to an unambiguous increase in their first-period consumption, since it allows the incumbents to appropriate the full first-period tax base for their own use rather than share it with new entrants to the farming sector. In addition, by allowing new labor-market participants to make the efficient choice to enter into the manufacturing sector, the incumbents may increase the size of the potential tax base to be used for second-period redistribution, which exerts a positive effect on second-period consumption for farmers. However, pursuit of this strategy (requesting transfers rather than price subsidies) will allow the manufacturing sector to grow in relative size over the course of the first period (via the socially efficient occupational choices of new entrants), which reduces the political influence of the farming sector over second-period redistributive politics and therefore exerts a negative effect on second-period consumption for farmers. For a range of parameter values, this last political economic consideration dominates the first two purely economic considerations, and incumbent farmers will choose rationally to lend their support to price subsidies in the first period. Notice that what matters to the incumbent farmers is not simply the welfare afforded by farming in absolute terms but also the welfare afforded by farming in relation to the welfare afforded by manufacturing, as the latter is the pertinent comparison for new entrants. Also, it sould be clear that the incentive for incumbent farmers to pursue distortionary subsidies would disappear—and the economy could obtain a Pareto improvement—if there existed mechanisms through which incumbent farmers could be guaranteed a certain level of second-period compensation.

Finally, Fernandez and Rodrik (1991) consider a prospective reform that is similar to the one discussed at the beginning of the previous section, for which there are absolute winners and losers, with the important exception that the winners' and losers' identities are not revealed until after the reform has been adopted. They study trade reform in a two-sector economy. If a trade liberalization is approved by majority vote, then real wages will fall in the first sector and rise in the second sector. Agents in the first sector can move into the second sector by incurring an individual-specific switching cost, but only the distribution of these costs is known at the time of the vote that determines whether the reform is to be adopted. In other words, some of the agents who are deciding whether to support a reform know their private returns from supporting it (those in the second sector), while the others are left to make an educated guess (those in the first sector). Given this setup, the principal result of the Fernandez and Rodrik model is that under certain conditions a reform that will eventually benefit a majority of agents ex post will be nevertheless opposed by a majority of rational agents ex ante.[2]

To clarify the issues at hand, first consider the following baseline example (see Drazen, 2000). Suppose that a large number of identical agents are contemplating adoption of a policy change. The policy change carries a per-capita cost of c and promises to generate a distribution of consumption gains across all agents in the economy, where x_i is the consumption gain accruing to agent i. Agents must decide on the policy knowing only the distribution of x_i. Assume that the representative agent will favor the policy change if and only if $E[u(x_i)] \geq c$, where $u(\cdot)$ is an individual agent's utility function. Further, since all agents are identical and have access to the same information, the policy change will be either unanimously opposed or unanimously supported. This is an important result that should be emphasized: in the presence of initial uncertainty across identical agents, there is a nonconvexity introduced by a system of majority voting; namely, small differences in the distribution of benefits accruing to a proposed reform may translate into either 100 percent support or 100 percent rejection of the reform. As is shown below, this result lies at the heart of the Fernandez and Rodrik model. But to close this baseline example, let us simply observe that socially desirable policy changes involving $E[x_i] \geq c$ will always be adopted when agents are risk-neutral, whereas certain socially desirable policy changes will not be adopted when agents are risk-averse.

Because Fernandez and Rodrik assume that a segment of the population stands to benefit from the policy change with certainty (those incumbent to the second sector), nonadoption of socially desirable policy changes may obtain even if the segment of the population facing uncertain returns is composed of risk-neutral agents. Specifically, provided that the segment of the population that stands to benefit with certainty contains strictly less than half of the total population, the median voter will belong to the group facing uncertain returns. However, this median voter will not represent the median preferences of the economy as a whole but will instead act as a representative agent

---

2. Even when (unlike in the Fernandez-Rodrik model) the government is allowed the ability to tax the winners to compensate the losers, Jain and Mukand (2003) show that reforms may still not be enacted if, under individual-specific uncertainty about the outcome of reform, the incumbent fears not only that it will turn out to be a loser but that the new government will be drawn from the ranks of winners, with no incentive to make compensatory transfers.

to the group facing uncertain returns. Using a numerical example, suppose that 60 percent of agents in the economy belong to some sector A and face the uncertain return x_i described above, while the remaining 40 percent belong to some sector B and face a certain return $y > c$. Further, suppose that x_i equals $1.5c$ with probability one-half and equals 0 otherwise. So $E[x_i] = 0.75c$, and all agents in sector A oppose the policy change. In this case, the policy change will receive only 40 percent popular support (the agents in sector B) even though everyone expects it to benefit 70 percent of the population (the agents in sector B plus half the agents in sector A).

5   Democracy and Poverty: The Peculiar Case of India

5.1

In the previous chapter we discussed the issue of accountability in connection with the theoretical literature in political economy on credible commitment. In this and the subsequent chapter, issues of accountability are examined largely in the empirical context of developing countries. This chapter begins with some mechanisms of accountability in a large functioning democracy (like India) and their relationship with the lives of poor people. To most theorists of democracy, India is an embarrassing anomaly and hence largely avoided. By most theoretical stipulations, India should not have survived as a democracy: it is too poor, its citizens are largely rural and uneducated, and its civic institutions are weak. Yet this country, with the world's largest electorate, keeps lumbering on decade after decade as a ramshackle, yet remarkably resilient, democratic polity. Bardhan (1987) offers an hypothesis about this survival as being rooted less in deep liberal values widely subscribed to by the citizenry and more in the functional value of democracy as an accepted mode of transactional negotiations among contending groups in an extremely heterogeneous society. In this chapter, however, we do not discuss this hypothesis any further; our intention is more to chart the *effects* of democracy on poverty and inequality in this large poor country with a view to gleaning some general ideas about the complex relationship between democracy and poverty.

A large empirical literature has tried to find a statistical relation between some measures of democracy and development[1] on the basis of cross-country regressions. I have in general found this empirical

---

1. This literature takes the narrow instrumental view of democracy, as does this chapter, not the broader concept of "development as freedom" used by Sen (1999).

literature unhelpful and unpersuasive. It is unhelpful because usually it does not give us much of a clue into the mechanisms through which democracy may help or hinder the process of development. It is generally unpersuasive because many of the studies are beset with serious methodological problems (like endogeneity of political regimes to economic performance, selection bias from the survival of particular regimes, and omitted variables) and the usual problems of data quality and comparability. My attempt here is to follow instead more old-fashioned methods of comparative-institutional analysis to understand the mechanisms involved. The focus is on contemporary India, and occasionally the discussion contrasts the development experiences in East Asia (which has been largely authoritarian in much of the last quarter of a century) and in largely democratic India. Over this period average economic performance, both in terms of reduction of consumption poverty and improvement in social indicators like literacy and longevity, has been substantially better in East Asia than in India. Yet it is possible to argue that authoritarianism may have been neither necessary nor sufficient for fostering the institutional mechanisms behind the differential economic performance. This chapter begins to probe the relationship (or the lack of it) between these mechanisms and the nature of political regime in a way that goes beyond a simple cross-country aggregative statistical correlation.

We should also mention that although in our subsequent analysis we shall not try to define democracy with any great precision, it is useful to keep a distinction between three aspects of democracy: basic minimum civil and political rights enjoyed by citizens, procedures of accountability in day-to-day administration under some overarching constitutional rules of the game, and periodic exercises in electoral representativeness. These aspects are of varying strength in different democracies, particularly in the few developing countries where democracy has been sustained over some period. A few authoritarian countries may display some degree of administrative accountability at certain levels of government and may also have periodic renewals through acclamatory or referendum-style elections. India's performance over the last half a century has been impressive in terms of elections (some electoral malpractices notwithstanding), but its performance in civil rights and accountability have been somewhat mixed, satisfactory in some respects but not in others, and as we'll comment below, there are some signs of accumulating tension between the participatory aspects of Indian democracy and its procedural aspects. Of course, different parts of India have had varying successes in these different aspects of democracy.[2]

5.2

The historical origins of democracy in India are sharply different in at least five ways from those in much of the West, and these differences are reflected in the current functioning of democracy in India, making it difficult to fit the Indian case to the canonical cases in the usual theories of democracy:

1. While in Europe democratic rights were won through continuous battles against aristocratic privileges and arbitrary powers of absolute monarchs, in India these battles were fought by a coalition of groups in an otherwise fractured society against the colonial masters. Even though part of the freedom struggle was associated with ongoing social movements to win land rights for peasants against the landed oligarchy, the dominant theme was to fight colonialism. In this fight, particularly under the leadership of Mohandas Gandhi, disparate groups were forged together to fight a common external enemy, and this required strenuous methods of consensus building and conflict management (rather than resolution) through coopting dissent and selective buyouts. Long before Independence, the Congress Party operated on consensual rather than majoritarian principles. The various methods of group bargaining, subsidies, and "reservations" for different social and economic categories that are common practice in India today can be traced to this history.

2. Unlike in western Europe, democracy came to India before any substantial industrial transformation of a predominantly rural economy and before literacy was widespread. This influenced the modes of political organization and mobilization, the nature of political discourse, and the excessive economic demands on the state. The democratic (and redistributive) aspirations of newly mobilized groups outstripped the surplus-generating capacity of the economy, and demand overloads sometimes even short-circuited the surplus-generation process itself.

3. In the West the power of the state was gradually hemmed in by a civil society dense with interest-based associations. In India groups are

2. For an account of the differing degrees of democracy within India, with high marks for Kerala, see Heller (2000).

based more on ethnic and other identities (caste, religion, language, and so on), although the exigencies of electoral politics have somewhat reshaped the boundaries of (and ways of aggregating) these identity groups. This has meant a much larger emphasis on group rights than on individual rights.[3] A perceived slight of a particular group (in, say, the speech or behavior of a political leader from another group) usually causes much more of a public uproar than crass violations of individual civil rights, even when many people across different groups suffer from the latter. The issues that catch public imagination are the group demands for preferential treatment (like reservation of public-sector jobs) and protection against unfavorable treatment. This is not surprising in a country where the self-assertion of hitherto subordinate groups in an extremely hierarchical society takes primarily the form of a quest for group dignity and protected group niches in public jobs.[4]

4. In Western history expansion of democracy gradually limited the power of the state. In India, on the other hand, democratic expansion has often meant an increase in the power of the state. The subordinate groups often appeal to the state for protection and relief. With the decline of hierarchical authority in the villages and with the moral and political environment of age-old deference to community norms changing, the state has moved into the institutional vacuum thus left in the social space. For example, shortly after Independence, popular demands for land-reform legislation (for rent control, security of tenure, and abolition of revenue intermediaries), however tardy and shallow those laws may have been in implementation, brought the state to the remotest corners of village society. In more recent days, with the progress of the state-supported Green Revolution (in loans, tubewells, fertilizers, seeds, agricultural extension, land records, and so on), the state is implicated in the texture of everyday village life in myriad ways. As hitherto backward groups capture state power with the advantage of numbers in electoral politics, they are not too keen to weaken it or to give up the loaves and fishes of office and the elaborate

---

3. One of the early leaders who carried in him the tension between individual and group rights was B. R. Ambedkar, who was a constitutional lawyer and a founding father of the Indian Constitution and also a major spokesperson for an oppressed caste group.

4. One of the triumphant slogans of the Bahujan Samaj Party (BSP), a major party mobilizing the historically oppressed low castes in North India, is "Vote se lenge PM/CM, arakshan se SP/DM" (We'll take the offices of prime minister and chief minister through votes; we'll take through reservation the offices of superintendent of police and district magistrate).

network of patronage and subsidies that come with state power.[5] This serves as a major political block to the recent (largely elite-driven) attempts at economic liberalization. Some of the new social groups coming to power have even suggested that all these years upper classes and castes have looted the state and that now it is their turn. If in the process they trample on some individual rights or some procedural aspects of democratic administration, the institutions that are supposed to restrain them are relatively weak.

5. By constitutional design, India differs from classical U.S. federalism in some essential features. The federal government in India more powerful than the states in many respects (including the power to dismiss state governments in extreme cases and to reconstitute new states out of an existing state in response to movements for regional autonomy) and has more obligation (through mandated fiscal transfers) to help out poor regions. In classical federalism the emphasis is on restraining the federal government through checks and balances; in India the emphasis is more on regional redistribution and political integration. Stepan (1999) has made a useful distinction between the "coming-together federalism" of the United States (where previously sovereign polities gave up a part of their sovereignty for efficiency gains from resource pooling and a common market) and the "holding-together federalism" of multinational democracies like India (where compensating transfers keep the contending nationalities together and where economic integration of regional markets is a distant goal, largely unachieved even in more than fifty years of federalism).

Given these social and historical differences in the evolution of democracy in India, its impact on poverty has been complex. The rest of this chapter delineates some of these complexities and brings out some of their general implications for the effects of democracy in a comparative-institutional framework.

5.3

In the history of western democracies, extension of the franchise has been associated with welfare measures for the poor. In recent data for a large number of countries, cross-country regressions have found a

---

5. In some sense this is familiar in the history of American municipal politics in big cities when one after another hitherto disadvantaged ethnic group captures the city administration and distributes patronage.

positive association between democracy and some human-development indicators (Przeworski, Alvarez, Cheibub, and Limongi, 2000) (relevant largely for the poor) or incomes of the lowest quintile of income distribution (Lundberg and Squire, 1999). (In the appendix to chapter 1 we have also found a positive association between political rights and human-development indicators.) After more than a half century of democracy in India, the percentage of people living below the poverty line has declined significantly, but India remains the largest single-country contributor to the pool of the world's extremely poor, illiterate people. Although antipoverty programs constitute a substantial part of the budgets of federal and state governments, it is widely noted that a large part of these funds do not reach the poor.

On the other hand, democracy has clearly brought about a kind of social revolution in India. It has spread out to the remote reaches of this far-flung country in ever-widening circles of political awareness and self-assertion of hitherto subordinate groups. These groups have increased faith in the efficacy of the political system, and they vigorously participate in larger numbers in the electoral process. In the National Election Study carried out by the Centre for the Study of Developing Societies, the percentage of respondents who answered positively to the question "Do you think your vote has an effect on how things are run in this country?" went up between 1971 and 1996 from 45.7 percent to 57.6 percent for "backward-caste" groups (designated as OBC—"other backward classes"—in India), from 42.2 percent to 60.3 percent for the lowest castes (designated as "scheduled castes"), from 49.9 percent to 60.3 percent for Muslims, and from 48.4 percent to 58.7 percent for all groups taken together (Yadav, 2000).

Yet this faith in the efficacy of the political system is inadequately translated into concrete economic progress for the median member of the poor disadvantaged groups. Let us explore this particular disjuncture between economics and politics in India a bit further. Endemic poverty is widely regarded among common people as a complex phenomenon with multiple causes, and they ascribe only limited responsibility to the government in this matter. The measures of government performance are rather noisy, particularly in a world of illiteracy and low levels of civic organization and formal communication on public issues. As indicated above, a perceived slight in the speech of a political leader felt by a particular ethnic group will usually cause much more of an uproar than if the same leader's policy neglect keeps thousands of children severely malnourished in the same ethnic group.[6] The same issue of group dignity comes up in the case of reservation of public-sector jobs for backward groups, which, as we have said before, fervently catches the public imagination of such groups, even though the overwhelming majority of the people in these groups have no chance of ever landing those jobs, as they and their children largely drop out of school by the fifth grade. Even when these public-sector job quotas help mainly the tiny elite in backward groups, they serve as symbols and possible objects of aspiration for their children and therefore perform a valuable function in attempts at group upliftment.

Particularly in North India the emerging lower-caste political groups seem to be preoccupied with symbolic victories. As Hasan (2000) points out with reference to BSP (Bahujan Samaj Party), a politically successful party of the oppressed in Uttar Pradesh, these groups seem less concerned about changing the economic-structural constraints under which most people in their community live and toil. Maybe this is just a matter of time. These social and political changes have come to North India rather late; in South India, where such changes took place several decades back, it may not be a coincidence that there has been a lot more effective performance in the matter of public expenditures on pro-poor projects like health, education, housing and drinking water. This reflects the fact that in South India there has been a long history of social movement against the exclusion of lower castes from the public sphere, and the attempts to improve their education and social status have been more sustained and broad-based than that in North India. One may also note that the upper-caste opposition to social transformation is somewhat stronger in North India, where upper castes constitute in general a larger percentage of the population than in most parts of South India. So new political victories of lower castes in North India get celebrated as defiant symbols of social redemption and recognition aimed at solidifying their as yet tentative victories rather than as committed attempts at changing the economic structure of deprivation.

While voters do not seem to penalize politicians for their endemic poverty, they are less forgiving when there is a sharp and concentrated deterioration in their economic condition. Sen (1983) has commented on the political sensitivity of democracies to the threat of famine, but to

6. For a formal analysis of the role of visibility in influencing government resource allocation across multiple public goods in an electoral framework, see Mani and Mukand (2000).

me the more commonplace example for this in India is the electorate's high degree of inflation sensitivity. It is a common presumption that a sustained double-digit annual inflation rate will be politically intolerable in India, and politicians universally support a conservative monetary policy to avoid this danger (even when the government stocks of food and foreign exchange are huge). The poor tend to make the government directly responsible for inflation and expect it to stop it in its tracks, even at the expense of cutting budgetary programs on infrastructure that would have helped the poor in the long run. As they say, contra Keynes, in the short run we are all dead when the country is poor (and incomes are largely unindexed in the face of high inflation).

One major way that democracy affects the lives of the poor is through local accountability mechanisms in the public delivery of services and antipoverty programs. Large-scale development projects directed from above by an insulated modernizing elite are often inappropriate technologically or environmentally and far removed from or insensitive to local community needs and concerns. Rather than involving the local people and tapping into the large reservoir of local information, ingenuity, and initiative, these projects often treat them simply as objects of the development process. They end up primarily as conduits of largesse for middlemen and contractors, and even when they reach the poor, they encourage widespread parasitism on the state.

However, no one-to-one relationship can be drawn between the strength of democracy at the national political level and the strength of institutions of accountability at the local level. Large parts of North India, for example, have a serious problem with absenteeism of salaried teachers in village public schools and of doctors in rural public health clinics.[7] The villagers are usually aware of the problem but do not have the institutional means of correcting it, as the state-funded teachers and doctors are not answerable to the villagers in the insufficiently decentralized system. On the other hand, in nondemocratic China the local Communist Party officials have sometimes been responsive to local needs (at least as long as they do not conflict with the Party's program), as the comparative study of two villages in China and India by Drèze and Saran (1995) show in the context of China's far better performance in the provision of primary education at the local level. (Similar accounts of more effective public pressure in rural basic education

---

7. See, for example, PROBE (1999) for an intensive survey of 234 randomly selected villages in north India carried out in 1996.

and health services in Cuba can be compared to accounts of less effective local pressure in some of the more democratic regimes in Latin America.) Of course, in many authoritarian countries, local accountability is completely absent, and the situation is much worse than it is in North India. Following the landmark constitutional amendments in India in 1993, some progress has been made in a few of the Indian states (most significantly in Kerala and West Bengal and modestly in Maharashtra, Karnataka, Madhya Pradesh, and Rajasthan) in terms of political, administrative, and financial devolution to lower-tier governments, but most states are far from satisfying the minimum requirements of a functioning local democracy.

Even in otherwise centralized bureaucracies, the nature of institutional design for the delegation of implementation tasks to local-level agencies is not uniquely related to the nature of the political regime at the national level. Wade (1997) points to interesting contrasts between the modes of operation of the South Korean and Indian irrigation bureaucracies (South Korea having been under an authoritarian regime in the recent past) and the clearly more locally effective performance of South Korea. The Indian canal systems are large, centralized hierarchies in charge of all functions—design, construction, operations, and maintenance. Their operations (including the rules for promoting and transferring officials that minimize identification between the irrigation patrollers and the local farmers and the frequent use of low-trust management and supervision methods) and sources of finance (most of the irrigation department's budget comes in the form of a grant from the state treasury) are insensitive to the need for developing and drawing on local networks and social relationships. In South Korea functionally separate organizations administer the canal systems. The implementation and routine maintenance tasks are delegated to the Farmland Improvement Associations, one per catchment area, which are staffed by local part-time farmers who are selected by the village chiefs, knowledgeable about changing local conditions, dependent for their salaries and operational budgets largely on the user fees paid by the farmers, and continually drawing on local trust relationships.

One reason that the Indian local irrigation bureaucracy is kept at arm's length from the local farmers is the constant suspicion of the "capture" of irrigation organization by the farmers. In general, local democracies are supposed to be more vulnerable to corruption than the national government. One of the central results of the literature on collective action is that small group size and proximity help collective action. Collusions are thus easier to organize and enforce in proximate groups, risks of being caught and reported are easier to manage, and the multiplex interlocking social and economic relationships among the local influential people act as formidable barriers to entry into these cozy rental havens. On the other hand, if institutions of local democracy and a vigorous opposition party and free press are firmly in place, the political process can be more transparent, and the theft of funds and the sale of influence become more visible compared to the system of centralized corruption. As Crook and Manor (1991) point out on the basis of indirect but strong evidence in the case of state of Karnataka in South India, this local democracy may reduce the overall amount of money and resources siphoned off through corruption: even though more hands are in the till, it is difficult for people to steal very much (in big central-government projects, on the other hand, a single transaction can yield very large bribes). Ironically, the increased openness and visibility of the system compared to the earlier centralized system have led local people to believe, often wrongly, that corruption has increased.

The "capture" problem of local democracies can have severe implications in areas with marked social and economic inequalities. In many situations, decentralization may leave the poor grievously exposed to the mercies of the local overlords and their malfeasance. Because there are certain fixed costs of organizing resistance groups or countervailing lobbies, the poor may sometimes be more unorganized at the local level than at the national level, where they can pool their organizing capacities. In these situations, they may even be able occasionally to play pivotal roles in national coalitions and get redistributive transfers in their favor under centralized systems. (These issues are discussed in more detail in chapters 6 and 7.) In the United States, for example, movements in favor of using "state rights" to diminish the power of the federal government have often been interpreted as regressive and working against poor minorities. The U.S. case also shows that in situations of inequality and decentralization of financing of local schools, neighborhoods deteriorate with the secession of the rich. In many developing countries this is already a big problem; public schools and health clinics decline as the elite (political or economic) do not utilize those services and as the structure of political support around them erodes. Advocates of "grassroots democracy" have to contend with the implications of this phenomenon of elite "capture" or "exit" for the quality and quantity of services to the poorest sections of the population.

5.4

While in the previous section we have largely commented upon how democracy may affect the poor as recipients of public anti-poverty or service delivery programs, the poor are, of course, affected also as workers, either self-employed or wage-employed, by the expansion of work opportunities under the general process of economic development, on which democracy may have an impact. The mechanisms through which democracy has this impact are, however, not clear-cut or independent of context. For example, there is a presumption in the literature that democracy fosters development since it is supposed to be better suited for providing a minimum legal and contractual structure and a set of well-defined and enforced property rights. But I agree with Przeworski and Limongi (1993, p. 52) when they say that "the idea that democracy protects property rights is a recent invention, and we think a far-fetched one." If the majority are poor and the democratic processes work, the property rights of the rich minority may always be under a threat. Democracy may be ideologically more hospitable to a rule of law, but for business predictability rather than legal accountability is really at stake, and authoritarian regimes can provide a framework for a predictable set of contracts or a reputation for keeping political promises. In the 1970s and 1980s, for example, the first family in Indonesia or the Kuo Ming Tang (KMT) leadership in Taiwan provided a reasonably predictable and durable (even though corrupt) contractual environment, and private business thrived without the procedural formalities of a democracy. Even today the largely authoritarian regimes of Singapore and Malaysia provide a more predictable business environment than democratic India. Also, in some democratic regimes, including India, for all the elaborate legal-contractual structure on paper, the courts (and the administrative arbitration machinery) are hopelessly clogged, and the businessperson values a connection with a durable politician much more than the legal niceties. The durability of a politician may vary wildly from one democracy to another (the incumbent legislator may have the edge, as in the United States, or the electorate may be more inclined to "throw the rascals out" with regular frequency, as in India) and also from an authoritarian regime to another (one may be more coup-prone than another).

The rule of law that a democracy is supposed to uphold does not by itself guarantee that the laws themselves are conducive to development. Even in some of the richest democracies of the world, the enforcement of laws may be better and subject to less corruption and arbitrariness than in developing countries, but the process of enacting those laws is subject to an enormous amount of influence peddling for campaign contributions and other perquisites for legislators. (The artificial distinction between bureaucratic and political corruption that is often made is linked to these two aspects of the rule of law). Over time this influence peddling has got worse in most democracies as elections grow increasingly expensive. When policies to be legislated are up for sale to the highest contributor to the campaign fund, development projects may not win out (the policy decision in the budget may go in favor of buying one more military aircraft rather than 100 rural health clinics), and being told that the policies thus legislated will be implemented well by the bureaucracy and the court system under a democracy is not much consolation. Nevertheless, in an open polity there may be more avenues for mobilizing public pressure against covert (but not always illegal) sales of public policy.

Not all cases of public pressure that democracy facilitates help development. Democracies may be particularly susceptible to populist pressures for immediate consumption, unproductive subsidies, autarchic trade policies, and other particularistic demands that may hamper long-run investment and growth. On the other hand, authoritarian rulers who may have the capacity to resist such pressures may instead be self-aggrandizing, plundering the surplus of the economy. In fact, historically, authoritarian regimes come in different kinds—some deriving their legitimacy from providing order and stability (like that of Franco in Spain or the military junta in Myanmar) and some from providing rapid growth (like Park Chung Hee in South Korea). Sah (1991) has argued that authoritarian regimes exhibit a larger variance in economic performance than democracies.

The East Asian success story in development over the 1960s, 1970s, and 1980s has convinced many that some degree of insulation of the bureaucracy (which is in charge of formulating long-run development policies and guiding their implementation) from the ravages of short-run pork-barrel politics is important. The successes of powerful semi-autonomous technocratic organizations like the Economic Planning Bureau in South Korea and the Industrial Development Bureau in Taiwan in this period clearly point in this direction. It is claimed that authoritarianism made it less difficult for the regimes in East Asia to sustain this insulation. Of course, one can point out that authoritarianism is neither necessary (even in East Asia, postwar Japan has successfully insulated parts of the bureaucracy without giving up on democracy), nor sufficient (even in East Asia, the dictatorship of Marcos in the Philippines is an obvious counterexample, not to speak of authoritarian regimes in many other parts of the world) for such insulation.

Among the enabling conditions for bureaucratic insulation in East Asia that Evans (1995) emphasizes are the Weberian characteristics of internal organization of the state like highly selective meritocratic recruitment and long-term career rewards for members of the bureaucracy. Such Weberian characteristics are present to a reasonable degree in the upper echelons of the Indian civil service, but over time the democratic political process has eroded some of the insulation. This is evident particularly in political decisions about transfers of civil servants: powerful politicians who cannot sack civil servants can make life unpleasant by getting them transferred to undesirable jobs and locations. In Latin America in general the appointments in the bureaucracy are more often matters of political patronage. Geddes (1994) in an analysis of the obstacles to building state capacity in Latin America shows how political leaders there have frequently faced a dilemma between their own need for immediate political survival, which leads them to buy political support with patronage in appointments to economic management positions, and their longer-run collective interests in economic performance and regime stability. In India, as well, administrative appointments outside the main civil service, like those to the boards of public-sector corporations in provincial governments, are often used as political sinecures to keep clamoring factions happy.

A more disturbing sign of the politicization of the internal organization of the government in a democracy is indicated by the slow but systematic erosion of the institutional independence of the police and the criminal-justice system in some states of North India in a way that is similar to Sicilian politics under the Christian Democrats. A significant number of elected politicians in these states have connections with the criminal underworld; they have figured out that once elected on a ruling-party ticket they can neutralize the police, who will not rush to press or pursue criminal charges against them. Given their organizational and financial resources, these elements have an edge over other politicians in winning elections, and the poor often are dedicated voters for them as they nurse their local constituency assiduously even as they loot from the system in general. Police officers (and sometimes even judges) are often rewarded (for example, with plum postings) if they do the elected politicians' bidding.[8] Another example of how the administrative system is exposed to the marauding forces of populist politics is the widespread presumption among borrowers (both rich and poor, but particularly the former) from government-owned or -controlled credit institutions in many countries that they can default on loans with impunity, as the politicians who have to depend on their support cannot afford to let bank officials be too harsh with them. This has been one of the major reasons for the massive failures of state intervention in credit in developing countries.

The systematic erosion of the institutional insulation in India of the administrative structure and public economic management has affected not just the ability to credibly commit to long-term decisions, but the whole fabric of governance itself. This is the tension between participatory and procedural aspects of democracy we have referred to before: the unfolding of the logic of populist democracy has itself become a threat to democratic governance. Kaviraj (1996, p. 119) has described this as a strange Tocquevillian paradox: "democratic government functioned smoothly in the early years after 1947 precisely because it was not taking place in a democratic society; as democratic society has slowly emerged, with the spread of a real sense of political equality, it has made the functioning of democratic government more difficult." Some people are not worried by this, and they regard it as part of the initial necessary turmoil of democratic movement forward and group self-assertion. The writer V. S. Naipaul (1997, p. 39), who is fascinated by the "million mutinies" in contemporary India, says, "When people start moving, the first loyalty, the first identity, is always a rather small one.... When the oppressed have the power to assert themselves, they will behave badly. It will need a couple of generations of security and knowledge of institutions and the knowledge that you can trust institutions—it will take at least a couple of generations before people in that situation begin to behave well."

I wish I could share in this optimistic belief in democratic teleology. Breakdowns in democratic governance and economic management structures are not easy to repair, and there are irreversibilities in

---

8. This police, politician, criminal nexus in India was examined authoritatively in the multivolume National Police Commission reports two decades back and more recently in the N. N. Vohra Committee Report, without much action being taken against it.

institutional decay. Besides, in India's multilayered social structure, by the time one self-aware group settles down and learns to play by the institutional rules, other newly assertive groups will come up and defy those rules, often in the name of group equity.

In the recent literature on the role of the state in economic development (for example, Bardhan, 1990; Rodrik, 1992), the issue of insulation or autonomy of the state has been formulated in terms of the notion of the ability to credibly precommit (an idea that is discussed in some detail in the previous chapter). The ruler in a "strong" state[9] is taken to be a Stackelberg leader: he maximizes his objective function subject to the reaction function of the ruled and in this process internalizes the economic costs of his impositions in accordance with that reaction function. In contrast, the "weak" state is a Stackelberg follower; it cannot commit to a particular policy and merely reacts to the independent actions of the private actors like special-interest groups. Thus compared to the strong state, the weak state will have too many undesirable interventions (creating distortions in the process of generating rent for lobbying groups) and, by the same logic, will have too few desirable interventions[10] (as may be necessary in the case of all kinds of market failures or the more general case of coordination failures), since the state does not take into account or internalize the effects of its own policies.

Elster (1994) has argued that to be credible and effective, precommitment requires democracy. The promises of a ruler are much more credible if well-established procedures exist for throwing the ruler out of office for failure to keep those promises. "To be effective, power must be divided": this is a central theme of much of the recent work on constitutional political economy. Similarly, as is mentioned in chapter

---

9. In any empirical exercise to explain growth performance in terms of state "strength" in this sense, the issue of reverse causality must be avoided. Economies in their most successful phases quite possibly might have less political conflict (most groups are doing well without political exertion, and the few losing groups are bribed), and therefore their governments might have an appearance of "strength." Their commitments are not challenged or reversed by political action. This is an important issue that needs to be examined with detailed historical data. The purposive and determined way that the South Korean state handled various macroeconomic crises in the 1970s (the two oil shocks, massive foreign debt, inflation) and even the financial crisis at the end of the 1990s suggests to me that the Korean state's "strength" has not been just a reflection of the success of the economy.

10. While the distinction between the strong and the weak state is thus qualitatively similar to the distinction Olson (1993) has drawn between the ruler as a "stationary bandit" and as a "roving bandit," he overlooks the case where the latter may have too little of desirable interventions.

2, North and Weingast (1989) have cited the historical case of the Glorious Revolution in England in 1688, which by strengthening political institutions that constrained the king enhanced his commitment to securing private property rights and thus fostered economic growth.

I am not fully convinced by this argument. Democracy is neither necessary nor sufficient for effective precommitments. This can be illustrated in the context of development by the case of infant-industry protection, which has been popular in developing countries, as it was in the early stages of industrialization in the United States and Germany. Such protection against foreign competition is to be granted for a short period until the industrial infant can stand on its own feet. But in most countries infant-industry protection inevitably runs up against the time-inconsistency problem. When the initial period of protection is about to expire, political pressures for its renewal become inexorable, and in this way the infant industry soon degenerates into a geriatric protection lobby. Given the concentration and visibility of benefits from the perpetuation of this protection and the diffuseness of its costs, in a democracy little popular pressure is organized against it. No conniving leader faces dismissal on this ground, making constitutional provisions for throwing out the ruler largely irrelevant here. Thus well-established procedures of democracy are not sufficient for credible commitments.

The most successful cases of infant-industry protection in recent history have taken place under some of the authoritarian regimes of East Asia, particularly Taiwan and South Korea. These regimes have seen some remarkable instances of the government holding steadfastly to its promise to withdraw protection from an industry after the lapse of a preannounced duration and let the industry sink or swim in international competition.[11] Democracy was not necessary to establish credibility of commitment.

As discussed earlier, the autonomy of the state has some costs in terms of economic efficiency, particularly if the balance between commitment and accountability is not maintained. Accountability mechanisms (like those associated with the democratic process, such as checks and balances in the allocation of control rights, standards of transparency, and auditing—"institutionalized suspicion") keep gross

---

11. For an example of how the government in Taiwan imposed an import ban on VCRs in 1982 to help two of its main domestic electronic companies and withdrew that ban after barely eighteen months when those companies failed to shape up to meet international standards, see Wade (1990).

abuses and wastes under control and keep elected leaders on their toes if there are electoral repercussions for their abuse of power and mistakes. Accountability mechanisms are particularly important in averting environmental disasters, as recent history in authoritarian countries has shown: in their absence major ecological damages in the former Soviet Union and Eastern Europe and a devastating famine in China went unchecked for too long.

Apart from accountability, lack of bureaucratic insulation also makes it difficult to attain flexibility in dealing with changes in technical and market conditions (and may thus discourage risk-taking) and also in correcting wrong decisions. This flexibility has been maintained in East Asia by fostering a dense network of ties between public officials and private entrepreneurs through deliberative councils (as in Japan or South Korea) or through the tightly knit party organizations (as in Taiwan under KMT), allowing operational space for negotiating and renegotiating goals and policies, sharing information and risks, and coordinating decisions (and mutual expectations) with remarkable speed. Such cozy government-business relations[12] are more difficult to achieve (or politically more suspect) in societies that are more heterogeneous and unequal, as in India.

In this chapter we have tried to understand the multi-dimensional process by which democracy tends to affect poverty, drawing examples from India. Contrary to the simplistic preachings about democracy that we are all familiar with, not all of this process is straightforward or pretty. There are important tensions between the procedural and participatory aspects of democracy and between the need for commitment and that for accountability. From the point of view of the poor the ultimate advantage of democracy is in its potential in terms of its healing powers or opportunities for correcting mistakes and abuses and for raising human dignity for the masses of people.

---

12. Such cozy relations have been a source of recent problems in the financial sector in East Asian countries.

6 Decentralization of Governance

All around the world in matters of governance decentralization is the rage. Even apart from the widely debated issues of subsidiarity and devolution in the European Union and states' rights in the U.S., it has been at the center stage of policy experiments in the last two decades in a large number of developing and transition economies in Latin America, Africa, and Asia. The World Bank, for example, has embraced it as one of the major governance reforms on its agenda (many of the World Development Reports of recent years as well as other Bank documents—for example, World Bank, 1999, 2000—give the matter a great deal of prominence). If one takes just the two largest countries of the world, China and India, decentralization has been regarded as the major institutional framework for the phenomenal industrial growth in the last two decades in China (taking place largely in the nonstate nonprivate sector); and in India a fundamental constitutional reform in favor of decentralization was ushered in around the same time that the country launched a major program of economic reform.

After many failures, the centralized state everywhere has lost a great deal of legitimacy, and decentralization is widely believed to promise a range of benefits—reducing the role of the state in general, fragmenting central authority, and introducing more intergovernmental competition and checks and balances. It is viewed as a way to make government more responsive and efficient. Technological changes have also made it somewhat easier to provide public services (like electricity and water supply) relatively efficiently in smaller market areas, and the lower levels of government now are better able to handle certain tasks. In a world of rampant ethnic conflicts and separatist movements, decentralization is also regarded as a way of diffusing social and political tensions and ensuring local cultural and political autonomy.

These potential benefits of decentralization have attracted a diverse range of supporters. For example, free-market economists tend to emphasize the benefits of reducing the power of the overextended or predatory state. In some international organizations that are pushing structural adjustment and transitional reform, decentralization has sometimes been used almost as a synonym for privatization. Similarly, in the literature on mechanism design, an informationally decentralized system of individual decisions coordinated by a price mechanism is pitted against a system of central commands and plans. Even those who are still convinced of the pervasiveness of market failures are increasingly turning for their resolution to the government at the local level, where the transaction costs are relatively low and the information problems that can contribute to central government failures are less acute. They are joined by a diverse array of social thinkers: postmodernists, multicultural advocates, grassroots environmental activists, and supporters of the cause of indigenous peoples and technologies. In the absence of a better unifying name, I describe this latter group as *anarcho-communitarians*. They are usually both antimarket and anticentralized state, and they energetically support assignment of control to local self-governing communities.

As is usually the case when a subject draws advocates from sharply different viewpoints, different people mean different things by decentralization. But this chapter focuses on a particular kind of decentralization in developing (and transition) economies—the devolution of political decision-making power to local-level small-scale entities. In countries with a long history of centralized control (as in the old empire states of Russia, China, or India), public administrators often use decentralization to mean the dispersion of some responsibilities to regional branch offices at the local level of implementation on a particular project. In this chapter, decentralization in the sense of devolution of political decision-making power is distinguished from such mere administrative delegation of functions of the central government to their local branches. Also the political and administrative aspects of decentralization need to be separated from those of fiscal decentralization, and the more numerous cases of decentralization of public expenditure need to be separated from those involving decentralization of both tax and expenditure assignments. We shall include cases where local community organizations get formally involved in the implementation of some centrally directed or funded projects. Not all these aspects of decentralization operate simultaneously in any particular case and it is quite possible that a given economy may be decentralized in some respects, not in others. It should also be clear that the effects of a policy of deliberate decentralization—which is our concern here—can be qualitatively different from those following from an anarchic erosion of central control either due to the collapse of the state (as has happened in some countries in Africa) or to the lack of administrative or fiscal capacity on the part of the central authority leading to abandonment of social-protection functions (as has happened in some transition economies). The latter case is also increasingly common in both developed and developing countries where a fiscal crisis leads the central government to devolve responsibilities for social-sector spending to local governments in the form of "unfunded mandates."

The territorial domain of subnational governments varies enormously from country to country. A typical province in India or China is larger (in size of population) than most countries in the world, and so federalism in the sense of devolution of power to the provincial state governments may still keep power over people fairly centralized. Unfortunately, data below the provincial government level are often scarce, and most quantitative studies of decentralization (for example, those based on share of the central government in total expenditure or revenues) do not pertain to issues at the local community level (even apart from the fact that the share of expenditure or revenues is not a good index of decision-making authority). Even at the latter level, the units are diverse (ranging from megacities to small villages), and boundaries are often determined by accidents of history and geography, not by concerns of decentralization of administration. In this chapter, the analytical focus of decentralization is generally confined to the governing authority at the local community level (say, village, municipality, or county level) of administration.

Our discussion in the rest of the chapter begins with a description of why decentralization poses some different issues in the institutional context of developing (and transition) countries and thus why it may sometimes be hazardous to draw lessons for them from, say, the experiences of U.S. states and city governments. We try to give the flavor of some new theoretical models, which extend the discussion to political agency problems that may resonate more in the context of developing and transition economies. We then refer to some of the ongoing empirical work in evaluating the impact of decentralization on delivery of public services and local business development.

Decentralization has undoubted merits and strengths. However, the idea of decentralization may need some protection against its own enthusiasts—both free-market advocates who see it as an opportunity to cripple the state and anarcho-communitarians who ignore the "community failures" that (as is pointed out at the end of chapter 1) may be as serious as the market failures or government failures that economists commonly analyze.

6.1 Departures from the Fiscal Federalism Literature

A large literature on decentralization, often referred to as "fiscal federalism," mostly relates to the case of the United States.[1] The principles discussed in this literature have been fruitfully applied to national-provincial relations in developing countries like Argentina, Brazil, Colombia, South Africa, India, and China, but in this chapter we shall go beyond this and stress the special issues that arise in decentralization in developing (and transition) economies primarily because the institutional contexts (and therefore the structures of incentives and organization) are in some respects qualitatively different from the classical U.S. case (or the recent case of the European Union).

Much of the fiscal-federalism literature focuses on the economic efficiency of intergovernmental competition, which often starts with a market metaphor that is rationalized by the well-worn Tiebout (1956) model. In this approach, different local governments offer different public tax-expenditure bundles, and mobile individuals are supposed to allocate themselves according to their preferences. The assumptions required for the Tiebout model are, however, much too stringent, particularly for poor countries.[2] The crucial assumption of population mobility (fully informed citizens who "vote with their feet" in response to differential public performance) that enables governments in the Tiebout framework to overcome the well-known problem of inducing citizens to reveal their preferences for public goods largely fails in poor countries.

In any case, many of the public goods in question are community- and site-specific, and it is often possible to exclude nonresidents. Resi-

---

1. Many of the issues have been well surveyed in the "Symposium on Fiscal Federalism" in the fall 1997 issue of the *Journal of Economic Perspectives*.
2. There are doubts about just how the Tiebout mechanism operates even in relatively mobile societies like that of the United States. For instance, few poor people move from state to state in search of higher welfare benefits (see Hanson and Hartman, 1994).

dents of rural communities of poor countries, in particular, are often face to face, and social norms sharply distinguish "outsiders" from "insiders," especially with respect to entitlement to community services.

Second, the information and accounting systems and mechanisms for monitoring public bureaucrats are much weaker in low-income countries. In the standard literature on decentralization and "fiscal federalism," the focus is on allocation of funds, and it is implicitly assumed that allocated funds automatically reach their intended beneficiaries. This assumption needs to be drastically qualified in developing countries, where attention must be paid to special incentives and devices to check bureaucratic corruption—and thus the differential efficacy of such mechanisms under centralization and decentralization.

Third, the institutions of local democracy and mechanisms of political accountability in the relatively few democratic developing countries are often weak. Thus, any discussion of delivery of public services has to grapple with issues of capture of governments at different tiers by elite groups more seriously than is usual in the traditional decentralization literature.

Fourth, the traditional literature on decentralization, even though not impervious to issues of distribution, is usually preoccupied with those of efficiency in public provision. When a major goal of decentralization in developing countries is to effectively reach out to the poor (or to diffuse unrest among disadvantaged minority groups), often in remote backward areas, targeting success in poverty-alleviation programs is a more important performance criterion than the efficiency of interregional resource allocation. In traditional discussions of decentralization and federalism, the focus is on how checks and balances can restrain the central government's power, whereas in many situations in developing countries the poor and the minorities are oppressed by the local power groups and may look to the central state for protection and relief. As is pointed out in the preceding chapter, Stepan (1999) has made a useful distinction between the "coming-together federalism" of the United States (where previously sovereign polities gave up part of their sovereignty for efficiency gains from resource pooling and a common market) and the "holding-together federalism" of multinational democracies such as India, Belgium, and Spain (where redistributive or compensating transfers keep the contending polities together). In heterogeneous societies, such redistributive pressures sometimes lead to fiscal decentralization, which allows for state and local borrowing that may be large enough to cause macroeconomic instability, which has happened in South Africa, Brazil, and Argentina.[3] Not all state-mandated redistribution, however, is inflationary or unproductive rent creation, as is usually presumed in the traditional literature. Some redistribution to disadvantaged groups or regions (say, in the form of decentralized delivery of health, education, or infrastructural services) need not be at the expense of efficiency and may even improve the potential for productive investment, innovation, and human-resource development on the part of communities long bypassed by the elite or the mainstream.

Fifth, the fiscal-federalism literature typically assumes that lower levels of government both collect taxes and spend funds, so localities can be classified as low-tax, low-service or as high-tax, high-service. This connection between local revenues and spending is rather tenuous. In most countries, much of the more elastic (and progressive) sources of tax revenue lie with the central government, and there is a built-in tendency toward vertical fiscal imbalance. Income is often geographically concentrated, both because of agglomeration economies and initial endowments of natural resources and infrastructural facilities. Thus, certain local areas will find it much easier to raise significant tax revenue than others. In addition, there are limits to interregional tax competition. In many low-income countries, the decentralization issues discussed there are primarily about providing centrally collected tax revenue to lower levels of government rather than about seeking to empower lower levels of government to collect taxes. The focus is on public-expenditure assignments, unaccompanied by any significant financial devolution.

Sixth, the decentralization literature typically assumes that different levels of government all have similar levels of technical and administrative capacity. This assumption is questionable for all countries. On account of agglomeration economies in attracting qualified people, in most countries central bureaucracies attract better talent. But the problem is especially severe in many developing countries, where the quality of staff in local bureaucracies—including basic tasks like accounting and record keeping—is very low. Even their more professional and technical people suffer from the disadvantages of isolation, poor train-

---

3. This chapter does not have much to say on the impact of decentralization on macroeconomic stabilization. For a game-theoretic model of how decentralization or local democratization may increase the level of central redistribution to prevent spirals of regional revolt and how the macroeconomic consequences depend on the initial levels of cultural division and decentralization, see Treisman (1999).

ing, and low interaction with other professionals. As Bird (1995) puts it, information asymmetry thus works both ways: the central government may not know *what* to do, and the local government may not know *how* to do it.[4] This problem is of differential importance in different services. Providing for street cleaning or garbage collection may not require sophisticated expertise, but power production and transmission, bulk supply of clean water, and public sanitation do. Decentralization to the local level will often work better in the former kind of services than the latter. There also is learning by doing in local administration, which improves the performance of local democracies. The following discussion of the issues of decentralization in developing countries takes into account these points of difference with the traditional literature.

6.2 Adapting the Theory of Decentralization for Developing Countries

The conventional wisdom in the fiscal-federalism literature, as in Oates (1972), is that decentralization is to be preferred when tastes are heterogeneous and there are no spillovers across jurisdictions. With spillovers and no heterogeneity, a central government that provides a common level of public goods and services for all localities is more efficient. With spillovers, decentralization leads to underprovision of local public goods, as local decision makers do not take into account benefits that go to other districts. The issue of spillovers is relevant to investment in highway transport, communication, public research and extension, pollution or epidemic control, and so on. Spillovers are less relevant when the public goods are more local, as in local roads, minor irrigation, health clinics, sanitation, identification of beneficiaries of public transfer programs, and so on.

Centralization can also exploit economies of scale better in the construction of overhead facilities, but these economies of scale are less

---

4. Occasionally, however, local people come up with ingenious low-cost solutions, whereas centralized systems use unnecessarily expensive services of specialized technicians. For some of the basic needs for poor people, local youths with some minimum training as primary health workers or primary schoolteachers can be adequate. In other, more technical projects there is a lot of scope for improving access to engineering, project design, and administrative skills. Organizations like the Agence d'Exécution des Travaux d'Intérêt Public (AGETIP) in Senegal or the Brazil-based Instituto Brasilero de Administración Municipal (IBAM) have in recent years been helpful in developing local technical capacity.

important in local management and maintenance. In a canal irrigation system—such as the one in South Korea described by Wade (1997)—construction was in the hands of a central authority, but maintenance was devolved to local communities. Similarly, while the local government may run the day-to-day functioning of primary schools, the upper-tier government can have the economies of scale in designing curricula and in prescribing and enforcing minimum quality standards. In the public delivery of electricity, economies of scale in generation and transmission may be the responsibility of centralized power plants and grids, while distribution may be decentralized to local governments.

The traditional theory of fiscal federalism is now being extended to a political-economy setting (by introducing transaction costs in the political markets, political agency problems between the ruler and the ruled, and agency problems between the politicians/bureaucrats and the electorate), and for reasons mentioned above these transaction and agency costs may be much more serious in developing countries. Local governments are usually presumed to have an information advantage over upper-tier governments. But a central government can procure for itself the same information advantage of proximity through local agents. In some countries the central government uses such representatives at the local level (like the *préfet* in France, the *prefetto* in Italy, or the *intendente* in Chile) for this purpose. The central government also can have economies of scope in the collection of information. But in practice, the local government still retains the informational advantage because of political accountability. In democratic countries local politicians may have more incentive than national or provincial politicians to use local information, since local politicians are answerable to local voters, whereas the national and provincial politicians have wider constituencies (so that local issues may get diluted).

Focusing on accountability rather than information leads to thinking about how the public can monitor and affect elected officials at different levels of government. Seabright (1996) discusses the problem of political accountability theoretically in terms of allocation of control rights in the context of incomplete contracts, where breaches of contract are observable—though not verifiable in administrative or judicial review—and are subject to periodic electoral review. His model includes both central and local elected officials. In his framework, centralization allows benefits from policy coordination, which is especially important if there are spillovers across jurisdictions. However, centralization has costs in terms of diminished accountability, in the sense of reduced probability that the welfare of a given locality can determine the reelection of the government. Elections are extremely blunt instruments of political accountability, and other institutional devices and unelected community organizations (like nongovernmental organizations) may be deployed to strengthen local accountability.

The mechanism of accountability may also be strengthened by "yardstick competition," where jurisdictions are compared to each other (Besley and Case, 1995). The effort or competence of public officials is not directly observable by citizens, and if poor results occur, public officials can always plead that they did the best that was possible under the circumstances. However, if the shocks that create a wedge between effort and outcomes are correlated across jurisdictions, then yardstick competition can act as an indicator of relative effort on the part of agents. As Seabright (1996) points out, this argument of yardstick competition under decentralization, which may help voters to know whether they should seek to replace their governments, is to be distinguished from his own argument that decentralization may increase their ability to do so.

The combination of decentralization and yardstick competition allows the possibility of experimentation in the way a given public service is provided, demonstration, and learning from others' jurisdictions. In the early years of China's market reforms, decentralization with jurisdictional competition allowed some coastal areas to experiment with institutional reform, the success of which showed the way for the rest of the country. Economic historians have pointed to the fragmentation and decentralization in early modern Europe—sometimes called "parcelized sovereignty"—as a source of strength, in enabling experimentation and competition, which led to technological and institutional innovations that helped Europe to ultimately overtake the more centralized empire states of Asia.

In comparing centralization and decentralization, Tommasi and Weinschelbaum (1999) pose the political-agency problem in terms of the number of principals (relative to agents). Citizens are viewed as principals, and their elected representatives as agents. The local government has better means (in the form of information) to be responsive and also better (electoral) incentives. In the case of centralization, principals are numerous and agents are few, whereas in the case of decentralization, there is one agent per locality. The larger the number of principals, the more serious is the problem of lack of coordination in contracting with agents. Decentralization is preferable to centralization when the problem of interjurisdictional externality is less important than the coordination effect.[5]

Besley and Coate (2000) focus on the importance of political aggregation mechanisms in the tradeoff between centralized and decentralized provision of local public goods. Under decentralization, public goods are selected by locally elected representatives, while under a centralized system, policy choices are determined by a legislature consisting of elected representatives from each district (so that conflicts of interest between citizens of different jurisdictions play out in the legislature). They then reconsider the traditional questions of the fiscal-federalism literature in terms of alternative models of legislative behavior—where the decisions are taken by a minimum winning coalition of representatives and where legislators reach a bargaining solution. They show that the familiar presumption that larger spillovers across jurisdictions help the case for centralization is not clear under such political-economy considerations.

Political accountability in poor countries is particulaly affected by the likelihood of corruption or capture by interest groups. While local governments may have better local information and accountability pressure, they may be more vulnerable to capture by local elites, who will then receive a disproportionate share of spending on public goods.[6] (This is in contrast to the Seabright, 1996, model, where political accountability is always greater at the local level.) On the other hand, the central bureaucrat who is in charge of the delivery of, say, an infrastructural service like electricity, telecommunication, or canal irrigation may be corrupt in a way that leads to cost-padding, targeting

---

5. The idea that fewer principals in smaller jurisdictions have more political control clearly resembles the relationship between group size and free-riding in the voluntary provision of a public good first discussed by Olson (1965). As is well known, this relationship can be ambiguous.

6. In the *Federalist Papers* (no. 10) James Madison (1961/1787, p. 63) comments on the notion that local governments are more prone to capture by elites and special interests:

"The smaller the society, the fewer probably will be the distinct parties and interests composing it; the fewer the distinct parties and interests, the more frequently will a majority be found of the same party; and the smaller the number of individuals composing a majority, and the smaller the compass within which they are placed, the more easily will they concert and execute their plans of oppression. Extend the sphere and you take in a greater variety of parties and interests; you make it less probable that a majority of the whole will have a common motive to invade the rights of other citizens; or if such a common motive exists, it will be more difficult for all who feel it to discover their own strength and to act in unison with each other."

failures, and generally an inefficiently low and inequitable service delivery. The problem for the central government that employs the bureaucrat is that it has very little information about local needs, delivery costs, and the amount actually delivered. Many programs in developing countries have thus a large gap between a commitment of resources at the central level and delivery of services at the local level. For a particularly egregious example, see Reinikka and Svensson (2001), where they study the leakage in the flow of educational funds from the central government to schools in Uganda in 1991 to 1995. They found that only 13 percent of the total grant transferred from the central government for nonwage expenditures in schools (for items like textbooks and instructional materials) actually reached the schools. The majority of schools actually received no money at all from the central transfers for nonwage expenditures.

Bardhan and Mookherjee (2000a) develop a simple analytical framework that formalizes the tradeoff between these conflicting aspects of centralized and decentralized delivery systems. Decentralization, by shifting control rights from the central bureaucrat (who otherwise acts like an unregulated monopolist) to a local government, typically tends to expand service deliveries as authority goes to those more responsive to user needs. But with capture of the local government (in the sense of having elites receive a larger weight in the local government's objective function, which is a weighted sum of welfare), there is a tendency for the service to be overprovided to local elites at the expense of the nonelite. The extent of such inefficient and inequitable cross-subsidization will depend on the extent of local capture and on the degree of fiscal autonomy of the local government. On the latter question, three different financing mechanisms for local governments are considered: local taxes, user fees, and central grants. With local tax financing there is the risk that the captured local government may resort to a regressive financing pattern whereby the nonelite bear the tax burden of providing services to the elite. Restrictions on the ability of local governments to levy taxes may then be desirable, even at the cost of reducing flexibility of service provision to local need.

User charges may be a useful compromise between matching provision to local needs and avoiding an unduly heavy burden on the local poor. Since no user is compelled to use the service, this imposes a limit on the extent of cross-subsidization foisted on the poor. So with user-fee financing, decentralization unambiguously welfare-dominates centralization as well as local tax-financed decentralization, irrespective of the extent of local capture. Central-grant financing, on the other hand, may encourage local governments to claim higher local need or cost, leading to a restriction of the level of service delivery; the welfare implications are ambiguous, depending on a range of relevant political and financing parameters.

User charges cannot, however, be used to finance antipoverty programs (like targeted public distribution of food, education, or health services) that by their very nature are targeted at groups that do not have the ability to pay for the service (or pay bribes to the central bureaucrats). In such cases, as is shown in Bardhan and Mookherjee (2000b), the extent of capture of local governments relative to that of the central government is a critical determinant of the welfare impact of decentralization. If local governments are equally or less vulnerable to capture than the central government, then decentralization is likely to improve both efficiency and equity. But the opposite may be the case when capture at the local level is much greater than at the central level.

Even though the extent of relative capture of governments at different levels is crucial in understanding the likely impact of decentralization initiatives, there has been very little work on the subject, either theoretical[7] or empirical. The extent of capture of local governments by local elites depends on levels of social and economic inequality within communities, traditions of political participation and voter awareness, fairness and regularity of elections, transparency in local decision-making processes and government accounts, media attention, and so on. These vary widely across communities and countries, as documented in numerous case studies (for example, Crook and Manor, 1998; Conning and Kevane, 2001). Central governments are also subject to capture, and this may be true more than at the local level on account of the larger importance of campaign funds in national elections and better information about candidates and issues in local elections based on informal sources. On the other hand, particularly in large heterogeneous societies, the elites are usually more divided at the national level, with more competing and heterogeneous groups

---

7. For a theoretical analysis of the problem, see Bardhan and Mookherjee (2000b) and the next chapter. The overall comparison of capture at central and local levels in a democracy would arguably depend on the interplay of a large number of underlying institutional factors, such as relative degrees of voter awareness and cohesiveness of special-interest groups, extent of heterogeneity across districts, and nature of the national electoral system, and so the issue is ultimately context- and system-specific.

neutralizing one another. At the local level in situations of high inequality, collusion may be easier to organize and enforce in small proximate groups (involving officials, politicians, contractors, and interest groups), risks of being caught and reported are easier to manage, and the multiplex interlocking social and economic relationships among the local influential people may act as formidable barriers to entry into these cozy rental havens. At the central level in democratic countries, more institutional mechanisms for checks and balances are usually at place: these include various constitutional forms of separation of powers and adjudicatory systems in some countries, more regular auditing of public accounts, and more vigilance by national media, which are often absent or highly ineffective at the local level.

Even in undemocratic but largely egalitarian societies, the problem of local capture may be less acute. In the widely noted success story of decentralized rural-industrial development of China, it is generally overlooked that the decollectivization of agriculture since 1978 has represented one of the world's most egalitarian distributions of land-cultivation rights (with the size of land cultivated by a household assigned almost always strictly in terms of its demographic size), and this may have substantially mitigated the problem of capture of local governments and other institutions by the oligarchic owners of immobile factors of production (like land), which afflicts other rural economies (for example, India).

When the potential for capture of local governments is serious, decentralization programs have to focus a great deal of attention on strengthening local accountability mechanisms. In fact, in policy debates that consider the costs and benefits of redistributive policies (like land reforms, public health campaigns, or literacy movements), the substantial positive spillover effects (in terms of enlarging the stake of large numbers of the poor in the system and strengthening the institutions of local democracy) are often ignored. Comparing across the various states in India, local democracy and institutions of decentralization are more effective in the states (like Kerala and West Bengal) where land reforms and mass movements for raising political awareness have been more active. The 1996 National Election Survey data in India (see, for example, Mitra and Singh, 1999) suggest that in West Bengal 51 percent of the respondent voters expressed a high level of trust in their local government, whereas in the adjoining state of Bihar (where both land reforms and local democracy institutions have been weak) the corresponding figure is 30 percent. Near-universal literacy in Kerala has helped sustain widespread newspaper readership, which has encouraged a vigilant press on issues like corruption in local governments.

In both Kerala and West Bengal it has also been observed that theft and corruption at the local level are more effectively resisted if regular local elections to select representatives in the local bodies are supplemented by an institutionalized system of periodic public hearings on items of major public expenditure. But even hearings are inadequate if the complaints made in public are not acted on by the ruling party. There is evidence that sometimes the opposition parties or minority factions stop attending the village council meetings or the public hearings, as they perceive that they cannot do much about the ruling party's spending of public funds on widespread patronage (like "jobs for the boys" or what Italians call *lottizzazione*), which sometimes consolidates the party's electoral advantage. It is important to install public-accounts committees at the local legislative level with their leading members taken from the opposition party (as is the case at the central parliamentary committees in India or Britain). In general, the auditing process at the local level is extremely deficient, not always by design but by the sheer dearth in the villages of technical capacity for accounting, record keeping, and auditing.

In sum, considering the theory of decentralization in developing countries requires moving beyond the traditional tradeoff between centralization for dealing with spillovers and decentralization for dealing with heterogeneity. It is necessary to delve into political-economy issues of institutional process and accountability at both the local and central levels.

6.3 Empirical Evaluation of Decentralized Delivery of Public Services

Various attempts have been made to empirically evaluate the impact of decentralization on the delivery of social services in developing countries. Even though decentralization experiments are being implemented in many of these countries, hard quantitative evidence on their impact is rather scarce. There are a number of scattered studies which we will try to arrange in terms of the nature of empirical methodology.

In two successful cases of decentralization in Latin America there is some evidence available on the before-after comparison of service-delivery outcomes. One is the widely noted case of participatory budgeting in municipal government in the city of Porto Alegre in Brazil, and the other is the less well-known but dramatic success of the post-1994 decentralization initiative in Bolivia. In Porto Alegre, where assembly meetings of local citizens and neighborhood associations in different regions discuss investment priorities, review accounts, and elect representatives to a citywide council (Conference of the Parties, COP) that allocates available resources across wards, impressive results have followed. Between 1989 and 1996 access to basic sanitation (water and sewage) as well as enrollment in elementary or secondary schools nearly doubled, while revenue collection increased by 48 percent (see Santos, 1998). Although it is difficult from this study to isolate the impact of participatory budgeting reforms from the effects of other ongoing changes, it seems likely that there has been a substantial impact on the pattern of resource allocation across localities, particularly to poor ones, and decreased misappropriations of resources compared to the past and to other areas in Brazil.

In Bolivia in 1994 the number of municipalities as well as the share of national tax revenue allocated to municipalities doubled, along with devolution to the municipalities of administrative authority, investment responsibility, and title to local infrastructural facilities. This has been associated with a massive shift of public resources in favor of the smaller and poorer municipalities and from large-scale production to social sectors. Faguet (2001) finds that public investment in education, water, and sanitation rose significantly in three-quarters of all municipalities and that investments responded to measures of local need (for example, the expansion in public education spending was larger on average in municipalities with a lower literacy rate or with fewer private schools). Faguet's analysis is in terms of levels of public spending rather than outcome variables like school enrollments, school performance, or access to water and sanitation services. In the studies of Porto Allegre or Bolivia there is not much information available on the allocation of resources within a community across households in different socioeconomic classes. This means that issues like cost effectiveness of programs, targeting performance, or the extent of capture of local governments cannot be addressed.[8] Without household-level data on access to public services, these crucial aspects of the impact of decentralization cannot be properly assessed.

---

8. The other problem in empirical studies is that the index of decentralization used in these studies or in before-after comparison does not fully capture the multidimensional nature of decentralization, which involves various aspects of devolution of power.

The literature has hardly any household-level analysis of the comparative effects of centralized versus decentralized delivery. One detailed study of targeting performance of a decentralized program using household-level information in a developing country is that of Galasso and Ravallion (2001) studying a decentralized food-for-education program in Bangladesh. In this central government program, in which two million children participated in 1995 and 1996, the identification of beneficiary households within a selected community was made typically by a local school-management committee (consisting of parents, teachers, education specialists, and school donors). Galasso and Ravallion use data from a 1995 to 1996 Household Expenditure Survey to assess the targeting performance of the program. They find that the program was mildly pro-poor: taking all villages, a somewhat larger fraction of the poor received benefits from the program than the nonpoor. But they also find some evidence of local capture. For example, within the set of participating villages, targeting performance was worse in communities with larger land inequality or in remote locations. But the targeting improved as the program expanded, suggesting that the program shifted the balance of power in favor of the poor. It is also clearly the case that the level of targeting *within* communities was superior to that achieved *across* communities by central allocation, thus offering little support for the view that the central government is more accountable to the poor than local communities. This is in some contrast to the experience of the widely acclaimed antipoverty transfer program of PROGRESA (Programa de Educación, Salud y Alimentación) in Mexico. The program follows a two-stage targeting process. Coady (2001) finds that most of PROGRESA's targeting effectiveness is achieved at the first stage, when poor localities are selected. In the second stage, households are selected within localities—not on the basis of identification of beneficiaries by local communities (as in the food-for-education program in Bangladesh) but on the basis of information collected from a census undertaken for this purpose.

Alderman (1998) examines, on the basis of a household survey conducted in 1996, a targeted social-assistance program (Ndihme Ekonomika) in Albania that was decentralized in 1995. He finds that modest gains have been made in targeting efficiency and cost effectiveness following decentralization, that local authorities use some additional information in allocating program benefits among households, and that the central allocation of social-assistance funds to local authorities is ad hoc and not strongly correlated with the level of poverty in the local communities. He does not find evidence that the decentralization initiative caused the benefits of the program to be captured by the well-off members of the community.

There is some quantitative evidence on the impact of mandated representations of historically disadvantaged groups like women in leadership positions in local governance in India. Since 1998 one-third of all positions of chief of the village councils in India have been reserved for women: only women may be candidates for the position of chief in a reserved village council and the latter is selected randomly. Taking advantage of this random assignment (thus avoiding an econometric problem in usual cross-section studies on this question that communities which are more likely to take women's needs into account may also be more willing to let them be in leadership positions), Chattopadhyay and Duflo (2001) have measured the impact of this political reservation policy on outcomes of decentralization with data collected from a survey of all investments in local public goods made by village councils in one district in West Bengal. They find that the women leaders of village councils invest more in infrastructure that is directly relevant to the needs of rural women (drinking water, fuel, and roads) and that village women are more likely to participate in the policy-making process if the leader of their village council is a woman. However, without direct evidence on the nature of women's preferences relative to men's and since women's reservation in the leadership positions in local government was not linked to the distribution of women in the village, this study does not quite address how local democracy affects the ability of underrepresented groups in the village to implement their desired outcomes.

Foster and Rosenzweig (2001) use a panel dataset of villages across India to examine the consequences of democratization and fiscal decentralization. They find that an increase in the demographic weight of the landless households in a village under democratic decentralization has a positive effect on allocation of public resources to road construction (which, according to them, benefits primarily the landless workers) and a negative effect on allocation of public resources to irrigation facilities (which benefit primarily the landed). But their dataset does not contain the many severe institutional lapses in the implementation of decentralization across India (particularly in manipulations of the local electoral process and in the range of authority and finances devolved to local governments, making democratic decentralization not yet a reality in most parts of India). It is not clear, for example, how much leeway elected local village councils have in matters of allocation to projects like road construction (which are often centrally sponsored, are bureaucratically controlled from above, and involve the local government at most only in the decisions about where to locate the road and how to identify the beneficiary workers).

Some case studies on the effects of decentralization in different parts of the world provide descriptive and suggestive correlations but not enough to clinch any hypothesis. Azfar et al. (2002) survey households and government officials at municipal and provincial levels in the Philippines with respect to the stated public-investment priorities in a given locality. Stated priorities of officials at the municipal level turned out to weakly match those of local residents, while those of officials at the provincial level did not, suggesting that decentralization may improve the quality of information used in public-investment decisions. Some evidence in the survey also suggests that more perceived corruption exists at the central level than at the local level. A similar survey was carried out by Azfar et al. (2002) in Uganda with qualitatively similar results. They also find in Uganda a greater reliance on community leaders for news concerning local corruption and local elections than for national news, which they interpret as evidence of greater potential for local capture.

In the 1990s Nicaragua started a program of transferring key management tasks in public schools from central authorities to local councils involving parents. An evaluation of this program by King and Ozler (1998) on the basis of school and household surveys and student achievement tests suggests that de facto autonomy has been given to only a few councils but that it has had a significant positive effect on student performance in those communities.

The World Development Report 1994 on Infrastructure cited several cases of quality improvement and cost savings in infrastructure projects after local communities were given part of the responsibility in management. A review of World Bank data for forty-two developing countries found that where road maintenance was decentralized, backlogs were lower and the condition of roads better. Data for a group of developing countries revealed that per-capita costs of water in World Bank–funded water projects were four times higher in centralized systems than they were in fully decentralized systems. A study of 121 completed rural water-supply projects, financed by various agencies, showed that projects with high community participation in project selection and design were much more likely to have the water supply maintained in good condition than projects with more centralized decision making.

In Chapter 5 we have already referred to Wade's (1997) contrasting account of the operations of irrigation bureaucracy in South Korea and in South India that brings out the importance of local accountability in delivery of infrastructural services. We have also given examples there that there is no one-to-one relationship between the strength of democracy at the national political level and the strength of institutions of accountability at the local level.

Taken as a group, these studies suggest generally positive effects of decentralization, but it is hard to draw conclusive lessons. Many of the studies are largely descriptive, not analytical, and often suggest correlations rather than causal processes. Most of them are not based on household survey data, making the comparative impact of centralized versus decentralized programs on different socioeconomic groups of households difficult to assess.

6.4   Decentralization and Local Business Development

Most of the cases of decentralization in developing countries that are examined in the theoretical and empirical literature relate to the delivery of social services. But in recent years the traditional literature on federalism has been extended to examine the role of local government in promoting local business development, particularly in the context of transition economies especially China, and this has potential implications for developing countries where public-delivery issues have been prominent. In Qian and Weingast (1997) and Qian and Roland (1998), for example, decentralization of information and authority and inter-jurisdictional competition have been considered as commitment devices on the part of the central or provincial government to provide market incentives, both the "positive" incentive that rewards economic success at the local level and the "negative" incentive that punishes economic failure. The local government-run township and village enterprises (TVEs) that have served as the engine of growth in China for over two decades have been cited as a major example of the outcome of a successful "market-preserving federalism." In terms of "positive" market incentives the TVE's had full control over their assets and they were largely left alone (as a residual claimant) to "get rich gloriously," and the limited knowledge of the upper-tier governments about the "extrabudget" and "off-budget" accounts of local governments acted as check on the formers' interventionism. In contrast, an econometric study of the fiscal relations between local and regional governments in Russia by Zhuravskaya (2000) examined a panel dataset for thirty-five large cities and found that local governments could retain only about 10 percent of their revenues at the margin, thus providing only weak incentives to foster local business development and increase their tax base. In terms of the negative incentive, Chinese upper-tier governments deny bailout to many failing TVEs to enforce a dynamic commitment. Having no access to state banks and facing mobility of capital across jurisdictions raised the opportunity costs of local governments for rescuing inefficient firms, thus leading to the endogenous emergence of a hard budget constraint.

Without denying the importance of these market incentives, however, it is possible to argue that market-preserving federalism is institutionally underspecified in these studies. Depending on the political-institutional complex in different countries, the same market incentives may have different efficacy. As Rodden and Rose-Ackerman (1997) have pointed out in a critique of market-preserving federalism, the institutional milieu determines whether political leaders of a local government respond to highly mobile investors or instead pay more attention to the demands of strong distributive coalitions dominated by owners of less mobile factors. Owners of capital vary widely in the specificity of their assets, and institutional incentives facing political leaders may vary even for the same jurisdictional competitive pressure. Even in a democracy, not to speak of authoritarian systems, electoral competition does not necessarily punish local leaders who fail to respond to exit threats of mobile asset owners and are instead more responsive to coalition building and well-organized lobbies. As has been noted above, local capture by the oligarchic owners of immobile factors of production like land has been a problem in rural India, whereas in China the lack of such strong rural lobbies (owing largely to egalitarian land distribution) may have made a difference in the local governments' vigorous pursuit of rural industrialization.[9] In Russia many have pointed out that over much of the 1990s local governments showed features of being captured by former rent holders and old firms that sometimes blocked the rise of new firms that could compete

---

9. Even in India, in areas where land distribution is relatively egalitarian and local democracy is more solidaristic, as in Kerala, there are now some instances of municipal governments taking a leading role, in collaboration with bankers and social groups, in local business development. For some examples, see Das (2000).

away their rents.[10] Even in China, by some accounts (for example, Shirk, 1993), local officials have often used their financial authority under decentralization to build political machines, collecting rents in exchange for selective benefits and patronage distribution, and federalism may not always have been that market preserving.

Jurisdictional competition does not seem to be enough to explain the emergence of endogenous hard budget constraints for local governments. More specification of the local political process is necessary. Even ignoring the lobbies of land oligarchies, in some countries (democratic or otherwise) if a local business fails, threatening the livelihood of thousands of poor people, it is difficult for the local government (or if the latter is bankrupt, upper-tier governments) to ignore the political pressure that will be generated in favor of bailing out the firm. Wildasin (1997) has rightly pointed out that federal grants to local governments may be less "soft" in the small jurisdictions than in the large (which are "too big to fail"), but even small jurisdictions may have key politicians representing (or lobbying for) them, and in any case coming to their rescue can be done inexpensively.

6.5 Conclusion

It is quite plausible to argue that in the matter of service deliveries as well as in local business development control rights in governance structures should be assigned to people who have the requisite information and incentives but at the same time will bear responsibility for the political and economic consequences of their decisions. In many situations this calls for more devolution of power to local authorities and communities. But at the same time, structures of local accountability are not in place in many developing countries, and local governments are often at the mercy of local power elites, who may frustrate the goal of public delivery to the general populace of social services, infrastructure facilities, and conditions conducive to local business development. This means that decentralization to be really effective has to be accompanied by serious attempts to change the existing structures of power within communities, to improve the opportunities for participation and voice, and to engage the hitherto disadvantaged or

---

10. Attributing China's relative success to political centralization (Blanchard and Shleifer, 2000) does not seem plausible. A strong central political authority can punish local governments (reducing the risk of their capture and the scope of their rent seeking), but a benevolent nonrentier central authority is required.

disenfranchised in the political process. This important indirect effect of redistributive reforms (like land reform or mass education campaigns) is usually ignored in studies that assess the effects of these reforms. Participation or enfranchisement has its own feedback effects in terms of energizing awareness and involvement on the part of a hitherto silent or apathetic majority and building local capacity.

After all, the logic behind decentralization is not just about weakening the central authority or about preferring local elites to central authority but is fundamentally about making governance at the local level more responsive to the needs of the large majority of the population. To facilitate this responsiveness, the state, far from retreating into the minimalist role of classical liberalism, may sometimes have to play an activist role in enabling (if only as a catalyst) mobilization of people in local participatory development, neutralizing the power of local oligarchs, providing supralocal support in the form of pump-priming local finance, supplying technical and professional services toward building local capacity, acting as a watchdog for service-quality standards, auditing and performing evaluations, investing in larger infrastructures, and providing some coordination in the face of externalities across localities.

The literature on decentralization in the context of development is still in its infancy. On the theoretical side, perhaps the key challenge is to find better ways to model the complex organizational and incentive problems that are involved in a situation with pervasive problems of monitoring and enforcement. On the empirical side, there is a great deal of scope for rigorous work in evaluating the impact of ongoing decentralization initiatives, using detailed household and community surveys and comparing decentralization with centralization experiences or some other counterfactual. In such empirical work, several econometric problems can arise. One issue is that some of the data involved in evaluating community participation and project performance may be subjective. For instance, some investigators start with the prior belief that participation is good, which creates a "halo effect" in their observations. A second problem is one of simultaneity: better beneficiary participation may cause improved project performance, but improved project performance often also encourages higher participation.[11] Finally, there is the commonly encountered endogeneity

---

11. For an attempt to take this latter set of econometric problems into account in an evaluation of 121 rural water projects, see Isham, Narayan, and Pritchett (1995).

problem. Before being too quick to claim that decentralization brought about certain outcomes, it is worth considering that decentralization may have resulted from ongoing political and economic changes that also affected these same outcomes. Separating decentralization from its political and economic causes, so that decentralization is not just a proxy for an ill-defined broad package of social and economic reforms, is a delicate problem.

The literature on public choice and political economy is characterized by numerous theoretical analyses of capture of the democratic process by special-interest groups. It is surprising, therefore, that this literature rarely addresses the question of relative capture at central and local levels of government. Yet there are some common presumptions on this matter in the general realm of public discussion, going back to James Madison in the *Federalist Papers* (no. 10). One view is that the lower the level of government, the greater the extent of capture by vested interests is, and the less protected minorities and the poor tend to be. In the United States, this view has been common in the discussion of the need for federal intervention in the protection of minorities in the U.S. civil rights years or of the putative regressive consequences of the movement in favor of "state rights." As is pointed out in the previous chapter, this view is central to discussions of decentralized mechanisms of "community targeting" in developing countries, in which the responsibility for composition and delivery of public services and for identification of local beneficiaries is transferred to local governments. If the conventional presumption is correct, the advantage of decentralizing delivery mechanisms to local governments with access to superior local information would be compromised by greater capture of these programs by local elites. The case for such forms of decentralization would then depend on the resulting tradeoff between these two effects.

Despite the importance of this issue, not much systematic research appears to have been devoted to assessing the relative susceptibility of national and local governments to interest-group capture. This chapter's model of two-party electoral competition with "probabilistic" voting behavior and lobbying by special-interest groups (based on Baron,

1994, and Grossman and Helpman, 1996) helps identify determinants of relative capture at different levels of government.[1] These include relative levels of voter awareness and interest-group cohesiveness, electoral uncertainty, electoral competition, heterogeneity of districts with respect to inequality, and the electoral system. While some of these determinants uphold the traditional Madisonian presumption, others are likely to create a tendency for lower capture at the local level, so the net effect is theoretically ambiguous. This suggests that the extent of relative capture may be context-specific and needs to be assessed empirically.

7.1   The Model*

We briefly set out the features of our extension of the Baron-Grossman-Helpman model. There are n districts each with an identical number of voters, divided into three classes: poor (p), middle income (m), and rich (r). Districts differ in demographic composition across the three classes: the proportion of voters in the population of district i are denoted by β_p^i, β_m^i and $\beta_r^i = 1 - \beta_p^i - \beta_m^i$, respectively. A fraction α_c of voters in class c are *informed* or politically aware and vote for different parties partly on the basis of the levels of welfare they expect to achieve under their respective policies. Political awareness is closely related to socioeconomic position and education level, so $\alpha_r \geq \alpha_m > \alpha_p$.[2] An increase in the fraction of the population that is poor will accordingly imply a lower fraction of informed voters in the population as a whole. This will also be the result of increased inequality in general if political awareness is a "concave" function of economic position, in the sense that $\alpha_r - \alpha_m \leq \alpha_m - \alpha_p$.[3]

The welfare level of any member of class $c = p, m, r$ is a function $U_c(\pi)$ of policy π. There are two parties, denoted A and B, selecting policy platforms π^A, π^B, respectively. Informed voter j in district i votes for party A if

$$U_{c(j)}(\pi^A) - U_{c(j)}(\pi^B) + a + a_i + \varepsilon_{ij} \geq 0, \tag{7.1}$$

*This section and section 7.3 introduce formal models. Readers who are not interested in the technical details may skip these sections.

1. Further details of this model are available in Bardhan and Mookherjee (1999).

2. Delli Carpini and Keeter (1996, ch. 4) present significant empirical evidence in support of this assumption for the United States.

3. This assumption is also consistent with the results reported in Delli Carpini and Keeter (1996, table 4.9 and figures 4.1 and 4.2).

where $c(j)$ denotes the class that voter j belongs to. Voter loyalty to party A is the sum of three independent random components: a nationwide preference a, a zero mean district-specific preference a_i, and a voter-specific preference ε_{ij} that is uniformly distributed within each district on the range $[-1/2f, 1/2f]$, where $f > 0$ is small. Uninformed voters are swayed by campaign spending C_i^A, C_i^B of the two parties: an uninformed voter j will vote for party A as long as

$$h[C_i^A - C_i^B] + a + a_i + \varepsilon_{ij} \geq 0, \tag{7.2}$$

where $h > 0$ is an exogenous parameter.

In the Downsian tradition, parties announce policies prior to the election and are assumed to credibly commit to these once elected. There is a single organized lobby, comprised only of the rich.[4] An exogenous fraction l of the set of rich citizens in the district actively contribute financially to the lobby, while the remaining members of this class free-ride on the contributors. The lobby contributes to the campaign finances of the two parties, conditional on their policy platforms. Given these contribution strategies, each party selects a policy to maximize its probability of winning the election.

Consider first an election to a local government in a given district i. Standard arguments can be employed to show that party k has a dominant strategy to maximize the objective function $V^i(\pi^k, C_i^k) \equiv W_I^i(\pi^k) + \chi_i C_i^k$, where $W_I^i(\pi^k)$ denotes the average welfare of informed voters $\beta_p^i \alpha_p U_p(\pi^k) + \beta_m^i \alpha_m U_m(\pi^k) + \beta_r^i \alpha_r U_r(\pi^k)$, $k = A, B$, and χ_i denotes $h\{1 - \beta_r^i \alpha_r - \beta_m^i \alpha_m - \beta_p^i \alpha_p\}$, the effectiveness of campaign spending in winning voter support. Moreover, the equilibrium policy choice π^k of party $k = A, B$ maximizes

$$V^{ik} = \beta_p^i \alpha_p U_p(\pi^k) + \beta_m^i \alpha_m U_m(\pi^k) + \beta_r^i \{\alpha_r + l\chi_i G_i^k\} U_r(\pi^k), \tag{7.3}$$

treating G_i^k, the equilibrium probability of party k winning, as parametrically given.

The implicit welfare weights in expression (7.3) neatly summarize the effects of the political system. In the case where all voters are informed, $\alpha_c = 1$, all c, χ_i equals 0 and (7.3) reduces to the expression for average (utilitarian) welfare. Policy biases arise from the existence of uninformed voters, which increase the weight on the interests of wealthier classes. Specifically, the model identifies a number of

---

4. Rosenstone and Hansen (1993, table 8-2) present evidence that the propensity to contribute money, attend meetings, and work on campaigns increases sharply with family income in the United States between 1952 and 1988.

determinants of capture: lack of effective electoral competition, resulting from loyalty biases in favor of one party, represented by a higher win probability for the favored party; electoral uncertainty, represented by the variability of voter loyalties (the riskiness of the swing factor $a + a_i$), which also affects the the equilibrium win probability; interest-group cohesiveness, represented by l, the fraction of the class of rich citizens that contribute to their lobby; average level of political awareness, represented by the parameter χ_i, which is increasing in the fraction of uninformed voters in the district; and disparity in awareness levels across classes, represented by the fractions of voters α_c in different classes that are informed. The last two factors explain why capture increases with illiteracy, poverty, and inequality.

Turn now to electoral competition at the level of the national government. Suppose that the policy space is the same as at the local level. Moreover, assume that owing to reasons of horizontal equity or to the lack of suitable information regarding differences across districts, national governments are constrained to select the same policy across all districts—that is, $\pi_i^k = \pi^k$, all i. With decentralization to local governments, this constraint no longer operates, allowing greater "flexibility" with respect to local conditions.

In a majoritarian system of national elections, party objectives turn out to be simple aggregate versions of their objectives in local elections, under certain supplementary assumptions. These include either a single nationwide voting district or an election of representatives from each district on a "first-past-the-post" system to a national assembly, with the party gaining a majority in the assembly forming the national government. Specifically, in the latter case suppose there are a finite number of *types* of districts $i = 1, 2, \ldots$, where different districts of the same type are homogeneous with respect to party loyalties: loyalty toward party A in district d of type i is given by $a + a_i + a_d$, where a_d has an i.i.d. uniform distribution on the range $[-1/2m, 1/2m]$. Then with a large enough number of districts within each type to permit application of the law of large numbers, the overall fraction of all assembly seats won by party A equals $1/2 + m[a + \Sigma_i \gamma_i a_i + \Sigma_i \gamma_i \{V^{iA} - V^{iB}\}]$, where γ_i denotes the fraction of districts of type i in the country. The objective of party k will be to maximize $\bar{V}^k \equiv \Sigma_i \gamma_i V^{ik}$, which aggregates its objective in local elections across the districts. A characterization of equilibrium-policy platforms analogous to that at the local level can then be derived, thus allowing comparisons of the extent of policy biases at the two levels.

Such simple expressions do not obtain in other electoral systems at the national level, such as in proportional representation or in power sharing between multiple parties as manifested in coalition governments or separation of powers between executive and legislative branches. The consequences of this will be noted below in section 7.3.

7.2   Basic Results

We first provide a benchmark case under which the outcomes of national and local elections exactly coincide. Suppose that (a) all districts are ex ante as well as ex post identical; in particular, they have the same socioeconomic composition, and the swings in different districts are perfectly correlated; (b) national elections are majoritarian; (c) the same proportions of voters in all classes are informed about local and national elections; and (d) the rich are well organized equally at the national and local levels. Then the outcome of local and (majoritarian) national elections will coincide exactly in terms of policy platforms, campaign spending, and winning probabilities. This result follows directly from expressions obtained above for the objectives of the parties in elections at the two levels.

Now suppose that assumptions (c) and (d) are modified: voters are better informed at the national level (owing to greater media attention), or the rich are less well organized at the national level (owing to the greater size and heterogeneity of the group or to their larger communication and coordination costs). Then assuming that conditions (a) and (b) continue to hold, there will be more capture at the local level. In particular, the dropping of assumption (d) in the manner echoes exactly the Madisonian argument. To identify other determinants of relative capture, we therefore subsequently assume that (c) and (d) hold.

Consider, for instance, possible differences in the nature of electoral competition at national and local elections. Suppose that two parties contest both national and local elections and that independent district-specific swings may exist but are drawn from the same distribution across all districts. Moreover, the districts have the same socioeconomic composition, so they are homogeneous. The existence of district-specific swings implies that electoral uncertainty is greater at the local level in the sense of a mean-preserving increase in spread of the swing factor. Under a regularity condition on its distribution (satisfied by a wide class of distributions, including uniform and normal distributions), this turns out to imply *less* capture of the dominant party at the local level. The essential reason is that the dominant party A is less likely to win at the local level, reducing the incentive of the lobby to contribute to its campaign funds.

The preceding result relies on the assumption that the districts are ex ante homogeneous in all respects. Suppose instead there are two types of districts, with sharply opposing party loyalties. Voters in the first type of district exhibit a marked preference for party A, while those in the second type favor B strongly. Local elections within these two types of districts will result in very uneven competition, with the contest being heavily weighted in favor of the locally favored party. The level of capture of local government will be high in both districts. If at the national level there are equal numbers of the two types of districts, the electoral competition will be substantially more even, and the outcome less certain. Then there will be less capture at the national level.

Another source of differential capture may be differences in the number of competing parties at the national and local levels. This may result from higher political stakes in national elections or from interdistrict disparities in the strengths of different parties. It is frequently the case that local elections involve a contest between two parties, different party pairs compete in different districts, and all parties compete at the national level. In such contexts, examples can be constructed where there is greater capture at the local level, resulting again from the stronger incentive of the lobby to contribute to campaign funds of the locally favored party.

7.3 Extensions*

Return now to a two-party system at both levels but where districts vary with respect to inequality. This tends to increase capture in high-inequality districts, owing to the higher fraction of uninformed voters in such districts, creating disparities in the effectiveness of campaign funds across districts. These disparities also imply that in a national election parties will bias the allocation of campaign spending in favor of high inequality districts. Given a per district campaign budget of C^k in the national election, party k's electoral strategy consists of a platform π^k and an allocation of campaign spending across districts C_i^k to maximize $\Sigma_i \gamma_i [W_i^j(\pi^k) + \chi_i C_i^k]$, subject to the budget constraint $\Sigma_i \gamma_i C_i^k \leq C^k$. Parties will concentrate their entire spending on district type h with the greatest inequality: $C_h^k = (1/\gamma_H)C^k$, and zero in all other districts. The additional premium placed on the interests of the rich in expression (7.3) as a result of lobbying will be χ_h at the national level, compared with χ_i at the local level. In this case *capture at the national level equals the highest level of capture across all local governments*. The intuitive reason is that in a national campaign, the fungibility of election funds implies that they can be deployed more effectively than in local elections. This raises the value of campaign finance in a national election, allowing lobbies to purchase influence at a "cheaper" price. This conclusion is modified in the case of diminishing returns (in terms of support of uninformed voters) to campaign spending. In that case parties spend a larger fraction (rather than all) of their funds in districts with high inequality. The net outcome is that the national government is captured less than local governments in the highest-inequality districts but more than local governments in the low-inequality districts. In this more realistic scenario, decentralization will tend to raise capture in high-inequality districts and to lower it in low-inequality districts.

Finally, consider the implications of nonmajoritarian national elections in a setting with homogeneous districts. Suppose that the two parties share power in a coalition national government based on their relative strengths in the national assembly, with every district electing one representative to the legislature on the basis of majority voting. Assume that the policy space is an interval of the real line and that the actual policy that emerges in the coalition national government is a convex combination of the policy platforms of the two parties, with weights equal to relative strengths of the two parties in the legislature. In addition, suppose that each class has a single-peaked, strictly concave utility function over the policy space and that the ideal points p_c of the three classes $c = p, m, r$ are ordered $p_r < p_m < p_p$, as in the case of a welfare program financed by income or property taxes. In this case equilibrium-policy platforms diverge more at the national than local level, but the resulting policy of the national government is less subject to capture by the rich than the majority of local governments where the dominant party wins. Similar to the case of heterogeneous inequality, the level of capture of the national level is intermediate between the range of levels of capture of different local governments.

7.4   Conclusion

In summary, the relative proneness to capture of local governments depends on a multitude of diverse factors. Some of these provide support to the Madisonian presumption in favor of greater capture at the local level, such as greater cohesiveness of interest groups and higher levels of voter ignorance at the local level. But a number of other determinants of capture pull in different directions. These include relative extent of electoral competition, electoral uncertainty, and the value of campaign funds in local compared to national elections. Other relevant factors include heterogeneity among local districts with respect to intradistrict inequality and different electoral systems at the two levels. The contrasting roles of these diverse factors suggest that the extent of relative capture at the local level may well turn out to be context- and system-specific. This creates the need for empirical research to identify the nature of relative capture in any given setting to appraise the potential pitfalls of decentralization. We hope that our analysis will provide a useful framework for such empirical work.

8   Corruption

8.1   Introduction

Corruption is an ancient problem. In a treatise on public administration dating back to the fourth century B.C. in India, Kautilya writes in his *Arthasastra* (Kangle, 1972, p. 91),

Just as it is impossible not to taste the honey (or the poison) that finds itself at the tip of the tongue, so it is impossible for a government servant not to eat up, at least, a bit of the king's revenue. Just as fish moving under water cannot possibly be found out either as drinking or not drinking water, so government servants employed in the government work cannot be found out (while) taking money (for themselves).

In a passage of characteristically remarkable precision, Kautilya states that there are "forty ways of embezzlement" and then goes on to enumerate these ways.

While corruption in one form or another has always been with us, its incidence and consequences have varied at different times and different places. The tenacity with which it persists in some cases can lead to despair and resignation on the part of those who are concerned about it, but policy measures can make a significant dent in the problem. This chapter discusses some of the alternative denotations of the problem of corruption and considers the ways in which the damaging consequences of corruption operate in the economy, while not ignoring its putative redeeming features in some cases. The question of why corruption is perceptibly so different in different societies is examined, as are the feasible policy issues that arise. This chapter's approach is primarily analytical and speculative, given the inherent difficulties of collecting good empirical data on the subject of corruption. The usual cross-country empirical analysis on the basis of the data on some subjective ordinal rankings of countries in terms of corruption that are available in the international media is not very useful in my judgment, marred as those rankings are by perception biases (including the fact that actual economic performance of a country often colors our judgment about governance failure) and by the much too aggregative nature of the data. Recently, however, some data have started being collected at the micro level (see, for example, Hellman et al., 2000; di Tella and Schargrodsky, 2003; and Svensson, 2003).

In common usage the word *corruption* is used to mean different things in different contexts. Even in the strictly economic context (for example, avoiding cases where the ill-gotten gains are primarily in terms of political power), there are alternative denotations of economic corruption. In a majority of cases such corruption ordinarily refers to the use of public office for private gains, where an official entrusted with carrying out a task by the public engages in some sort of malfeasance for private enrichment, which is difficult to monitor. There are, of course, many everyday cases of other kinds corruption, some of which may take place entirely in the private sector. For example, a private seller sometimes rations the supply of a scarce good (instead of using the price mechanism to clear the market), and people can use various ways of bribing him or an agent to jump the queue (paying a higher price to a "scalper" for a sold-out theater show or a game, tipping a "bouncer" for entry into a crowded nightclub, using "connections"—some form of long-run gift exchange—to get a job, and so on).

Sometimes legality is invoked, and the words *corrupt* and *illicit* are used almost interchangeably in describing a transaction. But just as clearly not all illegal transactions are corrupt, not all instances of corruption or bribery are illegal[1] (as when you tip the maitre d' to be seated at a good table at a restaurant or in the much more important cases of gift-giving by lobbyists to politicians, campaign contributions to political action committees, or postretirement jobs in private firms to bureaucrats of agencies meant to regulate them). Similarly, a distinction should be maintained between *immoral* and *corrupt* transactions. When you pay a blackmailer, you may consider him immoral, but you are paying to stop him from revealing some information that may be unpleasant for you but that may be neither illegal nor corrupt. On the

---

1. As Adams (1981, p. 177) notes, U.S. Department of Defense directive 55007 allows gratuities when they are a "part of a customary exchange of social amenities between personal friends and relatives when motivated by such relationships and extended on a personal basis."

other hand, one can think of instances of corruption and bribery that some people may not regard as immoral (particularly those for whom the end justifies the means), as when someone bribes a policeman not to torture a suspect. Having referred to these alternative meanings of even economic corruption, let me state that in this chapter I shall mostly confine myself to the application of this term to imply the use of public office for private gain.

Even though this use of the term is common among economists, the term often is applied to many ambiguous situations. Does striving for private gain include policies that are primarily oriented to increasing the chances for remaining in office? The distinction between political and economic corruption can become blurred here. In addition, problems occur in the common comparative use of the term in the absence of any publicly available objective measures. A particular African country may be in some sense more corrupt than a particular East Asian country, even though the actual amount of bribe money exchanging hands may be much larger in the latter; this may be simply because rampant corruption may have choked off large parts of economic transactions in the former. In some cases, the bribe per unit of transaction (and the consequent inefficiency) may be higher (in the case of decentralized corruption, as is noted below) than in situations of centralized ("one-stop shopping") corruption, where the inefficiency may be less, even though the total amount of bribe paid may be larger.

8.2 Allocation Effects

The Efficiency Argument

There is a strand in the corruption literature that is contributed by both economists and noneconomists and suggests that, in the context of pervasive and cumbersome regulations in developing countries, corruption may actually improve efficiency and help growth. Economists have shown that in a second-best world with preexisting policy-induced distortions, additional distortions in the form of black-marketeering and smuggling may actually improve welfare, even when some public resources have to be spent in policing such activities. The argument for efficiency-improving corruption is a simple extension of this idea. As Leff (1964, p. 11) puts it simply: "if the government has erred in its decision, the course made possible by corruption may well be the better one." As noneconomists usually point out, corruption is the much-needed grease for the squeaking wheels of a rigid administration. Huntington (1968, p. 386) states it bluntly: "In terms of economic growth, the only thing worse than a society with a rigid, over-centralized, dishonest bureaucracy is one with a rigid, over-centralized, honest bureaucracy."

Even without preexisting distortions, corruption may be viewed as part of a Coasean bargaining process in which a bureaucrat (who is in the illicit business of selling property rights in a public resource in the form of issuing permits and licenses) and a private agent (the prospective buyer) may negotiate their way[2] to an efficient outcome. If in a bribery game private firms engage in competitive bidding for a government procurement contract, and the corrupt official awards the contract to the highest bidder in bribes, then allocation efficiency is maintained, as only the lowest-cost firm can afford the largest bribe. (This, of course, assumes that other goals of the program are not violated: this bidding procedure is clearly not acceptable in the case of university admissions, for example.) That the producer surplus lines the pocket of the bureaucrat and does not go to the public treasury (as would have happened in an open auction for the contract) does not seemingly affect the allocation efficiency.

This argument is more complex when a briber does not have full information about the cost levels and therefore the bribing capacity of his competitors and when he has to take into account strategic considerations in making any particular offer of a bribe. But the situation can be modeled as an n-person symmetric game with incomplete information on the part of each player, and the theory of sealed-bid auctions can be drawn upon. In such a context Beck and Maher (1986) and Lien (1986) have shown that under the assumptions of the model, the lowest-cost firm is always the winner of the contract, and thus bribery can reproduce the efficiency consequences of competitive bidding procedures under imperfect information. Inefficiency may result if the official is influenced by considerations other than just the size of the bribe (for example, favoritism for a particular client or nepotism); when the briber can get away with supplying a low-quality good at a high-quality price, and the official lets in unqualified applicants with a

---

2. Where a firm is faced with a rent-maximizing public official and is forced to pay to stay in business, two firm-specific features are likely to affect the magnitude of the bribe: the firm's ability to pay and its refusal power (the cost of not paying or its outside options). From a micro dataset containing quantitative information on bribe payments of 176 firms in Uganda in 1998 and other financial data about these firms, Svensson (2003) tests that these two factors explain a large part of the variation in bribes across graft-reporting firms.

high willingness to pay; or when bribery is used to limit the competition (as in the case of bribing the police or tax inspectors to harass rival firms).[3]

Another efficiency argument in favor of corruption is to view it as "speed money" (for which there are distinct terms in different countries, like *lagay* in the Philippines), which reduces delay in moving files in administrative offices and in getting ahead in slow-moving queues for public services. Queuing models that have received some attention in the theoretical literature allow the possibility for the corrupt bureaucrat to practice price discrimination among clients with different time preferences. In an interesting equilibrium queuing model with some special assumptions, Lui (1985) derives bribing functions where the size of the bribe (decided by the briber, not the server of the queue) is linked to the opportunity costs of time for the individual client and shows that the bribing strategies will form a Nash equilibrium of this noncooperative game that will minimize the waiting costs associated with the queue, thereby reducing the inefficiency in public administration. (The model can also be useful in designing schedules of incentive payments in the pay structure of civil servants.)

One does not have to take a moralist position on corruption to see that some of these arguments above in favor of the efficiency effects of corruption are fraught with general problems, even though in individual instances some redeeming features of corruption may be present. For example, in the second-best case made above, it is usually presumed that a given set of distortions is mitigated or circumvented by the effects of corruption, but quite often these distortions and corruption are caused or at least preserved or aggravated by the same common factors. The distortions are not exogenous to the system and are instead often part of the built-in corrupt practices of a patron-client political system. As is indicated above, bidding procedures in such a system may still end up in allocational inefficiency.

Models that view corruption as a pure transfer with no effect on economic allocation also ignore that it may cause exit of firms. This may be particularly important for small firms that operate on thin margins and that find the bribe demanded by an inspector to be too much to bear. Bliss and Di Tella (1997) have a model that focuses on the effect of corruption on the number of firms in a free-entry equilibrium. They also point to the fact that the possibility of exit may limit

---

3. For an account of many such harmful effects of corruption, see Rose-Ackerman (1996).

the bribe demand and that the welfare effect of corruption is ambiguous, depending on what the optimum number of firms in an industry with fixed costs and imperfect competition is.

As for speed money, Myrdal (1968), citing the 1964 Santhanam Committee on the Prevention of Corruption appointed by the government of India, has argued that corrupt officials may, instead of speeding up, actually cause administrative delays to attract more bribes. (I am told in Russia there is a clear terminological distinction between *mzdoimstvo*, taking a remuneration to do what you are supposed to do anyway, and *likhoimstvo*, taking a remuneration for what you are not supposed to do.) Lui's equilibrium queuing model is meant to question the validity of Myrdal's hypothesis at the theoretical level. But as Andvig (1991) points out, from the point of view of imperfect information and strategic considerations, queues as allocation mechanisms are more complex and many-sided than has been recognized in the literature, and different ways of organizing the queue may give rise to different outcomes on the average waiting time. In Lui's otherwise interesting model, for example, both sides in the corrupt transaction are honest in the sense that they stick to a deal, that no new bribe offers are made by the waiting clients after the new entrants have arrived, that there is no moral hazard about the reliability of the sale by the server of a priority in the queue, and so on. The model's results may not be robust to these kinds of considerations.

An interesting question is why corrupt bureaucracies tend to be also associated with a great deal of red tape. Banerjee (1997) examines situations where bureaucrats create red tape and use it to screen clients of different types. In his model a socially minded government employs a selfishly minded bureaucrat to allocate a fixed number of scarce government-provided goods to credit-constrained citizens varying in type in their valuation of those goods. The bureaucrat has two mechanisms at his disposal—prices (bribe) and red tape—and is penalized by his employer for goods misallocated to low-valuation-type citizens. One of the interesting results is that a lower level of citizens' ability to pay the price forces the bureaucrat to use more red tape. With lower ability to pay, low-type citizens become more tempted to proclaim themselves as high types to secure the good. The bureaucrat will then counteract this incentive effect by increasing the amount of red tape against high types. This implies that there may be an efficiency-based reason for government agencies in poor countries to inflict comparatively more red tape on their customers. Guriev (2003) has a model of red tape that differs from Banerjee (1997) in three important respects: there are externalities rather than cash constraints; red tape is informative about the agent's type rather than a purely dissipative sorting device; and the main innovation is in the contrast between ex ante corruption (bribes paid to the bureaucrat to reduce the amount of red tape or testing or auditing) and ex post corruption[4] (bribes paid to suppress unfavorable results coming out of the red tape). While the former tends to reduce red tape, the latter gives incentives for more red tape. Guriev shows that the latter effect dominates and that in equilibrium there is socially excessive red tape.

The part of the literature that views bribes simply as side payments in a Coasean bargaining process between officials or politicians and firms has some obvious problems to grapple with (even apart from the agency problem that the bribee is not representing the interests of the principal, the public). The briber and the bribee may fail to agree on the appropriate size of the bribe on account of bargaining in a situation of asymmetric information, and collective-action problems arise when several firms have to get together to bribe a single politician or bureaucrat. But more important than these problems, corruption contracts are not enforceable in courts, and there is many a slip between the bribing transaction and the actual delivery of the good or the service involved (Boycko, Shleifer, and Vishny, 1995). The control rights on delivery are often arbitrary and uncertain, leaving a lot of leeway for the bribee to renege on his understanding with the briber or to come back and demand another bribe. (It used to be said of General Manuel Noriega of Panama that he could not be bought; he could only be rented.) Of course, the bribee may have to worry about his reputation for keeping promises (but many corrupt politicians have a short time horizon), or sometimes the briber can hire hoodlums to discipline the bribee (but the transaction costs for such enforcement can be high).

Centralization of Bribery
Sometimes the bribee cannot deliver not because he wants to cheat but because a multiple-veto-power system, makes centralized collection of bribes in exchange for guaranteed favors very difficult. One high official in New Delhi is reported to have told a friend: "If you want me to move a file faster, I am not sure if I can help you. But if you want me to

---

4. This is similar to the distinction made by Shleifer and Vishny (1993) between what they call "corruption without theft" and "corruption with theft."

stop a file, I can do it immediately." This ability to "stop a file" at multiple points (a system often installed to keep corrupt officials in check) may result in increasing the inefficiency as well as the rate of bribes. In general, centralized corruption has fewer adverse consequences for efficiency than decentralized bribe taking has, since in the former case the bribee will internalize some of the distortionary effects of corruption (assuming similar powers at all levels to determine the overall rents in the system).

Shleifer and Vishny (1993) illustrate this point with an elementary model that compares two cases—a case of independent monopolists (where different public agencies provide complementary government goods or services independently) and a case of a joint monopolist agency providing the same goods or services. Suppose that a customer in the first case needs two permits or two complementary inputs from two different agencies. Each agency as an independent monopolist will take the other agency's sales as given, and so the bureaucrat in charge of the agency will set the bribe-inclusive price in a way that marginal revenue is equal to the marginal cost, the bribe per unit of sale being the difference between the price and the monopolist's marginal cost (the official price of the good supplied). The joint monopolist, on the other hand, takes into account the effect of an extra unit sold on the sales of the complementary good and thus on the revenue from bribes from the other source as well, so that in equilibrium the marginal revenue in the supply of each good is less than the marginal cost. So the per-unit bribe is higher, and the supply of each good is lower in the independent monopolist case than in the case of collusion.[5] The aggregate revenue from bribes is larger in the latter case, but the customer gets a larger supply of both inputs. The problem is made much worse when complementarity can be artificially created (just when you think you have bribed the two agencies that will give you the required two permits, another independent monopolist comes along and tells you that you need a third permit from her to get your business in place) and when corruption opportunities stimulate the entry of permit dispensers armed with new regulations. Free entry in this game allows officials to "overfish" in the "commons" or the rental havens.

---

5. In an extension of the model, Waller, Verdier, and Gardner (1999) consider the case of imperfect coordination under centralization between the top ruler and the lower-level officials, where the latter may deviate from the former's mandated bribe per permit. If the threshold at or above which the lower-level officials do not have the incentive to deviate is sufficiently low, centralization will tend to be efficiency-enhancing.

Shleifer and Vishny would explain the increase in the inefficiency flowing from corruption in post-Communist Russia in comparison with Communist Russia in these terms. Formerly, the Communist Party used to centralize the collection of bribes and effectively monitored (sometimes with the help of the KGB) deviations from agreed-upon patterns of corruption. Now different ministries, agencies, and levels of local government all set their own bribes independently in a decentralized attempt to maximize their own revenue. It is usually suggested that the regulatory state is at the root of the inefficiency due to corruption spawned by the regulations; the above analysis suggests that a weak central government with its inability to stop the setting up of independent corruption rackets (a kind of economic warlordism) makes the problem of inefficiency particularly acute. This may be relevant in a comparison of corruption in, say, Indonesia with that in India. In the 1980s and the early 1990s the relative ranking of corruption in the data from Business International suggests, for whatever it is worth, that in the perception of foreign businessmen Indonesia under Suharto was, if anything, more corrupt than India, and yet the economic performance by most accounts had been much better in Indonesia in that period. Could it be that Indonesian corruption was more centralized (controlled largely by the first family and the top military leadership in cahoots with the ethnic Chinese-run conglomerates) and thus somewhat more predictable, whereas in India corruption was (and is) a more fragmented, often anarchic, system of bribery, as is suspected to be the case in post-Suharto Indonesia?

Centralization of the political machine also makes it possible to have a system approximating "lump-sum" corruption, without distorting too many decisions at the margin. It has been suggested, for example, corruption in countries like South Korea during the military regime may have been more in the form of lump-sum contributions by the major business leaders to the president's campaign slush fund, which avoids taxing economic activity at the margin. The important question here is how the ruler can credibly promise to keep the contributions lump sum and not come back again for individual quid pro quo deals at the margin. This ability to credibly commit is a feature of "strong" states that very few developing countries have.

The idea of the differential efficiency effects of centralized versus decentralized corruption is akin to Olson's (1993) idea of smaller distortionary effects of the tax impositions of the state as a "stationary bandit" (having thus an "encompassing interest" in the domain over which its rent-exacting power is exercised) as opposed to those of the "roving bandit." Even centralized corruption is more distortionary than taxation (not to speak of the extra burden of taxes that public-revenue losses from corruption may necessitate). This is because of the need to keep corruption secret, as Shleifer and Vishny (1993) point out. Efforts to avoid detection and punishment cause corruption to be more distortionary than taxation. Since different activities have different chances of detection for bribes, there will be some substitution effect following from corruption by which corrupt officials will try to induce investment and transactions in the direction of lower-detection activities (or contractors who are less likely to squeal, even though they may be less efficient). Bureaucrats in poor countries may, for example, opt for imports of complex technology or goods (where detecting improper valuation or overinvoicing is more difficult) in preference to more standardized, but possibly more appropriate, technology or goods. For similar reasons, allocating government funds to a few large defense contracts may look more attractive to the officials involved than spending the money on building numerous small rural health clinics. To preserve the secrecy of deals, a small elite group may also try to raise entry barriers for outsiders, which in many situations has the effect of discouraging the flow of new ideas and innovations. Secret payments, particularly by foreign companies, also tend to be accumulated and spent not inside the country but abroad.

Bribes Relative to Rents

Before we leave the subject of costs of corruption, it may be useful to comment on the magnitude of bribes in relation to that of the rent they are supposed to procure for the briber. The early literature on rent seeking (as in Krueger, 1974) assumed a process of competitive bidding by the rent seekers that resulted in a complete dissipation of the rent. Since then models have been proposed of barriers to entry in the rent-seeking sector (including models of dynamic games of moves and countermoves of the contending rent seekers) and of the various transaction costs and risks that the rent seekers have to face. But what is still astonishing is the small size of the usual bribe compared to the rent collected. Tullock (1980) pointed this out quite early, and the phenomenon is sometimes referred to in the public-choice literature as the "Tullock paradox." The anecdotes are endless. Tullock (1990) cites the case of Mario Biaggi, the New York congressman who manipulated the federal government to save from bankruptcy an enormous Brooklyn dockyard, for which he received three Florida vacations worth $3,000. Spiro Agnew had to resign as Richard Nixon's vice president for continuing to take bribes of a trifling amount from an arrangement made earlier in his political career. Most such anecdotes are from democratic polities. On the other hand, there are anecdotes of corrupt income running to billions of dollars for authoritarian rulers in much poorer countries, like Mobutu sese Seko in Zaire or Ferdinand Marcos in the Philippines. This may point to a particular coordination problem in bribe collection in democratic polities that Rasmusen and Ramseyer (1994) have tried to model.

They use a coordination game among wealth-maximizing legislators to show that if the legislators cannot coordinate their actions, they may supply private-interest statutes for bribes even less than the costs they incur. Only when they can enforce agreements with one another, solving a prisoner's-dilemma problem, will they come close to collecting the full benefits of the statutes they pass. Rasmusen and Ramsayer (1994) have a simple example to illustrate the differences between democratic and autocratic governments in this context. Suppose that private-interest statute S14 would provide a benefit of 14 for a lobbyist and would cost an autocratic government 50 because of, say, an increased probability of public discontent or even rebellion. The autocrat will supply this statute only if offered at least 50, which the lobbyist will be unwilling to offer, so S14 will not pass. Suppose that a second statute, S80, would cost the autocrat 50 but benefit the lobbyist by 80; the autocrat will supply this statute for a bribe anywhere between 50 and 80.

Now take a democracy where five legislators vote on statutes S14 and S80. For each statute, each legislator loses 5 by voting yes when the others vote no but loses 10 if the statute passes. The government thus loses (again in terms of public discontent) a total of 50 if a statute passes, exactly the same cost as in the case of the autocratic government. Take first the statute S14. If each legislator thinks that the others will vote no, then all voting no will be the equilibrium. The lobbyist could overcome these expectations by offering a bribe of 5 to three legislators, but that is too costly for her for a statute worth 14. But if each legislator thinks the others will vote yes, then each may as well vote yes for an infinitesimally small bribe, since she will lose 10, no matter how she votes (so that her marginal cost of voting yes is 0). Thus a democratic government may sell a private-interest statute at below cost when the autocratic government would not. Consider now the statute S80. Here too there is an equilibrium in which the statute passes in the democratic legislature with an infinitesimally small bribe, when the autocrat would do it only for a large bribe.

It is often said that autocratic rulers are more corrupt than democratic ones because the former do not have to worry about reelection. (This is not quite true as elections have become very expensive, and dispensing favors in exchange for campaign contributions is a major source of corruption in democratic regimes.) In the example above, the cost of corruption is deliberately kept the same for both autocratic and democratic governments, and yet the equilibrium bribe amount is larger under the former. The essential problem results from an externality that each democratic legislator's vote potentially imposes on every other legislator when they cannot coordinate their votes to demand a bribe that compensates them for that externality. In some actual democratic polities, such coordination problems are reduced by committee systems, disciplined factions, and party political machines.[6] It is reported that in the postwar decades Japan's Liberal Democratic Party (particularly its so-called Policy Affairs Research Council, where important policies were made and payoffs were coordinated behind closed doors) was quite successful in centralizing bribery and raking off billions of dollars in the process.

8.3   The Growth Process

Corruption has adverse effects not just on static efficiency but also on investment and growth. A payment of bribes to get an investment license clearly reduces the incentive to invest (even apart from affecting the composition of investment, in view of the considerations of secrecy and uncertainty alluded to above). In the taxation system of many countries, negative profits (losses) can be deducted from taxable investment income, but there is no corresponding loss offset for bribes, so that the latter are particularly harmful for risk taking in the context of innovation.

Similarly, when public resources meant for building productivity-enhancing infrastructure are diverted for politicians' private consumption (cement for public roads or dams used for luxury homes), growth rates will be adversely affected. Another growth effect follows from the fact that higher bribes imply declining profitability on produc-

---

6. Rose-Ackerman (1978) has noted that well-organized legislators may be able to extort larger amounts than disorganized legislators.

tive investments relative to rent-seeking investments, thus tending to crowd out the former. As Murphy, Shleifer, and Vishny (1993) point out, there are many reasons why there are increasing returns to rent-seeking, so that an increase in rent-seeking lowers the cost of further rent-seeking relative to that of productive investment. In general, when there is slow growth, the returns to entrepreneurship (particularly in production of new goods) fall relative to those to rent seeking, and the ensuing increase in the pace of rent-seeking activities further slows growth. Besides, innovators are particularly at the mercy of corrupt public officials, since new producers need government-supplied goods like permits and licenses more than established producers. In any case, as Romer (1994) has suggested, corruption as a tax on profits may in general stifle entry of new goods or technologies that require an initial fixed-cost investment.

Some of these growth effects have been statistically corroborated from cross-country data. On the basis of corruption-rankings data assembled from the Business International correspondents[7] in seventy countries in the early 1980s, Mauro (1995) finds a significant negative association between the corruption index and the investment rate or the rate of growth (even after controlling for some other determinants of the latter and correcting for a possible endogeneity bias in the data). A one-standard-deviation improvement in the corruption index is estimated to be associated with an increase in the investment rate by about 3 percent of GDP.[8] The negative relation seems to hold even in subsamples of countries where bureaucratic regulations are reported to be cumbersome, indicating that corruption as a way of bypassing these regulations may not have been very beneficial.

Historians point to many cases where a great deal of corruption in dispensing licenses, loans, or mining and land concessions has been associated with (and may have even helped in) the emergence of an

---

7. As has been mentioned, this dataset is based on the perception of foreign business-people, whose experience of corruption may be different from what domestic business-men face in a country. The former may have less insider knowledge about the intricacies of the indigenous bureaucracy and even less patience with its slow processes. So they may end up paying much larger bribes than what the latter settle for at the end of long negotiations and endless cups of coffee in familiar terrain. This discrepancy may vary from country to country and thus bias the results of statistical analysis on the basis of this dataset.

8. These results are confirmed in Mauro (1996) with a larger and more up-to-date dataset. In a smaller sample of thirty-two countries, Ades and Di Tella (1997) estimate that in the presence of corruption, the total effect of an active industrial policy on investment ranges between 84 percent and 56 percent of the direct impact.

entrepreneurial class. In European history the latter class grew out of the sales of monopoly rights, tax farms, and other forms of privileged access to public resources. In the U.S. "gilded age" of the 1860s and 1870s, the widespread corruption of state legislatures and city governments by business interests and those seeking franchises for public utilities is reported to have helped rather than hindered economic growth.[9] More generally, corruption may have historically played some role in undermining the sway of collective passions that used to fuel internecine group warfare. As Wraith and Simpkins (1963, p. 60) say of English history: "For two hundred and fifty years before 1688, Englishmen had been killing each other to obtain power.... The settlements of 1660 and 1688 inaugurated the Age of Reason, and substituted a system of patronage, bribery, and corruption for the previous method of bloodletting." In the twentieth century, the highly corrupt system institutionalized in the PRI (Partido Revolucionario Institucional) enabled Mexico to transcend the decade of bloodletting that followed the revolution. Without denying the positive role that corruption may have played in history in some situations, however, in many developing countries today corruption is perceived to be so pervasive and endemic that it is unlikely to have good net effects—on grounds discussed earlier in this section, because corruption tends to feed on itself (as is discussed in the next section), and because corruption is impossible to confine to areas of relative beneficial effects.

What about the effects of the growth process on the extent of corruption? Although the requisite time-series evidence in terms of hard data is absent, circumstantial evidence suggests that over the last hundred years or so corruption has generally declined with economic growth in most rich countries (and in some developing countries, like Singapore, it is reported to have declined quite fast in recent decades). While the historical relationship between economic growth and corruption is thus likely to have been negative in general, it is possible to envisage some nonlinearities in this relationship. In particular, with the process of modernization and growth in some countries, corruption may have got worse for some time before getting better. What kinds of forces work toward possibly increasing corruption at the early stages of economic growth? As the economy expands and becomes more complex, public officials see more opportunities for making money from their decisions, which now go beyond simple functions like

9. See Theobald (1990) for a discussion.

maintaining law and order and collecting land revenue. As the markets in many new products are "thin" for quite some time, this gives scope for those officials to milk the process of granting monopoly rights and franchises. In the process of transition from controlled to market economy in Eastern Europe, China, and Vietnam, it has often been observed that some special factors increase corruption even as income grows. For a considerable period of time the transition economy is on a dual-track system: a part of output is still under obligatory delivery at controlled prices, while the rest is allowed to be sold at market prices. This creates all kinds of new opportunities for corruption. The process of privatization of state-owned enterprises in many countries has also given rise to opportunities for public officials to get kickbacks from "crony-capitalist" buyers of those enterprises and contractors.

Yet it is probably correct to say that the process of economic growth ultimately generates enough forces to reduce corruption. Rewards to entrepreneurship and productive investment relative to rent-seeking investment rise in the presence of sustained growth. A prospering economy can also afford to pay its civil servants well, reducing their motivation for corruption. And to the extent that prosperity in the long run brings more demand (at least on the part of the middle classes) for democratic reforms, the latter may install institutions that check corruption. Not merely is the coordination problem in bribe collection among legislators rendered more difficult under democracy (as is discussed at the end of the preceding section), but, more important, democratic institutions build mechanisms of accountability and transparency at different levels, which makes it difficult for the networks of corruption to be sustained for long. A qualifier to this argument relates, as we have noted before, to campaign finance in democratic elections, which leads to influence peddling on the part of politicians. Thus while rich democracies have been successful in better *enforcement* of laws, they have been in some cases less successful in reducing the influence of money on the process of *enactment* of those laws.

8.4   Factors behind Differential Incidence and Persistence

Why is the incidence of corruption so palpably different in different countries, and why in some cases is corruption so persistent? Liberal economists have an easy answer to this: the regulatory state with its elaborate system of permits and licenses spawns corruption, and different countries with different degrees of insertion of the regulatory state in the economy give rise to varying amounts of corruption. This explanation is no doubt valid to a large extent, but it is inadequate. It cannot, for example, explain why corruption, in the judgment of many perceptive observers, may have increased in post-Communist Russia or in post-market-reform China. Comparing across countries on the basis of Business International survey data for the early 1980s, this answer cannot explain why corruption is supposed to be so much more in Mexico than in, say, South Korea or Taiwan in the early 1980s (when in the latter countries the state was not much less interventionist than in Mexico).

Another common explanation for differential corruption, popular among sociologists, is that social norms vary in different countries. What is regarded in one culture as corrupt may be considered a part of routine transaction in another. But a more important issue is involved. It is widely recognized that in developing countries gift exchange is a major social norm in business transactions, and allegience to kinship-based or clan-based loyalties often takes precedence over public duties even for salaried public officials. Under such circumstances, use of public resources to cater to particularistic loyalties become common and routinely expected. At the same time, concern about public corruption is not peculiarly Western. In most of the same developing countries, public-opinion polls indicate that corruption is usually at the top of the list of problems cited by respondents. But there is a certain schizophrenia in this voicing of concern: the same people who are most vocal and genuinely worried about widespread corruption and fraud in the public arena do not hesitate at all in abusing public resources when it comes to helping people who belong to their own kinship network. (It is a bit like the U.S. congressmen who condemn the rampant pork-barrel politics they see all around them but fiercely protect the "pork" they bring to their own constituencies.) Banfield (1958) comments on the prevalence of what he calls "amoral familism" in the Mezzogiorno in Italy, but Putnam (1993) observes in his study of comparative civicness in the regions of Italy that the amoral individuals in the less civic regions clamor most for sterner law enforcement. Yang (1989) notes how people in China generally condemn the widespread use of *guanxi* (connections) in securing public resources but at the same time admire the ingenuity of individual exploits among their acquaintances in its use.

A major problem with norm-based explanations is that they can easily become tautological ("a country has more corruption because its

norms are more favorable to corruption"). A more satisfactory explanation has to describe how otherwise similar countries (or regions in
the same country, like the north and south in Italy) may settle with
different social norms in equilibrium (in, say, a repeated-game framework) and how a country may sometimes shift from one equilibrium
into another (as has happened in the case of today's developed countries in recent history with respect to corruption).

The idea of multiple equilibria in the incidence of corruption is
salient in some economic theorists' recent explanations. The basic idea
is that corruption represents an example of what are called *frequency-
dependent equilibria*, and the expected gain from corruption depends
crucially on the number of other people who are expected to be corrupt. At a simple level the idea may be illustrated, as in Andvig (1991),
with a so-called Schelling diagram (shown in figure 8.1). The distance
between the origin and any point on the horizontal axis represents the
proportion of a given total number of officials (or transactions) that are
known to be corrupt, so that the point of origin is when no one is corrupt, and the end point *n* is when everyone is corrupt. The curves *M*
and *N* represent the marginal benefit for a corrupt and a noncorrupt
official, respectively, for all different allocations of the remaining officials in the two categories. The way the curve *N* is drawn, the benefit of

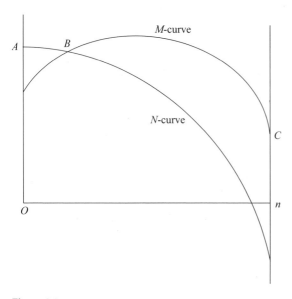

Figure 8.1

a noncorrupt official is higher than that of a corrupt official when very few officials are corrupt, declines as the proportion of corrupt officials increases, and ultimately becomes even negative when almost all others are corrupt. The M curve goes up at the beginning when more and more officials are corrupt (for the marginal corrupt official, lower reputation loss when detected, lower chance of detection, lower search cost in finding a briber, and so on) but ultimately declines (when the size of bribe is bid down by too many competing bribers, for example), even though at the end point the payoff for a corrupt official remains positive. In figure 8.1 there are three equilibrium points, A, B, and C. A and C are stable, but B is not. At point A all are noncorrupt, and it does not pay to be corrupt for anyone contemplating to be a corrupt official. At C all are corrupt, and it does not pay to be noncorrupt. At B, any given official is indifferent between being corrupt and noncorrupt, but if only one more official is corrupt, it pays to become corrupt; on the other hand, if one fewer is corrupt, the marginal official will choose to be noncorrupt. So initial conditions are important: if the economy starts with (or gets jolted into) a high average level of corruption, it will move toward the high-corruption stable equilibrium C; if the initial average corruption is low, the economy gravitates toward the honest equilibrium A. The diagram illustrates in an elementary way how two otherwise similar countries (both in socioeconomic structures and in moral attitudes) may end up with two very different equilibrium levels of corruption and also how small changes may have a large impact on corruption if one starts out at points close to B.

The problem with such simple diagrams is that the mechanisms through which the economy reaches one or the other equilibrium are not fully spelled out. Several theoretical models in the literature try to do that rigorously and also get away from the naive informational presumptions implicit in the diagram. Cadot (1987) has a model of corruption as a gamble, where every time an official asks for a bribe in a bilateral situation, there is a risk of being reported to and sacked by a superior officer. The optimal Nash strategy of a corrupt official is derived under alternative assumptions about the information structure. The comparative-static results show that a higher time-discount rate, a lower degree of risk aversion and a lower wage rate will induce him, under certain conditions, to be more corrupt. Then Cadot goes on to introduce corruption also at the level of the superior officer who can be bribed (beyond a certain threshold) to cover up lower-level corruption. The interaction of corruption at different hierarchical levels of administration leads to multiple equilibria (one with only petty corruption and the other with more pervasive corruption), as the probability of being sacked diminishes with the general level of corruption in the civil service, and corruption at each level feeds on the other. In the rent-seeking literature it has been pointed out by Hillman and Katz (1987) that there are extra social costs when a hierarchical structure is such that a lowly customs official is obliged to pay a part of his take of bribes to a superior. The usual presumption of that literature (which is, in any case, questionable)—that bribes used in contesting a rent do not entail a social cost since they are only transfers—is seriously vitiated when multitiered rent seeking is taken into account, and the official positions to which the bribes accrue are themselves contested with real resources.

Andvig and Moene (1990) in their model assume (as in Cadot, 1987) that the expected punishment for corruption when detected declines as more officials become corrupt, since it is cheaper to be discovered by a corrupt rather than a noncorrupt superior. There is a bell-shaped frequency distribution of officials with respect to their costs of supplying corrupt services. On the demand side the potential bribers' demand for corrupt services decreases as the bribe size increases and as the fraction of officials who are corrupt decreases (raising the search cost for a potential bribee). This model generates two stable stationary equilibria of the Nash type and highlights how the profitability of corruption is positively related to its frequency and how temporary shifts may lead to permanent changes in corruption.

Sah (1999) has a model of corruption with intertemporal behavioral externalities in the context of overlapping generations and a Bayesian learning process in belief formation. The bureaucrats and citizens both start off with a subjective probability distribution that tells them how likely it is that they will meet a corrupt agent in a transaction. Corrupt (noncorrupt) agents would prefer meeting agents on the other side of the transaction who are similarly corrupt (noncorrupt). For each corrupt agent they meet, they will revise upward their subjective probability estimates of meeting corrupt people and are more likely to initiate a corrupt act in the next period. This is how beliefs about the nature of an economic environment that are formed on the basis of past experiences of dealing with that environment feed into the perpetuation of a culture of corruption. Again, there are multiple equilibria (except that Sah's model explicitly deals with dynamics that may induce multiple paths of evolution of corruption): two economies with an identical set of parameters can have significantly different levels of corruption, and the particular steady state to which the economy settles is influenced by the history of the economy preceding the steady state.

Sah's model admits the possibility that there may be discrepancies between beliefs about corruption frequency and its actual incidence. Oldenburg's (1987) account of the land-consolidation program in villages in Uttar Pradesh in Northern India provides an interesting case study in this context. A land-consolidation program involves a major reorganization of the mapping of the existing cultivation plots, their valuation, and the carving out of new plots in a village and thus provides a lot of scope for corruption for the petty officials in charge. But Oldenburg's field investigations found little evidence of actual *official* corruption. Complaints of corruption usually came from farmers who had not gotten precisely what they wanted, did not understand the process fully, and assumed that other farmers who in their perception did better must have bribed to get their way. Bribes were often paid to a middleman, who pocketed the money while telling the villagers that it was primarily meant to bribe the assistant consolidation officer (and even made a show of paying a visit to the officer). There may actually be more corruption in other cases, but Oldenburg makes a valid point that the middlemen in general have a vested interest in spreading (dis)information that "nothing gets done without bribing the officials," and when everybody believes that, it may even have the effect of inducing an official to indulge in corruption, as he is assumed to be corrupt anyway. This is a familiar self-fulfilling equilibrium of corruption.[10] (The middleman's role in corruption is similar to what Gambetta, 1988, observes in his study of the Italian Mafia: "the mafioso himself has an interest in *regulated injections of distrust* into the market to increase the demand for the product he sells—that is, protection.")

In an overlapping-generations framework with dynamic complementarity between past and future reputation, Tirole (1996) has argued that the persistence of corruption in a society may partly be explained by the bad collective reputation of previous generations: younger generations may inherit the reputation of their elders with the consequence that they may have no incentive to be honest themselves. This means that if for some temporary reasons (say, a war or some

---

10. Myrdal (1968, pp. 408–409) quotes Prime Minister Nehru: "Merely shouting from the house-tops that everybody is corrupt creates an atmosphere of corruption. People feel they live in a climate of corruption and they get corrupted themselves."

other disruption in the economic system) corruption in an economy increases, it has lasting effects: collective reputation once shattered is difficult to rebuild. Similarly, a one-shot reduction in corruption (through, say, an anticorruption campaign) may have no lasting effect: it may take a minimum number of periods without corruption to return to a path leading to the low-corruption steady state.

We have discussed in this section the reasons for the persistence of corruption that have to do with frequency-dependent equilibria or intertemporal externalities, but a simpler reason for persistence in the case of some types of corruption is that corruption can be mutually beneficial for both the official and his client. Neither the briber nor the bribee has an incentive to report or protest, for example, when a customs officer lets contraband through or a tax auditor purposely overlooks a case of tax evasion. Shleifer and Vishny (1993) call this *corruption with theft* (a better name may be *collusive corruption*), to distinguish it from cases where the official does not hide the transaction in which the client pays the requisite price, fee, or fine to the government but only charges something extra for himself (what Shleifer and Vishny call *corruption without theft*). The former type is more insidious, more difficult to detect, and therefore more persistent. This type also includes many cases of official relaxation of quality-control standards in inspection of safety in construction of buildings and bridges, in supplies of food and drugs, in pollution control, and so on.

8.5   Policy Issues

We now turn to policy issues arising from our analysis above. We shall in general avoid paying much attention to the policy positions taken by the "moralists" and the "fatalists" on corruption, even though it is sometimes tempting to take their side. The 'moralists' emphasize that without fundamental changes in values and norms of honesty in public life—a kind of ethic cleansing through active moral-reform campaigns—no big dent in the corrosive effects of corruption is likely to be achieved. The fatalists are more cynical and claim that we have reached a point of no return in many developing countries where the corruption is so pervasive and well-entrenched that for all practical purposes nothing much can be done about it. The previous section's discussion of the history-dependence of the high-corruption equilibrium and the forces that tend to perpetuate it does point to the difficulties of getting out of the rut, but some examples exist of success in controlling corruption even in the recent history of developing countries. Klitgaard (1988) cites several examples, of which the cases of the Hong Kong Police Department and the Singapore Customs and Excise Department are the most successful, but in some sense the valiant efforts by one tax commissioner to fight pervasive corruption in the Bureau of Internal Revenue and the substantial impact he made in the 1970s in a hopelessly corrupt country like the Philippines under Marcos provide the most striking case. Without minimizing the importance of moral exhortations in anticorruption campaigns, the focus here is on incentive structures that may induce even opportunists to forgo corrupt practices and on the general problems and prospects of implementing them.

The first point that is commonly made, no doubt with a great deal of justification, is that regulations and bureaucratic allocation of scarce public resources breed corruption, and so the immediate task is to get rid of them. In some sense the simplest and the most radical way of eliminating corruption is to legalize the activity that was formerly prohibited or controlled. As Klitgaard (1988) notes, when Hong Kong legalized off-track betting, police corruption fell significantly, and as Singapore allowed more imported products duty free, corruption in customs went down. Sometimes, however, turning over a government agency's functions to the market implies essentially a shift from a public monopoly to a private monopoly, with a corresponding transfer of the rent[11] but without much of an improvement in allocational efficiency (except that due to a removal of the distortion caused by secrecy, discussed in the second section in this chapter).

While regulations designed primarily to serve the patronage-dispensing power of politicians and bureaucrats are common, many regulations serve some other valued social objectives, and there may be a tradeoff between these objectives and the objective of reducing corruption through deregulation.[12] Suppose that a scarce but essential consumer good (like food) in a poor country is currently rationed by the government so that the poor people can have some access to it. The

---

11. The history of privatization in the last few years in many developing countries is replete with instances of corrupt transfers to cronies of politicians.

12. In a theoretical exploration of this tradeoff, Acemoglu and Verdier (2000) derive conditions under which an optimal allocation of resources will involve some corruption. As they point out, there are many cases where corruption opportunities arise because government intervention is essentially trying to redress some of the problems of unregulated equilibria, not because it is intentionally creating rents to appropriate. In Guriev (2003) red tape has a positive role in overcoming market failures.

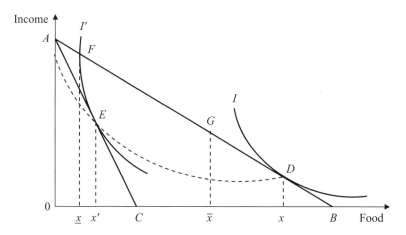

Figure 8.2

rations are administered by corrupt officials. What will be the welfare consequences for the poor of replacing this system by the market?[13] To simplify, assume that the government is the only source of food under the rationing scheme, that food obtained under ration cannot be resold, and that corruption takes the form of the official charging a price higher than the stipulated ration price. In figure 8.2 the ration price p is given by the slope of AB and the consumer's income by OA. The ration $\bar{x}$ is binding in the sense that the consumer with income OA and ration price p would like to buy x, which is more than $\bar{x}$. If there were no corruption, the consumer's rationed consumption equilibrium will be at some point G on the line AB to the left of D. Suppose the alternative nonrationed market equilibrium is given by point E, where the market-price line, which is the slope of AC, is tangent to indifference curve I', and the consumption is given by x'. As long as G is to the right of F (where the indifference curve through E intersects AB), the consumer prefers the uncorrupt ration scheme to the market system. Now suppose that the corrupt official charges a price higher than the ration price while distributing a stipulated total amount of food. The broken curve in figure 8.2 is the locus of points of tangency on the indifference map as the price line is rotated with A as its focus starting at AB and converging to the vertical axis. This locus is also the locus of consumption points to which the consumer is driven to by the corrupt

---

13. For a taxonomic analysis of different cases for this question, see Gordon (1994). The idea for figure 8.2 is from T. N. Srinivasan.

official as the ration is reduced from $\bar{x}$ to zero, since at each point on the locus the slope of the indifference curve represents the maximum price the consumer is willing to pay for the associated ration. As long as the ration exceeds x', the consumer will prefer the corrupt ration scheme to the market system. The basic point is simple, although it can be made with more complicated models and should be brought to the attention of those who in their zeal for deregulation and the market system with a view to reducing corruption lose sight of the social objective that the regulation was supposed to serve. (It is not an accident that getting rid of the corrupt public-distribution systems in food under structural adjustment programs in developing countries has been politically so unpopular.) In general, the literature on corruption often overlooks the distributional implications of corruption (apart from noting that the poor do not have the resources or the "connections" to be able to bribe their way through).[14] In particular, there are many cases of corrupt law-enforcement officers (in collusion with the rich) extorting from the poor, who have few means of protection and are less informed about their rights.

The general presumption in the literature is that an increase in product market competition (say, through trade liberalization) reduces corruption by reducing the rents to be appropriated.[15] Bliss and Di Tella (1997), however, caution that in a model where corruption affects the number of firms in a free-entry equilibrium, an exogenous increase in competition can have an ambiguous effect on corrupt payments per firm, depending on the structure of the uncertainty about the firms' overhead costs that faces the corrupt official. Competition reduces the level of profits per firm available to pay overhead costs plus bribe, but this does not imply that the amount of the smaller total going to bribe might not increase. The increase in competition could take the marginal firm to a region of the probability distribution of overhead costs where marginal increases in bribe demands are relatively less likely to induce exit.

With competition among officials, one way of reducing bureaucratic corruption is to reduce the monopoly power of the bureaucrat when a client faces him or her in trying to get a license or some subsidy or

14. In some cases the poor may not be completely left out. They get the rationed good after waiting in line (unless the good is extremely scarce), while the rich bribe to jump the queue.

15. For example, Ades and Di Tella (1999) estimate that almost a third of the corruption gap between Italy and Austria may be explained by Italy's lower exposure to foreign competition.

transfer.[16] Rose-Ackerman (1978) has suggested that instead of giving each official a clearly defined sphere of influence over which he or she has monopoly control, officials should be given competing jurisdictions so that a client who is not well served by one official can go to another. When collusion among several officials is difficult, competition will tend to drive the level of bribes to zero. Without an appropriate incentive payment system, this can encourage laziness in some officials, since clients who are tired of waiting can turn to another official instead of complaining to the official's superior. Also, in cases of ex post or collusive corruption, competitive pressure might increase theft from the government (including relaxation of minimum quality standards) at the same time as it reduces bribes. So in such cases, competition in the provision of government services has to be accompanied by more intensive monitoring and auditing to prevent theft. Rose-Ackerman (1994) has suggested that multiple officials with overlapping jurisdictions may also help in such cases, since the potential briber has to face the prospect of "persuading" all the officials involved, which raises costs and uncertainty for the corrupt project.[17] (It has been reported that in the United States the overlapping involvement of local, state, and federal agencies in controlling illegal drugs has reduced police corruption.) In the case of legitimate business projects, however, this raises the multiple-veto-power problem discussed in the second section of this chapter.

In some cases with large fixed costs, indivisibilities, and coordination problems, bureaucratic competition through overlapping jurisdictions is not feasible (nor desirable, if bargaining advantages are to be pressed), as in the case of large defense contracts or when the government buys in bulk in world commodity markets (say, in petroleum) or expensive single items like aircrafts. Not surprisingly, some of the major corruption scandals in developing countries (with substantial kickbacks from foreign contractors) involve politicians and bureaucrats in charge of such large procurement cases. On the bribe givers' side, when competition among the foreign contractors is intense, few

---

16. In an agency model of corruption, Laffont and N'Guessan (1999) show that the effect of greater competition on corruption depends on the complementarity or substitutability of the two instruments available to lower information rents (low-powered incentives and greater competition).

17. Laffont and Meleu (2001) model separation of powers among regulatory officials as an instrument against corruption, more specifically as a way to decrease the costs of collusion-proofness, but recognize that implementation of such arrangements may be particularly costly in developing countries.

governments of industrially advanced countries discourage (at least not until recently) the bribing of officials in the purchasing countries (in fact, tax deductibility of bribes by the companies used to make the taxpayers complicit in the payment of such bribes). Even in the exceptional case of the United States, where the 1977 Foreign Corrupt Practices Act forbids American companies from making payments to foreign officials, what are described as "grease payments" to speed up transactions are not ruled out. (In fact, the 1988 amendments to the Act expand the range of such payments allowed.)

Many countries launch periodic "spring cleaning" through anticorruption campaigns. Their effectiveness varies. To be effective, they have to be credible and sustained. As suggested by the frequency-dependent equilibrium models, a critical mass of opportunist individuals have to be convinced over a long enough period that corruption is not cost-effective. But as has happened many times in the recent history of Africa or China, anticorruption campaigns are usually ad hoc and targeted at political enemies or at best at small fry, exempting the big fish or the important cronies and accomplices of the political rulers. Short-lived campaigns and repeated amnesties to offenders (designed to wipe the slate clean) only increase the cynicism about the next round and give out the wrong signals. As is discussed in connection with Tirole's (1996) intertemporal collective reputation model, trust takes several periods to reestablish itself. It is important to institutionalize various kinds of accountability mechanisms—like an independent office of public auditing, an election commission to limit and enforce rules on campaign contributions in democratic elections, independent investigating agencies (like the Hong Kong Independent Committee against Corruption, which reports directly to the governor general), an office of local ombudsman with some control over the bureaucracy, citizens' watchdog committees providing information and monitoring services and pursuing public-interest litigation, a vigorous and independent, even muckraking, press, less stringent libel laws or laws protecting official secrecy, and so on.[18] The watchdog committees need to unearth and publicize egregious cases of public corruption and also highlight credible cases where the automatic and cynical presumptions of the local people that the officials are corrupt turn out to be gross exaggerations, thus cutting down on the feedback effects of rumors and designs of middlemen.

---

18. For a discussion of some of the "countervailing actions" that victims of corruption can undertake, see Alam (1995).

In many countries institutions like ombudsmen or grievance committees allow aggrieved parties to air their complaints, but more often than not these committees do not have the clout or resources to follow through, particularly if the complaints are against politically well-connected officials. Also, such committees usually consider only individual cases and are not authorized to launch large-scale investigations on the general problem of which the individual case may just be the tip of the iceberg. In any case, one general problem in detecting or proving corruption by such institutions is that acts of misallocation of public funds motivated by corruption on the part of bureaucrats are sometimes indistinguishable from outcomes of simple ineptitude on their part. In many acts of corruption both the briber and the bribee gain illicitly from the noncompliance or evasion of the law so that the complaints have to come from others. So well-established procedures of encouraging "whistle blowers" and guaranteeing their anonymity are important.

Many other measures of reform within public administration have been suggested. One measure involves cutting down on the proliferating functions of government departments (using vouchers and competition with private suppliers to serve a public need when customers can "vote" with their feet) and concentrating these functions largely in areas where, on account of elements of natural monopoly or a public good or quality standards not easily discernible to the customers, a voucher plan is not an efficient way of providing the service. Other measures include making supervisors answerable for gross acts of malfeasance by their subordinates; authorizing periodic probing of ostensible but "unexplainable assets" of officials; working in teams (for example, in Singapore customs agents were asked to work in pairs) when lower bureaucrats face a customer instead of one-on-one so that there is some check in the bargaining process (this is a simpler form of the overlapping jurisdictions case discussed above); creating well-defined career paths in civil service that are not dependent on the incumbent politicians' favor; periodically rotating jobs so that a bureaucrat does not become too cozy with a customer over a long period; more elaborately codifying civil service rules that reduce the official's discretion in granting favors; and so on.

In many of these cases, one can also argue on the opposite side. Too many rules rather than discretion may have the perverse effect of providing opportunities for corruption simply to circumvent mindless inflexibilities. Overzealous watchdog agencies discourage risk taking in bureaucratic decisions. In some investment-related public-sector jobs the top officers need to take dynamic entrepreneurial decisions, and some of these decisions are bound to fail. If some private parties gain from such a failure, it will be difficult to disentangle cases of genuine failures in risky decisions on the part of an officer from cases where he or she may have been influenced by interested private parties. The practice of frequent job rotation may provide an incentive to officials for maximum loot[19] in the shortest possible time, discourage learning on the job, and in general provide the politician (or the senior officer) a weapon to transfer an honest official bent on rocking the boat of existing patronage distribution. The opportunity to probe the private finances of an official is sometimes abused against rivals and political opponents. Working in teams when facing a customer may sometimes encourage unnecessary delays or collusion in demands for larger bribes. And so on.

8.6   Incentive Payments for Civil Servants

The important policy issue of an incentive pay structure in public administration is often cited as one of the most effective ways of fighting corruption. In imperial China under the Ch'ing dynasty, district magistrates were paid an extra allowance called *yang-lien yin* ("money to nourish honesty"). Klitgaard (1988, p. 81) cites a quote from the historian Thomas Babington Macaulay's account of Robert Clive's attempt to reduce the corruption rampant in the British East India Company in 1765: "Clive saw clearly that it was absurd to give men power, and to require them to live in penury. He justly concluded that no reform could be effectual which should not be coupled with a plan for liberally remunerating the civil servants of the Company." In recent times both Singapore and Hong Kong have followed an incentive wage policy for public officials with a great deal of success. Current reforms in tax enforcement in many countries, which include a bonus to the tax officer based on the amount of taxes he or she collects, have often been associated with significant improvements in tax compliance.[20] In some cases (like in Singapore) a wage premium above private-sector salaries

---

19. In Wade's (1985) case study in South India, an executive engineer in charge of irrigation may pay as bribe up to fourteen times his annual salary to obtain a two-year tenure at a particular location. This suggests the lower bound of how much he expects to earn in bribes in two years.

20. See Das-Gupta and Mookherjee (1998) for details of some of these reforms.

has been found useful, consistent with the efficiency wage theory. The potential cost of job loss (including the wage premium and seniority benefits) on detection may stiffen official resistance to temptation for corruption. International agencies pushing for structural adjustment policies sometimes ignore that while deregulation reduces opportunities for corruption, another part of the same policy package aimed at drastic reductions of public spending may result in lower real wages for civil servants, increasing their motivation for corruption. When today's rich countries had beaten the worst of corruption in their history, the average salary of an official was many times that of officials in most poor countries.

There is some dispute in the literature about the cost effectiveness of wage policy in eliminating corruption. When bribe levels relative to wages are high or the probability of enforcement or detection is low (for example, the civil service code or public employees' unions in many countries makes punishing and dismissing civil servants difficult), the usual "shirking" models of efficiency wage theory point out that the wage necessary to eliminate corruption may be too high.[21] But those who use "fair-wage" models find wage policy to be more cost effective, depending on the civil servants' standards of fairness in a local context. On the basis of data on wages in civil service relative to those in manufacturing covering thirty-one developing countries and low-income OECD (Organisation for Economic Co-operation and Development) countries over the period 1982 to 1994, Van Rijckeghem and Weder (2001) find a significant negative relation between relative wage and the corruption indicator of a country. (An alternate dataset that uses scores given by experts in a number of less developed countries on the level of civil service wages relative to comparable private-sector employment also confirms their result.) But their estimate of the level of the relative wage that will bring about a quasi-eradication of corruption is more than what one would expect from the fair-wage models but less than that predicted by shirking models. Di Tella and Schargrodsky (2003) estimate in their analysis of micropanel data from public hospitals in Buenos Aires that a doubling of wages would cause a more than 20 percent decline in the prices paid by hospitals in procuring basic supplies; monitoring policies act as a complement to raising salaries in curbing procurement corruption.

---

21. Besley and McLaren (1993) show that in the case of tax collectors who are heterogeneous in their corruptibility, the revenue authority may sometimes prefer to tolerate a regime of corruption among the tax collectors than to pay them efficiency wages.

While these empirical results support the argument for incentive payment, the relationship between public-compensation policy and corruption can sometimes be quite complex. This is because the objective is not merely to reduce corruption in an official agency but, at the same time, not to harm the objective for which the agency was deployed in the first place. Much of the theory of rent seeking does not worry about this because the presumption often is that government is nothing but organized theft and the less of it the better. But as already has been shown in the case of rationed distribution of food to the poor, if there is another valued social objective, there may be cases where the corrupt administered system is preferable to the market. The compensation policy for corruptible enforcers of a regulation that has a valued social purpose may have to take this into account. Let us take, for example, the case of public inspectors charged with monitoring pollution from a factory. We shall follow the theoretical model of Mookherjee and Png (1995) to understand the nature of the tradeoff among corruption, pollution, and enforcement effort and consider the consequences of strategic interaction between the polluting factory and the corruptible inspector.

Suppose the regulator can directly control neither the inspector's monitoring effort nor his underreporting of the factory's pollution for which he gets bribed, a double moral-hazard problem in a principal-agent model. The regulator has three instruments: a rate of reward r for the inspector (a percentage commission based on the fines for pollution collected from the factory), a penalty p (depending on the amount of underreporting of pollution) on the inspector when corruption is discovered, and a penalty q (a markup over the usual fine for the evaded pollution) on the factory for bribing the inspector. The probability that the inspector will unearth the factory's true pollution level (assuming that he will not overreport) depends on the monitoring effort exerted by the inspector. There is also an exogenous probability that the inspector's underreporting and the bribe paid are discovered by the regulator. Given the regulator's policy package (r, p, q), the factory and the inspector simultaneously choose the pollution level and the monitoring intensity, respectively. The two parties (assumed risk-neutral) then jointly determine the bribe, if any, as part of a Nash bargaining solution.

Suppose that the factory has polluted and the inspector has found out about it. If bribery is going on, then small increases in r or p may merely raise the level of the bribe: a compensation policy whereby a large reward for the inspector or a high penalty for taking a bribe raises the cost borne by the inspector for underreporting pollution, leads the inspector to demand and receive a larger bribe, and corruption *increases*. Mookherjee and Png show that it takes a sufficiently large, discrete increase in the reward or the penalty to eliminate corruption (when the inspector's demand for bribe rises beyond the factory's willingness to pay). One way to reduce the bribe, however, is to raise q, the penalty on the bribe giver (making bribing more costly for him), while reducing the penalty p for the bribe taker (so that the latter does not demand a larger bribe): this contrasts with the typical practice of punishing bribe givers less severely than bribe takers.

What effect does the compensation policy have from the point of view of the primary objective of regulating pollution? A small increase in the reward rate r raises the bribe and hence the price of pollution and lowers the incentive for the factory to pollute. The larger bribe will increase the inspector's incentive to monitor, further deterring the factory. The reduction in pollution, on the other hand, will discourage the inspector from monitoring. In equilibrium the net effect is to reduce pollution. By contrast, when the regulator raises the penalty rate p on the inspector, this reduces his incentive to monitor; the reduction in monitoring can reduce the expected penalty for pollution for the factory, and hence the result may be more pollution. Thus although the inspector is risk-neutral, the carrot (reward for reporting pollution) and the stick (penalty for taking a bribe) can have opposite effects on the level of pollution.[22] All this is presented not to discourage a suitable incentive payment system in the context of corruption but to point to the nature of the complexities involved. The analysis also suggests that the reward system should be more geared to the incidence of the primary harm that the regulator is supposed to control. (This indicates that in the case of controlling corruption in the customs department the value of paying rewards to customs officials should be assessed by their effect on the open-market price of the product subject to import controls). Also, as Das-Gupta and Mookherjee (1998) emphasize, incentive reforms in general are more likely to succeed if concomitant

---

22. A potential drawback of bonus-based incentives ignored by the preceding analysis is that they may increase extortion-based bribery where the inspector harasses the factory owner by threatening to overreport pollution (or the tax collector harasses the taxpayer by threatening to overassess taxes). A system of cross-checking, such as the one that was instituted by the Mexican reform of tax administration in 1988 to 1992, that establishes a separate auditor who hears appeals of any judgments by tax agents and any cases of overassessments may be useful in checking such extortion.

organizational changes occur within public bureaucracies, including changes in supervision systems, information and control procedures, staffing policy, degree of autonomy, and accountability at all levels.

Finally, policy issues on corruption cannot be discussed without involving the larger question of the nature of the state that is supposed to carry out the policies. This is related to the larger topic of the role of the state discussed in chapters 1, 4, 5, 6, and 10, but nevertheless, assuming that all states are predatory (as is customary in much of the public-choice literature in the context of developing countries) does not help explain why corruption is more prevalent in some countries than in others (even with similar extent of state intervention) and why countries with similar overall levels of corruption differ in its effect on productivity and growth. It is noted in the third section in this chapter that political competition can reduce corruption (unless the transaction costs in the political market in the form, say, of campaign finances are too large), but what is particularly important in deciding the economic consequences of corruption is the extent of centralization in the rent-collection machinery and the mechanisms of monitoring and detection. Weak and fragmented governments (even under authoritarian rulers) with rampant economic warlordism can let loose a regime of de-centralized looting that is particularly harmful for static and dynamic efficiency.

Some African states in recent history became predatory in their rent extraction not because they were strong but because they were weak: the state could not enforce the laws and property rights that provide the minimum underpinnings of a market economy and thus lost respect; disrespect quickly led to disloyalty and thievery among public officials. The strong states of East Asia with their centralized rent-collection machinery and their dense "encompassing" network with business interests stand in sharp contrast, even though by some measures corruption has been substantial. As is emphasized in the discussion of "lump-sum corruption" in the second section in this chapter, the ability to precommit credibly may have been an important feature of the "strength" of such states. This is not to deny that getting rid of many of the dysfunctional regulations remains a major first step in anticorruption policy, whatever the nature of the state. In addition, it is imperative to institutionalize the various kinds of accountability mechanisms at different levels of the government as part of the agenda for any meaningful policy reform in this context.

9   Ethnic Conflicts: Method in
                   the Madness?

9.1   Introduction

A specter has been haunting much of the world in recent decades—
that of ethnic and sectarian conflicts. Particularly in countries with less
developed or transitional economies, the ethnic cauldron frequently
seems to be boiling over, leading to much distress and devastation. In
this chapter the word *ethnic* is used as a generic label to include all
racial, tribal, religious, or linguistic groupings. The Center for Defense
Information publishes every year a list of ongoing "significant" (with
over 1,000 casualties so far) conflicts in the world, and its list at the beginning of 2002 includes at least twenty-six such conflicts that may be
described as ethnic in origin in this chapter's sense of the term.

In the face of this inexorable tragedy, members of the international
policy-making and intellectual communities are often prone to throw
up their hands in utter despair. As their eyes glaze over television
images of massacres in different, sometimes remote, parts of the world,
some tend to attribute all this turmoil to the historical memories of
primordial hatred among ethnic groups. Yet it is not uncommon to
see communities sharing some historical animosities coexisting peace-
fully (sometimes even intermarrying) for generations (Serbs, Croats,
and Muslims in the former Yugoslavia, for example), and then something snaps and intercommunity violence erupts. Understanding these
eruptions requires us to go beyond pointing to primordial antago-
nisms, examine the nature of that crucial "something," and see if it can
be placed within some meaningful framework.

Horowitz (1998) finds that existing theories of ethnic conflicts are
often characterized by two sharply distinguished views of ethnicity—
the "hard" view, which sees ethnicity as a primordial condition that

evokes intense passion and takes ethnic groups as exogenously defined, and the "soft" view, which takes a more strategic constructivist approach where ethnicity is subject to interests and calculation and the group boundaries are somewhat malleable. While in our political economy analysis we will emphasize the aspect of interests rather than passions, I generally agree with Horowitz that in reality both aspects may be involved in a given ethnic situation. Loyalty to some group causes, sometimes even at the expense of extreme individual sacrifice, cannot be translated in terms of mere interests, and reservoirs of accumulated passion often attract organization and manipulation by political entrepreneurs.

Radical sociologists and historians often attribute postcolonial communal (in the sense of intercommunity) conflicts to colonial machinations of divide-and-rule. Many colonial rulers undoubtedly exploited preexisting cultural cleavages to their advantage or constructed a communal divide as a master narrative to explain away all public disturbances,[1] but some of the nationalist or subnationalist ideology (for example, that behind Tamil secessionism in Sri Lanka, the Sikh rebellion in India, or the successful secession of the Bengalis from the former Pakistan) is actually more modern. Violent ethnic conflicts in the city of Karachi in Pakistan or in the state of Assam in India—in both cases between the locals and recent migrants—have also very little to do *directly* with the distorting legacies of colonial administration. Economists in their turn often associate sectarian conflicts with precapitalism and expect these to fade away with the development of markets, modern technology, and capitalist institutions. Yet in some cases (such as the frequent communal riots in recent years in Mumbai, the booming financial capital of India, or in Ahmedabad, a leading industrial center), capitalism and communalism have moved together. It is thus important to look for some clear patterns in the horrendous complexities of ethnic and sectarian conflicts (without denying the historical, geopolitical, and societal particularities in individual cases) to learn how political and economic factors in particular situations may make ethnicity more salient and to see if these patterns suggest ways of mitigating conflicts (without being glib about prescriptions for "conflict management"). This chapter is a partial attempt in this direction, in general from the political-economy point of view.

---

1. See, for example, the argument in Pandey (1990) for colonial North India.

9.2 Intergroup Economic Competition

The literature on ethnic conflicts often claims that a straightforward relationship between ethnic conflicts and conflicts of economic interest is difficult to establish. People often find it more fruitful to try to understand the cultural roots of identity formation and exclusivity and the social process of escalation into violence. But many important economic factors often lurk in the background, even though explanations for the origin of ethnic preferences, the level and intensity of hostilities, or the group dynamics of their spinning out of control one may have to look elsewhere. We shall start with an enumeration of some of these economic factors.

Many of these economic factors have to do with aspects of interethnic competition, which may take place at various levels: within the working class, between middleman minorities and their customers, within the professional elite, among producers, traders, and other operators, between "ethnoclasses," and between regions. These six levels of competition are discussed below.

A common area of conflict is in the low-skill job market. This is familiar in Western Europe and North America, where a rising tide of anti-immigrant politics reflects the working-class fear of being undercut by alien low-wage workers, particularly when unemployment and job insecurity are rampant and prolonged. Analogous conflicts arise in poor countries, as well—in colonial Guyana and Trinidad, between the Creoles and the descendants of indentured laborers brought from India; in Côte d'Ivoire between the Mossi immigrants and the locals; in parts of India in recent years, between the Muslim Bangladeshi immigrants and locals; in different parts of Southeast Asia, between the Vietnamese "boat people" and locals; and so on. But as Horowitz (1985) points out, the ethnic segmentation of the labor market that usually takes place—with poorer immigrants taking jobs that the locals by and large choose to move away from—keeps the interethnic competition from being as acute as it otherwise could be. Even so, as the anti-immigrant tensions in Western Europe show, things can turn nasty in spite of a marked ethnic division of labor.

Historically, the better known intergroup economic conflicts are between certain middleman minority groups (in occupations like moneylending, trading, or renting out) and their resentful customers. The Chinese in Southeast Asia, the Indians in East Africa, and the Jews in prewar Europe are well-known targets of such ethnic resentment.

In the Hindu-Muslim conflicts of pre-Partition India and in the more recent Hindu-Sikh conflicts in Punjab, the stereotypical image of the Hindu that was resented was often that of a *bania* (trader) or a landlord. Horowitz (1985) refers to a study that asked African university students about their attitudes to the trading minorities in their countries—Indians in Uganda, Lebanese in Nigeria, Ghana, and Senegal, and Armenians in Ethiopia. These students were generally hostile to the trading groups, most often on economic grounds, and described them as "exploiting," "money-minded," or "dishonest." Such hostile attitudes on the part of the members of the elite may not always be shared by the common people, as Horowitz points out, but more often than not elite opinion may have disproportionate influence in fomenting conflicts.

What has been sometimes described as the "tribalism of the elite" pertains particularly to competition for jobs in the government service (and admission to higher education, which acts as a passport to those jobs). This tribalism can actually be more vicious and protracted compared to traditional tribal conflicts because the booty in question is access to the resources of a much more powerful agency, the government. Even when the private sector pays more, the public sector ensures more job security and opportunities for corrupt income, and in many poor countries the government is the major employer in the formal sector. Besides, ethnic representation in government service is part of the symbolic prestige (and a matter of opportunity and aspiration) for even the nonelite members of a community. This provides the background for many of the ethnic conflicts in the world in recent years—the very effective *bumiputera* (son of the soil) movement in Malaysia and Indonesia against the Chinese and the Indians; the perceived overrepresentation of Tamils in professional jobs that initially spurred Sinhalese militancy and the resultant policies of discrimination against Tamils in Sri Lanka; the struggle between "backward" and "forward" castes on the issue of caste quotas in government jobs in India; the agitations against the non-Maharastrians in Mumbai, against the Ibos in Nigeria, against the Kewri in Mauritania, against northerners in Southern Sudan, against southerners in Northern Chad; and so on. Professional careerist aspirations sometimes fuel separatist sentiment among the elite of backward or disadvantaged communities.[2]

---

2. The Muslim separatist movement that resulted in the Partition of India in 1947 was led by a secular elite (under the leadership of a thoroughly Westernized M. A. Jinnah) and not by the religious elite.

Economic rivalries among producers, traders, and other operators sometimes take the form of ethnic conflicts. In some North or West Indian towns, clashes lead to riots between Hindu businesspeople and the new traders and small manufacturerers from the Muslim community who are trying to break the dominance of the former. (Sometimes during religious festivals, outbreaks of ethnic violence are associated with rituals of public self-assertion by the upwardly mobile sections of both communities.) In Kenya many of the restrictive measures against Indian traders in the past were sponsored by an active lobbying group, the Kenya African Wholesalers and Distributors. Similarly, in Uganda the petty traders largely from the Baganda community were active against the Indian traders. The Malaya and Filipino business groups have instigated government action against Chinese merchants in Malaysia and the Philippines, respectively. The minority trading groups then utilize various in-house and guild techniques to raise barriers to entry in some lines of business and form ethnic cartels.

Among farmers land has been a major source of ethnic contention throughout history. Even in recent years ethnic conflicts have erupted with encroachments of the cultivating and grazing lands of the indigenous or tribal people by migrants and settlers from other communities (as in Assam, Tripura, Mizoram, and the Chittagong Hills in the eastern part of the Indian subcontinent or in Guatemala and Northern Brazil or in central Nigeria). Disputes in sharing of water have caused ethnic tensions (as between Palestinians and Israelis, between Tamils and Kannadas in South India, and between Jat Sikhs in Punjab and Jats in Haryana and Rajasthan in North India). Irrigation dams and hydroelectric projects have led to ethnic agitations among displaced tribal people in different parts of India. Disputes over the rights of tribal people to forests and mineral resources have led to ethnic conflicts and successful demands for a tribal homeland known as Jharkhand in Central-East India.

Ethnic riots are sometimes a part of turf battles over valuable resources between rival gangs belonging to different communities. Oil, gold, cobalt, and diamonds have been among the resources over which different ethnic groups have waged civil wars in Africa for many years.[3]

---

3. With a dataset on civil wars that took place from 1960 to 1999, Collier and Hoeffler (2003) show that the risk of outbreak of civil war increases significantly with the ability to fund rebellion from sources like access to natural resources and primary commodities. In the ultimate analysis, it is, however, difficult to resolve whether it is the "demand" for conflicts (born out of grievance, inequality, and tensions) or its "supply" (depending on the costs of carrying out conflicts) that determines the equilibrium outcome.

In urban protection rackets, smuggling, and other illegal activities, in strike breaking (on behalf of industrial magnates), or in real estate speculation, groups in organized crime have sometimes used local animosities against members of other ethnic communities to keep their rivals' economic operations in check, as various investigative studies of Hindu-Muslim riots in Indian cities have sometimes indicated.[4] Ethnic strife may thus be a part of the policy of restrictive business practices by the neighborhood mafia. It has also been observed that in Indian cities with rent control and high real estate prices (as in Mumbai), ethnic riots provide an opportunity for slumlords and their agents to use arson and other terror tactics to carry out tenant eviction and slum clearance where the tenants primarily belong particularly to a victimized community.

The term *ethnoclasses* refers to situations where there is a large overlap between ethnic stratification and class division. In Rwanda and Burundi, the ethnic warfare over many years between the Tutsi minority (which was generally wealthier in terms of cattle and land) and the numerically larger Hutu has had many of the characteristics of class warfare. In the conflict between the Maronite Christians and the impoverished Shi'is in Lebanon or between Thakurs and other upper-caste landlords and the landless Chamars and other low-caste groups in Uttar Pradesh and Bihar in North India, ethnic and class struggle often go together.

Interregional competition sometimes takes the form of ethnic conflicts. In extreme cases it contributes to secessionist movements and in some unusual cases to irredentism (attempts to retrieve ethnic kinsmen across territorial borders, as in the case of the Kurds, who straddle Iraq, Iran, Turkey, and Syria). Interregional economic disparity is a pervasive fact of life, particularly in countries of any significant size.

---

4. See the detailed and painstaking reports and analysis of Engineer (1989, pp. 13, 230). Here are two typical examples: "The rivalry between two illicit liquor gangs led respectively by a Hindu and a Muslim erupted in the form of communal riots in Baroda during September–October 1982. One of the gangs led by Shiva Kahar enjoyed the support of a section of the ruling party.... politicians today need both money and muscle power of the underworld gangs to finance and win elections. They in turn provide them with immunity against any action."

On the Moradabad riots of 1980: "The higher wages in the brass industry and entrepreneurship brought about not only greater prosperity among the Muslims; it also began to lessen the importance of the middleman, often Hindu, in business transactions. Some of the Muslim entrepreneurs even managed to get direct orders from West Asian countries. The Hindu middlemen thus edged out began to rally round the Jan Sangh (now BJP), which has its base among petty businessmen."

Groups in backward regions usually complain of unfair treatment and object to "internal colonialism" that extracts resources for the benefit of and investment in other regions and that discriminates against them in jobs, education, and subsidies. This, for example, used to be a major source of disgruntlement for the Bengalis in Pakistan. Groups in advanced regions in turn complain about their having to unduly subsidize backward regions. For example, the better-off regions like Croatia and Slovenia in the former Yugoslavia increasingly and vehemently objected to the redistributive policy of the Federal Fund for the Accelerated Development of the Underdeveloped Republics and Kosovo. Protest songs, like the one among the industrially advanced Basques that used to describe Spain as "a cow with its muzzle in the Basque country and its udder in Madrid," are quite common.

Horowitz (1985) categorizes potentially secessionist groups in different parts of the world by their advanced or backward status and by their location in advanced or backward regions. For the advanced groups in advanced regions, if one looks at economic factors alone, it is a trade-off between the benefits of continuing to participate in a larger state (like economies of scale in the provision of public goods and in catering to a larger market) and the burden of subsidizing poorer regions. Economic factors are unlikely to be the only or even the most important consideration in a group contemplating secession. But if the balance in this tradeoff calculation turns out to be substantially positive, it is likely to act as a damper on separatist sentiment. This may be reinforced if the advanced group has, as is frequently the case, spread itself beyond its own region and developed its business and professional interests in far-flung corners of the country: a prosperous cross-regional diaspora may thus act as an insurance against rampant secessionism. Examples of this are provided by the Yorubas in Nigeria, by the Baganda in Uganda, by the Luo in Kenya, and by the Lozi in Zambia.

For similar reasons the advanced groups from backward regions are usually ambivalent about separatism. The cases of the Ibos in Nigeria in the 1960s and more recently of the Tamils in Sri Lanka are those where these groups were driven to desperate actions like secessionist movements only after long years of discrimination and violence against them, herding many of them back to their not-so-advanced home regions.

Separatism most frequently is promoted by backward groups, particularly in backward regions. A major instigating factor is the calculation of the elite in these groups, who are currently outcompeted, that they stand to gain from the creation of new opportunities in civil-service jobs and in business, even in a smaller and poorer state. The nonelite—who have much to lose from the potential withdrawal of central subsidies and of the skills and capital of the advanced migrant groups in their midst—are sometimes overpowered by their anxiety about domination by outsiders, particularly if the latter operate with heavy-handed repressiveness (as the West Pakistanis did in East Pakistan, the Indonesians did in East Timor, the Arab northerners did and do in Southern Sudan, and the Chinese did and do in Tibet).

9.3 Markets, Adjustments, and Ethnic Tensions

The various levels of interethnic economic competition discussed above delineate the arenas of conflict, but two general economic issues have played particularly prominent roles in these arenas in recent years. One relates to cases of failed economic policy, and the other to the more general question of the impact of expansion of the market and global economic integration.

Failed economic policies often provide the context of despair and desperation that encourage channeling of frustrations on ethnic lines. In Yugoslavia toward the end of the 1980s, the leader of the discredited old economic regime, Slobodan Milosevic, forestalled economic and political reforms that would have swept him out of power by a systematic ethnification of politics. In Tadzhikistan the struggle for power between the *nomenklatura* who controlled the levers of political and economic power in the old policy regime and the excluded local Muslims has taken the form of ethnic hostilities. In North Africa the failure of the old economic regime of state control, nationalization, and import-substituting industrialization and particularly the corruption and the privileged life of the elite that this failure has nurtured have spawned powerful Islamic movements that are popular among the lower classes. This in turn has had an adverse impact on ethnic minorities (like the Berbers in Algeria and the Copts in Egypt). In many cases in North Africa and South Asia as the inept and corrupt state agencies have failed to deliver basic public services (like education and health), sectarian organizations have sometimes filled in the void for the deprived poor (the proliferation of *madrasas* is only one example). Economic malaise also implies that there are fewer avenues open for economic advancement, and this encourages in some people particularistic attempts to seek ways of climbing up that are more tightly dependent on ethnic connections.

Failed economic policies bring in their wake domestic and international pressures for some, by now standard, stringent measures to be imposed. In this context it has sometimes been suggested that the ethnic tensions have been exacerbated by the hardships of the stabilization and structural adjustment programs often imposed on debt-ridden countries by the international financial institutions like the International Monetary Fund and the World Bank. There is no doubt that the policies of fiscal austerity that these programs bring about make ethnic accommodation and compromise through selective subsidies and patronage distribution more difficult and that they thus tend to undermine the preexisting social contract and unravel long-standing political coalitions. Furthermore, given the political realities (of weak and fragmented organization of the poor), the budgetary axe often falls more heavily on social and economic programs for the poor, which include some of the already disadvantaged minorities (in Latin America, for example, the indigenous people are among the poorest of the poor). Of course, in eruptions of violence the urban lower-middle classes often take the leadership. These and other sections of the urban population may be hit hard by wage cuts, by unemployment and retrenchment in the existing overmanned and inefficient industries, often in the public sector, and by price rises for essential consumer goods and important services (like public transportation) induced by the withdrawal of subsidies and by devaluation. The exchange-rate policies and trade liberalization that form part of the adjustment package may lead to a contraction of the nontraded sector, which includes the informal services sector where many of the lower-income groups earn their livelihood. But in many cases the fiscal and debt crisis is brought about in the first place by economic mismanagement and domestic profligacy on the part of the government and its various ways of subsidizing the rich. This is not to exculpate the role of the international banking community in promoting the profligate and unproductive borrowing that precipitates catastrophe in many countries.

On the general question of the impact of markets on ethnic tensions, there are again arguments on both sides. On the one hand, markets may weaken ethnicity on several grounds. Markets and profit opportunities give salience to incentives at the individual level and thus may undermine the hold of collective passions. As Keynes (1936, p. 374) says in a somewhat different context,[5] "Dangerous human proclivities can be canalized into comparatively harmless channels by the existence of opportunity for money-making and private wealth." Markets also make it possible for the separation of the economic from the political-cultural spheres of existence, which are usually merged in precapitalist formations and thus tend to delimit the influence of ethnicity. As markets develop (particularly for credit, insurance, and information), dependence on kinship or clan networks for these essential functions declines. This means that even individuals who are proud of their ethnic identity can more easily switch to other modes of social interaction in a portfolio of crosscutting affiliations that they usually carry, thus reducing the salience of the ethnic affiliation alone. Besides, by improving outside opportunities and exit options for individual members of an ethnic group, markets may reduce the effectiveness of the group's social sanctions, norms, and cohesiveness, resulting in a devaluation of ethnic networking and exclusiveness. Markets also make ethnic discrimination more costly for the perpetrator of discrimination. Finally, to the extent that the expansion of markets at the expense of restrictive controls and regulations helps economic growth, the enlargement of the pie facilitates ethnic compromises. At the same time a reduction in the size of the rent (generated by these regulations) to be contested may reduce rent-seeking efforts and conflicts, as the literature on contested rent starting with Tullock (1980) suggests.

On the other hand, market expansion may accentuate ethnic problems by increasing inequality, polarization, dislocation, social fragmentation, and the attendant group anxieties. When a country moves to a market system from a system of controls and regulations or from a traditional patron-client system, the consequent resource reallocation rewards the more enterprising and the more efficient (and often the already better endowed) and leaves behind other individuals and groups. Even when the winners can afford to compensate the losers, in the actual political process they seldom do. In this reallocation process there are inevitable dislocations from declining industries, occupations, and regions, and some groups do not have the skills, the human capital, and the access to credit, information, and connections to make easy adjustments to the new technologies, locations, and opportunities. At

5. For a more sophisticated discussion of the opposition of passions and interest-motivated behavior in earlier European thought, see Hirschman (1977).

the same time, the reduced role of the government diminishes its ability to insure the losing groups against these hardships and other external shocks and to assuage conflicts through redistributive transfers.

One of the frequent sources of ethnic conflict involves the market value of land and its possession. As the market expands, some of the land (on which peasants have carried out cultivation and grazing for generations under some informal rules of community control) increases in value, and pressures arise to "enclose" and privatize the property rights on that land. It is not uncommon in such cases for the poor minority groups to be dispossessed and deprived of their traditional communal rights on the land. The history of many countries is replete with instances of ethnic violence in such situations. One recent example in Africa is the conflict that began in 1989 as a consequence of the massive Senegal River Valley project: as land values in the river valley rose, the Mauritanian Arab elite passed new laws on land ownership that denied black Africans their traditional rights; the consequent eruptions of violence killed many people in both Mauritania and Senegal. Even in the urban sector, as land values rise, real estate racketeers in India sometimes use ethnic divisions to evict people (as noted above). In any case, as urban congestion drives more and more people, already cut off from their rural moorings, into overcrowded slums with appalling conditions of amenities, internecine violence often lurks just beneath the surface.

When there are increasing returns to scale, some of the low-fixed-cost, small-scale handicrafts produced by indigenous artisanship tend to be wiped out in the market by mass-produced manufactures, thus threatening the livelihood of some ethnic minorities and indigenous people. It has long been recognized in economic geography that when there are agglomeration economies of scale in manufacturing, the centripetal forces will lead to regional economic concentration and polarization. If the ethnic groups in a country are territorially distinct, then the market process may thus accentuate existing ethnic inequalities, which can be a source of discontent. In human-resource development (like investment in education for children) and in general socialization (acquiring "cultural capital"), minority ethnic groups often face a cruel dilemma between the advantages of assimilation with the "mainstream" (that largely follow from scale economies and human-capital externalities) and the loss of group autonomy and dignity.

Going beyond national economies of scale, one should note that global economic integration by making small countries economically viable (drawing on the scale economies of the world market through international trade, particularly in components and semifinished products) may encourage ethnic separatism. The small island economy of Taiwan became a major economic powerhouse based to a large extent on international economies of scale and vertical specialization; in a less integrated international economy its political separation from the mainland would have been less viable. Many people have noticed the association between global integration and the rise of ethnic separatism in different parts of the world. Even in Europe many regional leaders now feel they can supersede their dependence on the national government and connect directly to the European Union. Alesina, Spolaore, and Wacziarg (2000) have a formal model of the relationship between openness and the equilibrium number and size of countries.

9.4   Ethnicity as a Political Mobilization Device

In the last two sections we have discussed the economic factors that may be at the background of ethnic conflicts. We shall now discuss the political factors that provide the agency as well as the mechanism of ethnic mobilization.

Western countries went through long periods of absolutism and formation of powerful states before the appearance of nationalist ideology. In many (though not all) of the former European colonies in Asia and Africa, however, nationalist ideologies were forged out of a struggle for political identity based on diverse indigenous cultural roots, sometimes even before modern state building got underway. (To some extent this is also true in Eastern Europe, the Balkans, and Central Asia, where diverse cultural formations took political shape out of the dissolution of the Hapsburg, Ottoman, and tsarist empires in the early decades of the twentieth century and that of the Soviet empire in its last decade or so.) Many of the postcolonial states, particularly in Africa, were artificial: they were cartographically carved up in the state rooms of Europe, had juridical and military trappings, but lacked an embedded and encapsulating political and administrative structure or integrated national markets. Their writ often did not run very far into the society. In some cases the territorial expansion of the polity and the economy under colonial rule had helped somewhat in enlarging the transactional network of preexisting small communities and forming ethnic amalgams out of them (as in the case of the Kikuyu in

Kenya or the Bangala in Congo), but in most cases a transethnic historical mythology to provide legitimacy and ballast to the postcolonial state was missing. In some situations the relevant groups were never reconciled to unification under one state even at the beginning of its formation (as in the case of the southerners in Sudan, the Eritreans in Ethiopia, or the Karens in Myanmar), and the subsequent history was marked by endemic secessionism.

The ideology of identity politics is socially constructed as historical memories are adapted and traditions are often "invented" (the nineteenth-century French scholar, Ernest Renan once said: "getting its history wrong is part of being a nation").[6] There is a certain fluidity and malleability in the boundaries of community identity or in the mythology of ethnicity-based nationalities or subnationalities as "imagined communities."[7] This gives considerable leverage to political leaders bent on using ethnicity as a mobilization device.[8] As Ignatieff (1993, p. 3) comments in connection with the recent tragedy in the Balkans, "It is not how the past dictates to the present, but how the present manipulates the past that is decisive." In any case ethnic groups are often easier to organize and consolidate than interest groups since in the former the norms and loyalties restricting entry and exit are more powerful, the boundaries less fluid, and the defining characteristics more easily identifiable.

In India in recent years Hindu nationalist leaders have cynically and occasionally successfully manipulated religious mythology to mobilize electoral support, resulting in a substantial increase in communal divisiveness. Post-Independence India under the leadership of Nehru had established a nondenominational state based on a secular constitution and largely secularized laws, attempting to separate the private sphere of personal faith and the public arena of political legitimacy. But there has always been a great deal of tension between this secular state and the larger society where religious influence was pervasive. This tension

---

6. In fact, as Hobsbawm says in his introduction to Hobsbawm and Ranger (1983, p. 4), "we should expect [such invention] to occur more frequently when a rapid transformation of society weakens or destroys the social patterns for which 'old' traditions had been designed."

7. The major reference work on the political imagination in the formation of nationalities is Anderson (1983).

8. As Horowitz (1998) warns, the constraints of the field in which group interactions occur limit what political entrepreneurs can do and what interests they can pursue. Kakar (1996) points to the image of "evil politicians and innocent masses" as one that does little justice to the agency of ordinary people who participate in conflict behavior.

has been exacerbated by the exigencies of "vote-bank" politics: the then ruling Congress Party wooed the ethnically mobilized pockets of Muslim voters in some parts of the country, sometimes with distinctly non-secular concessions (for example, in the form of religiously based separate personal law for Muslims on matters of marriage, divorce, and inheritance), which made the charge of "appeasement" brought by Hindu fanatics look credible. The social and economic backwardness of Muslims in most areas and their understandable insecurities in a largely Hindu society made them particularly susceptible to such mobilization by sectarian and sometimes obscurantist leaders. To this was added the largely unsubstantiated (but widely shared among the Hindu community) demographic anxieties (about the larger population growth of Muslims through higher fertility and immigration) and the suspicion of extraterritorial loyalty of the Muslims (to the pan-Islamic movement, in general, and to the "enemy" country Pakistan, in particular). This was the context in which the Hindu nationalists' reconstruction of mythology and an attempted homogenization and semitization of Hinduism paid dividends for them in terms of popular support and communalization of politics. Communal violence became frequent in recent years after a period of *relative* quiet in Hindu-Muslim relations for the first three decades after Independence.

Not merely is it common in many countries to observe similar attempts by ethnic entrepreneurs to reorganize historical memory to serve a modernist political purpose, but the methods of mass mobilization used in ethnification of politics are often ultramodern in character. The revolutions in communications technology now enable the most atavistic rhetoric of the ethnic leader to reach a far wider audience and with a great deal more vividness than the old tribal chieftain could ever dream about. Ancient prejudices are transmitted through the most sophisticated media, just as ancient vendettas are carried out with the most modern military weaponry. The channels of access to resources, technology, and arms for even the remotest secessionist group have been globalized to an unprecedented extent.

The intensity of ethnic mobilization sometimes betrays some anxiety about intragroup cohesiveness. For example, the religious revivalist groups, like their counterparts on the radical left, are always worried about heretics and renegades in their midst. They become more aggressive in their exclusivist positions if they perceive their unity to be precarious or if a group identity crisis looms large. The gerontocracy in some ethnic groups (mindful of the need to safeguard their sunk ethnic-specific investments) is worried about the temptations of their young to stray from their old customs and defy their old leadership as they become exposed to outside values and mores with the process of modernization. But the foot soldiers in ethnic movements are usually provided by the young, who are drawn from the ranks of the demoralized unemployed and are looking for faith, hope, and arms-toting bravado.

Sometimes intraethnic competition hardens ethnic posturing as a political aggregation device.[9] In India the Hindu nationalists have used this device to paper over the many fissures in Hindu society along caste and class lines. They usually have a large following among sections of the vernacular middle class who resent the influence of the more sophisticated and usually the more affluent Westernized elite. (This is somewhat similar to the resentment of the liberal Westernized elite among the Muslim militants in the Arab world or in Iran, who try to use political Islam as an aggregation device.) In general, intraethnic animosities make interethnic compromises more difficult as the moderates are afraid of their conciliatory actions being decried as a "sell-out" by the extremists.

9.5   Ethnic Composition, Political Structure, and Eruptions of Violence

Intraethnic competition in chauvinism is encouraged by certain characteristics of the electoral and the party system. Ethnically based parties in a winner-take-all (or first-past-the-post) electoral system tend to push the parties to extreme ethnic demands. Under such a system in Sri Lanka for the first three decades after independence, the two main Sinhalese parties—the United National Party (UNP) and the Sri Lanka Freedom Party (SLFP)—vied with each other in pandering to Sinhalese ethnic sentiments against Tamils, which pushed the Tamils ultimately to take to arms, a process that the later constitutional changes in the system were unable to avert. One of the stabilizing factors of democracy is to provide opportunities for inclusiveness in a divided society. But when one group is permanently excluded as a consequence of the electoral and the party system, as has happened frequently in Africa,

---

9. Fearon and Laitin (2000) emphasize that elites sometimes provoke conflict with other groups to resolve within-group power struggles.

the legitimacy of democracy is undermined, and violence is seen as the only alternative by that group.[10]

The incentives provided by electoral arithmetic and the composition of the constituencies also a play a role in helping or hindering multi-ethnic coalitions. In Sri Lanka the parliamentary constituencies are highly polarized. Even in the early 1970s, in four-fifths of the total number of constituencies the Tamil vote was insignificant; on the other hand, in the small number of constituencies in which the Tamils had a plurality, they usually had an overwhelming majority. In such a situation an ethnic group does not have much to offer electorally to the moderates in a party of an opposing ethnic group, whereas each party caught in intraethnic competition has an incentive to pander to its extreme wings. In contrast, in Malaysia the non-Malay minorities (Chinese and Indian) are numerically much larger than the Sinhalese Tamils, they are not regionally concentrated, and they form significant proportions of the electorate in an overwhelming majority of the constituencies. So in many constituencies the minorities have the power to punish Malay extremists and reward moderates. This kind of heterogeneity in the composition of the electorate facilitates interethnic coalitions on the basis of exchange of votes between the partners.[11] These issues are not captured in the simple negative correlation in cross-country data (as reported in Mauro, 1995) between the index of ethno-

---

10. Bates (1973) finds that ethnic conflict in Africa tends to be maximized when the largest ethnic group just barely achieves dominance. Following Dion (1997), the underlying argument may be given a formal structure as follows. Suppose that the world consists of many heterogeneous agents who are randomly paired as trading partners. Also suppose that the world consists of type As in proportion α and type Bs in proportion $(1 - \alpha)$. Finally, suppose that any individual who transacts with a rival type becomes agitated with probability p and that an episode of interethnic violence breaks out whenever two interethnic trading partners become agitated. Therefore, and as can be easily verified, the frequency of interethnic interaction in the economy will be equal to

$$2\alpha(1 - \alpha),$$

and the per capita incidence of interethnic violence will be equal to

$$2p^2\alpha(1 - \alpha).$$

Clearly, this last expression is monotonically increasing in the frequency of interethnic interaction and reaches a global maximum at $\alpha = 0.5$.

11. For a more detailed comparative study of Sri Lanka and Malayasia on this point, see Horowitz (1989). In nondemocratic setups the ethnic composition of the military compared to the general social composition of the population is also important, as the case of Rwanda with the dominance of the minority Tutsis in the army in a Hutu-majority country has shown repeatedly and disastrously. For a discussion of the military as an instrument for advancement of ethnic claims to power, see Horowitz (1985).

linguistic fragmentation (computed in Taylor and Hudson, 1972) and an index of political stability computed from Business International data.

In general, ethnically dispersed societies tend to have such safe-guards originating from the mutual vulnerability of groups, which fosters interethnic compromises in the polity even in the absence of general goodwill. Large, ethnically dispersed societies (like India or Nigeria) may also have some latitude in localizing and containing ethnic conflicts without necessarily putting the whole state apparatus on the line. The postcolonial state in India has had to fight ethnic brush fires almost all the time—separatist movements occasionally in the south, often in the northeast, and more recently in the northwest and periodic eruptions of Hindu-Muslim riots. But more often than not, these could be dealt with one at a time, without the fires totally engulfing and wrecking the whole state (as they sometimes have in smaller, more ethnically polarized, societies in Africa). There is thus a kind of economies of scale (and of heterogeneity) in ethnic firefighting.

We have commented above on how ethnically based parties can widen and deepen ethnic cleavages. But we should also note that a party in general can act as a useful mediating institution between civil society and the state. In multiethnic plural societies, parties can act as conduits for group demands and can moderate and regulate them. We have noted above that there was a relative quiet in Hindu-Muslim vio-lence in India in the first three decades after Independence. India in that period had also a relatively successful experience of containing in-tense conflicts of linguistic groups in a polyglot country. This period also was characterized by the effective operation of a massive coun-trywide organization, the Congress Party, that had an elaborate but resilient network of transactional negotiations and a political machine much larger than even the formidable organizations of the Liberal Democratic Party (LDP) in Japan or the Christian Democrats in Italy at that time. Many political observers in India associate the rise in ethnic violence with the decline in this huge mediating institution, along with other decaying governance structures[12] (including the politicization of the bureaucracy and the police and the growing nexus between pol-iticians and the criminal underworld). When such mediating institu-tions fail in their functions, the organizational channels of demand

---

12. For a detailed account of the erosion of established political authority in India and of the institutional capacity to absorb conflicts, see Kohli (1990).

articulation and conflict resolution are easily clogged, and group tensions spill over into the streets with increasing frequency in agitational politics, anomic violence, and intransigent extremism. The Sikhs in Punjab are a relatively prosperous group with dispersed interests in other parts of India that should have worked against separatism, but complications in their situation arose from international factors like support from adjoining Pakistan. The origin of the Sikh rebellion (now suppressed through largely brutal means) had much to do with the diminished institutional capacity of the ruling party to negotiate compromises in time and in general to follow the policies of inclusive accommodation that paid good dividends elsewhere in India during earlier decades. Instead, through short-sighted manipulative politics, what was essentially a movement for regional autonomy was allowed to spin out of control.

Political party is only one among many civic organizations (business associations, trade unions, professional groups, and sports clubs are others) that can play a role in moderating ethnic conflicts. In a comparison of riot-prone and peaceful cities in Hindu-Muslim rioting in India, Varshney (2002) has found that ethnically integrated civic organizations are very effective in controlling or preventing conflict. One problem with such comparative empirical studies is that both integrated civic organizations and peace may be jointly determined by a third set of omitted variables.

In general, the battered but as yet remarkably resilient structures of democratic negotiations in most parts of India still offer some means for interethnic accommodation. The political-institutional failures are much more severe in many other countries, particularly in Africa. The extreme cases in recent history are provided by Lebanon (where for a prolonged period in an organizational vacuum without functioning political parties, the armed private militias ruled the roost) and more recently by Somalia, Liberia, Sierra Leone, Rwanda, Burundi, and Congo (where the governance structures basically collapsed).

Reciprocal vulnerability in electoral fortunes may help interethnic compromises. But when democratic institutions and credible mechanisms of commitment and arbitration collapse, the ethnic composition in different regions may lead to reciprocal vulnerability to violence. In such situations each group is afraid of being victimized, and sometimes this fear drives them to strike first in a preemptive move to minimize damage. As Weingast (1994) argues with a game-theoretic example applied to the process of disintegration of Yugoslavia, the damage from victimhood is often so large that even small probabilities that the other group will act aggressively can induce the first group to initiate violence, even when the latter would have preferred to live in peaceful coexistence. Ethnic hatred is thus not adequate to explain this strategic recourse to violence against the best of intentions. Block (1993, p. 10) quotes a young Croatian at Mostar: "I really don't hate Muslims—but because of the situation I want to kill them all." This young man originally intended to sit the war out, but the "situation" in Mostar caught up with him; he had to choose to fight and pre-emptively kill or leave his community like a traitor or a coward. This also suggests opportunities for extremists in each group to influence their mobilization of the initially reluctant moderates: preemptive strikes by the former against the rival ethnic group and the anticipated retaliation against the whole group are often successful in enlisting the moderates in the extremist cause. De Figueiredo and Weingast (1999) model how in equilibrium unscrupulous extremist leaders are able to maintain power by using their informational advantages to play up moderates' fears of violent and indiscriminate victimization by the rival group (which is perceived to be costlier than war). Information asymmetries and manipulation of information by better-informed political elites also play a prominent role in Woodward's (1999) analysis of civil war in Bosnia-Herzegovina and in Jones's (1999) analysis of events in Rwanda.

Weingast (1994) also uses the same model to explain why it is often the case that after a long period of quiescence ethnic violence seems to erupt suddenly. The failure of mediating institutions in India during the spate of Hindu-Muslim riots in recent years after a long period of relative quiet is noted above. Weingast's model is also one of institutional failure: when there is a breakdown in some of the preexisting institutions of trust and commitment, a group reevaluates the probability of facing aggression from an opposing group, and when that probability exceeds a critical value (below which peace is maintained), fears of becoming a victim will induce the former group to initiate violence. (The revoking of federal concessions in Serbia and in Sudan leading to new violence may be cited as examples from recent history).

But the decision-making process of the individual member of a rampaging group still needs explanation. Why does he or she conform to the group decision? If this behavior is not to be written off simply as irrational zealotry, some alternative mechanisms must be at work. One is suggested by the case of the Croatian young man cited above—social sanctions on deviant behavior. There are now quite a few models in economics—Akerlof's (1984) is one of the best known—of a Nash equilibrium of individual conformity to unpleasant group behavior arising out of a mutually sustaining network of social sanctions; the sanctions diminish in effectiveness as the group size increases. Potential dissidents may be too pessimistic about the success of dissent, and the failure to challenge group behavior thus becomes a self-fulfilling prophecy. Then there are cases of strategic complementarities, whereby the more people adopt a particular behavior pattern, the more convenient it is for others to join the bandwagon, and as more people join in, the equilibrium "tips" over (to use Schelling's, 1960, idea of a "tipping equilibrium") from, say, an equilibrium of communal tolerance to one of hostilities. Kuran (1995) shows how individuals often engage in ethnic-preference falsification in an effort to accommodate perceived social pressures and how such interdependence among individuals can influence the pace and nature of ethnification.

But there is an additional, though related, element of fragility in uninformed mass behavior: small perturbations can frequently lead to large shifts. Anyone who has ever observed the formation of rumors and noted how important a role rumors (particularly about violence perpetrated by members of an opposed community) play in sparking communal riots in hitherto quiet neighborhoods has observed the dynamics of imitative decision processes—what has been called *informational cascades*. In a model of volatile fads and fashions, an informational cascade has been described by Bikhchandani, Hirshleifer, and Welch (1992) as a situation when an individual observes the actions of those ahead of him and finds it optimal to follow the behavior of the preceding individual rather than to obtain his or her own information. They show in their model of a sequential decision-making process under uncertainty that at some stage a decision maker will ignore his or her private information and act only on the information obtained from the previous decisions of others. (Thus, to apply this theory to the current context, a Hindu or a Serb will ignore private information about friendly Muslim neighbors and go by what others have told him or her about the aggressive propensities of Muslims.) Unlike mechanisms of conformity where the process becomes more robust as the number of followers increases, the "depth" of an informational cascade need not rise with the number of adopters: once a cascade has started, adoptions by more people are uninformative; a cascade aggregates the information of only a few early individuals' actions. Thus conformity in this case may be brittle and may break with arrival of new and credible information. The public-policy implications of this aspect of informational cascades are discussed in the last section in this chapter.

An alternative approach to ethnic relations has been developed by Fearon and Laitin (1996). According to them, existing scholarship on ethnic conflict has been geared too heavily toward explaining (highly visible) episodes of violence and has devoted too little effort toward understanding what underpins the more prevalent phenomena of peaceful coexistence and cooperation in the face of ethnic animosities—even when the state is inadequate in providing credible commitment mechanisms to support interethnic compromise. In particular, Fearon and Laitin emphasize an "in-group policing equilibrium" in a randomized social matching game with trigger-punishment strategies. The presumption is that intragroup information networks are more dense than intergroup ones and that individuals who transgress against ethnic rivals are punished by members of their own ethnic group. This is akin to the "community-responsibility system" and intragroup sanctions in long-distance trade and credit in early modern Europe discussed by Greif (1997). There are, however, serious limitations to in-group policing.

As Bhavnani and Backer (2000) argue, in-group policing can have an uglier side. Specifically, in-group policing can just as easily be used to sanction individuals who *do not* transgress against (or fight or massacre) their ethnic rivals. The presence of such "genocidal norms," as they term it, appears to be evident in the 1994 Rwandan tragedy, where it is estimated that between 10,000 and 30,000 Hutu moderates were killed for their refusal to participate in the massacre of their Tutsi countrymen.

That in-group policing can be insufficient to sustain cooperative outcomes even in less violent circumstances is demonstrated by Miguel and Gugerty (2002), who examine public-good investment in an ethnically diverse setting. In their model, self-interested households are allocated across two ethnic groups and must simultaneously decide whether to contribute to a public good that benefits all households uniformly. Household choices are observed ex post, and noncontributors may be punished by social sanction. The two critical assumptions are that households receive punishment only from their ethnic cohorts and that the size of the punishment is an increasing function of the number of own-group households that have contributed. This sets the stage for a "tipping" outcome: households in group A contribute to avoid heavy sanctions if they expect a sufficient number of other group A households to contribute, but they free-ride on the contributions of group B if few other group A households are expected to contribute. Miguel and Gugerty show that at low levels of ethnic diversity (where one group composes the overwhelming majority), the high-contribution outcome obtains for the majority ethnic group, while the low-contribution outcome obtains for the minority ethnic group. As ethnic diversity increases, the proportion of the total population made up of the contributing majority group shrinks, while the proportion made up of the free-riding minority group grows, leading to declining investment in the public good. At very high levels of ethnic diversity, where both groups are close to equal in size, the temptation to free-ride is too great for households in both groups, and so total contributions to the public good equal zero. Using microdata on school finance in Kenya, Miguel and Gugerty find empirical evidence to support these results.

9.6 Policy Isuues: Political Institutions of Commitment

We have discussed the economic factors that are sometimes at the background of ethnic turmoil, along with the political mechanisms of mobilization and the institutions of mediation and containment in situations of conflict. In this and the next section we shall try to draw some policy lessons from the above discussion. In the real world the actual situations of conflict are much too complex and enveloped in the particularities of history, culture, geopolitics, and personal ambitions of leaders to be amenable to neat policy prescriptions derived from structured and streamlined models of analysis. The complexities are sometimes so overwhelming that we tend to throw up our hands in despair or look away until the warring factions bleed themselves to exhaustion. It is the task of a political-economy analyst to discern some patterns, however oversimplified—some method in the madness—and look for ways of constructing incentives for conciliatory actions. Working toward an incentive structure that induces otherwise disaffected people to patch up and cooperate is more useful than mere exhortations or sermons about solidarity and fraternity or drastic measures like banning ethnic parties (which drive them underground and encourage violence). To be of sustained value these incentives are to be embodied in institutions, and institution building is easier said than done.

Various political institutions provide guarantees against fears of victimhood and subjugation (and the consequent preemptive agression) and also provide mechanisms of commitment on the part of the state as well as the contending groups in a plural society. In a democratic society this usually involves constitutional arrangements for checks and balances and separation of powers (with an independent judiciary to enforce these arrangements), and the constitution should be sufficiently difficult to amend, making the commitments credible.[13]

The separation of powers is to be installed among the executive, the legislature, and the judiciary, and each party with numerically significant seats in the legislature should have some veto power not on day-to-day legislation but on some predefined set of basic issues. Such a multiple-veto system reduces the flexibility of operation, apart from hardening ethnic distinctions, but in situations of preexisting deep distrust it may be an unavoidable price to be paid for allaying the suspicions of rival groups that they will be excluded on important matters. Power sharing—in the form of allowing leaders of major defeated parties to have some representation in a coalition government—needs to be institutionalized, even beyond the kind of consociational arrangements illustrated by Lijphart (1977) from the experience of small pluralistic societies in parts of Europe. Recent attempts in South Africa to share power between leaders of white and black groups have functioned reasonably well. Below the top leadership level, one important contentious issue arises from attempted ethnification of the police and the bureaucracy on the part of the majority ethnic party. One of the major factors that drove the Serbs in Croatia to initiate guerilla action was the decision by Croatia to remove Serbs from local police forces. The Hindu-Muslim conflicts and backward-caste/forward-caste conflicts in recent years in India have been exacerbated by politicization of the local police and bureaucracy by the ruling party in the state governments, with the victimized community in these conflict situations looking on the latter, with a great deal of justification, as partisans and accomplices rather than protectors. Institutional safeguards against such ethnification of the arms of the state and means of redress in cases of institutional violations are absolutely crucial in maintaining legitimacy of the state and reducing suspicion among ethnic groups.

---

13. As Singh and Wright (1995) emphasize, these constitutional safeguards are particularly important for small minority groups with low bargaining strength.

The electoral system has to give incentives for the formation of multiethnic coalitions and interethnic accommodation and to encourage the exchange of votes between moderates in contending ethnic parties. As shown above, the system in Sri Lanka used to be deficient in this respect compared to that in Malaysia. Many ethnically divided polities have noted the damaging effects of the first-past-the-post electoral rule in single-member constituencies, particularly if the ethnic groups are regionally polarized. Sri Lanka adopted, somewhat late, a preferential system of voting in presidential elections in which the second or third preferences of minorities might turn out to be important for the majority group. After the tragic war in Biafra, the Nigerian Second Republic devised a presidential electoral formula in which election to the presidency required a candidate to win a plurality of votes nationwide plus at least 25 percent of the vote in no fewer than two-thirds of the nineteen states. These attempts at confronting a structural incentive problem are important to study, even though they did not quite solve the problem in Sri Lanka or Nigeria. Similarly, the first-past-the-post rule, by giving the majority party a disproportionate number of seats, often causes frustration in a minority ethnic party. This may be assuaged by the proportional-representation rule. The latter may sometimes produce a proliferation of splinter parties and thus instability of another kind, but the evidence on this is mixed (and threshold size of a party can be required, as in Germany).

When ethnic groups are somewhat territorially distinct, devolution of power in the form of a federal structure and regional autonomy are important. Such devolutions fragment the support of some dominant majority groups (this has been the effect of Nigerian federalism on the dominance of the Hausa-Fulani), disperse the points of conflict, and compartmentalize the conflict in substate units or intraethnic groups.[14] As with the familiar Russian dolls, there are always groups within groups, and attention gets deflected from a dangerously overheated center. A larger number of states is usually better for such dispersal of tension. The nineteen states in the Nigerian Second Republic served that purpose.[15] With a similar goal in mind, the new constitution in Ethiopia drew up nine new regions so that in each, except the south,

---

14. To quote Horowitz (1985, p. 619), "Where groups are territorially concentrated, devolution may have utility, not because it provides 'self-determination' but because, once power is devolved, it becomes somewhat more difficult to determine who the self is."
15. The excessive fragmentation of states in the more recent history of Nigeria may have, however, been counterproductive.

one of the eight main ethnic groups dominates. Regional autonomy often diffuses ethnic separatism: relatively successful cases in recent years include that of the Miskitos in Nicaragua and the Moros in the Philippines. On the other hand, regional autonomy may block the prospects of civil-service jobs for advanced groups from backward regions outside their own regions and may be a source of discontent.

Federalism and regional autonomy imply both administrative and fiscal decentralization. From the point of view of ethnic conflicts decentralization deflects the focus of tension away from the center and reduces the power of the central bureaucracy, which is often uncoordinated and insensitive to local needs of particular groups. By increasing local accountability of officials and adjusting the delivery of public services to fit the diversity of preferences of different groups (this is, for example, culturally important in the case of children's education in terms of curriculum and language of instruction), decentralization can go a long way in helping to diffuse tensions.

But as is discussed in chapter 6, many administrative and fiscal constraints may reduce the expected benefits of decentralization. In particular, fiscal competition among the regions and mobility of capital seriously restrain the ability of the regional government to follow its own tax, expenditure, and regulatory options, much to the disgruntlement of the potential separatists. Furthermore, given the limited revenue-raising capacity as well as the pressures on expenditure of the subnational units of administration, there is often a built-in tendency toward vertical fiscal imbalance and dependence on central transfers. This has two major political-economic effects that can feed back onto ethnic conflicts. First, if the ethnic groups are territorially distinct, the majority ethnic party at the center can use the local units' dependence on central transfer to manipulate alliances against and inflict selective punishments on rival ethnic groups. Second, when the subnational governments are frequently bailed out by the center, the resultant fiscal indiscipline of the former may exacerbate the problem of fiscal deficit and macroeconomic instability for the country as a whole, which ultimately makes the adjustment problems (that some of the poorer groups bear the particular brunt of) much harder. In cases when the center tries to harden the budget constraint and let local units raise their resources (through taxes, borrowing, and foreign investment), the ensuing competition usually favors the regions with better endowments and infrastructure. In some countries, as part of the structural-adjustment program, the center has tried to shift the fiscal responsibility of some redistributive programs to the underfunded local units, with serious implications for poor ethnic groups in backward regions.

The political dilemma of announcing a policy of devolution of power has to do with its appropriate timing. If the government is considered to have yielded "too early" to sectarian agitations, a whole host of hitherto dormant movements in other regions and groups may be encouraged, and the state may soon be engulfed in them; this is the argument that usually persuades the leaders at the center to drag their feet. On the other hand, if the government is considered to have yielded "too late," the timing may signal the weakness or vacillation of a government reacting to separatist violence and may encourage a further escalation of violence and demands that spiral to secession. It requires a great deal of political acumen and confidence on the part of the central leadership to demonstrate sensitivity to local-level grievances by devolving power preemptively and effectively and at the same time to show credible commitment not to tolerate any compromise on the basic question of territorial integrity of the nation as a whole. The policy of power sharing has to be steered slowly and cautiously (so as not to trigger a backlash in parts of the dominant group) but persistently and without reneging on agreed concessions (so as not to give the militant factions in the minority groups a reason to defect). This is a delicate task.

9.7 Economic-Policy Issues

A major economic policy aimed at reduction of ethnic tension has been to provide preferential treatment to disadvantaged minorities in civil-service jobs, admission to higher education, business contracts and permits, and so on. Variants of this policy have been tried in Malaysia, India, the Southern Philippines, and elsewhere. Politicians who face ethnic turmoil are sometimes quick to adopt these policies as a low-cost strategy. But these policies, even when their immediate financial costs are low, may be costly in the long run: job quotas for minorities may splinter the labor market, distort allocation of labor between covered and other sectors, and seriously impede efficiency and morale. Since the quotas usually apply to public-sector jobs only, this further exacerbates the declining efficiency of the public as opposed to the private sector. Even the objective of reducing tensions is not achieved in all cases; in North India the job-"reservation" policy in favor of the so-called backward castes has produced a backlash among the upper castes and intensified intercaste tensions. The preferential policy for business permits and contracts are in some cases easily bypassed with appropriate deals and bribes: in Malaysia and Indonesia these deals used to be called Ali-Baba combinations, Ali being the Muslim *bumiputera* or *pribumi* front man and Baba the Chinese businessman. In general, the preferential policy, as under the New Economic Policy (NEP) in Malayasia, has resulted largely in a substantial transfer of rent to the politically well connected.

If, however, group-specific dynamic externalities and social capital (like peer effects and role models) are important determinants of economic success, as in the models of Benabou (1994) and Durlauf (1996), preferential policies can increase efficiency by changing the way that workers are sorted across occupations and firms. In addition, if employers hold negative-stereotype views about minority-worker productivity, and if in such cases the return to acquiring signals of ability is low or if signals are uninformative, preferential job policies for some time can help in eliminating stereotypes and thus improving incentives on the part of minority workers for skill acquisition, as Coate and Loury (1993) have pointed out. If continued for too long, the same policies can be a disincentive to skill acquisition among members of the quota-protected group.

To the extent that preferential policies are supposed to cope with a historical handicap, their economic rationale is akin to that behind the age-old argument for infant-industry protection in early stages of development. Some disadvantaged groups need temporary protection against competition so that they can participate in "learning by doing" and on-the-job skill formation before catching up with the others. Some of the standard arguments against infant-industry protection are also equally applicable against preferential policies. For example, the "infant," once protected, sometimes refuses to grow up: preferential policies, once adopted, are extremely difficult to reverse. The Indian constitution stipulated a specified duration for job reservation for the lowest castes and tribes in the social hierarchy. Not only has this been extended indefinitely, but the principle of reservation has now been extended to a large number of other castes. Another argument against infant-industry protection is that even when the goal is justifiable, it may be achieved more efficiently through other policies. For example, a disadvantaged group may be helped by a preferential investment policy or development programs in a region where the group is concentrated or with preferential loans, scholarships, job-training programs, and extension services for its members, instead of job quotas that bar qualified candidates who come from advanced groups. Such indirect policies of helping backward groups are less likely to generate resentment among advanced groups (particularly because in this case the burden may be shared more evenly, whereas in the case of job quotas the redistributive burden falls on a subset of the advanced group).

The ultimate rationale behind preferential policies in civil-service jobs has less to do with dynamic efficiency (as in the learning-by-doing argument for infant-industry protection) and more to do with institutionalized rent sharing. Civil-service jobs are looked on as sinecures, with salaries that are much above the reservation income of the employees, particularly when there is rampant unemployment even among the educated. At most levels these jobs come with a great deal of opportunity to earn various kinds of rental income arising out of the allocation of scarce permits and quotas or out of the various stages of implementation of policies of regulation. As governments have become more important in the economic life of many developing countries, this rent sector has become more prominent, and demands for rent sharing from more and more mobilized groups have become insistent. Even at the expense of inefficiency, some sharing of these spoils of office is to be tolerated for the sake of keeping ethnic envy and discontent under control. Privatization, contrary to popular belief, is not a complete solution to the problem. In the context of most of these countries, with limited competition in the market structure it is not unrealistic to expect privatization to replace a rent-generating public monopoly only with an almost equally invidious rent haven of oligarchic or crony capitalism: the pressures from different groups for capitalizing on political connections and contracts often continue unabated even after large-scale privatization.

Many other policies suggest themselves from an analysis of the factors behind ethnic conflicts. For example, the revolt and resistance of tribal and indigenous people in many parts of the world against encroachments on their traditional rights to land, forests, and mineral resources may be mitigated by stopping bureaucratic or commercial appropriation of the local commons and allowing the local communities to coordinate their management. There are several documented examples of successful and autonomous local-community-level cooperation in regulating the use of common property resources in different parts of the world. (This issue is discussed further in chapter 10.)

When big development projects uproot and dispossess many indigenous people from their traditional habitats and occupations, project designers, executors, and lenders need to be more sensitive to the social and economic costs of dislocation. Institutionalized mechanisms must allow the grievances of the oustees to be voiced and given sufficient weight in the project evaluation, the adequacy of compensation paid to them to be judged by an independent body, and plans for their resettlement with provisions for adjustment assistance, retraining for new occupations, credit, and information to be regularly monitored. Much too often the promises made to the displaced indigenous people by the government and private commercial interests before the project starts are subsequently breached with impunity.

Similarly, visible mechanisms need to make sure that the sacrifices necessitated by macroeconomic stabilization programs (including the slashing of social and welfare expenditures to reduce fiscal deficits) are equitably shared. In spite of all the talk about "safety nets" and "adjustment with a human face," much too often some disadvantaged groups find that agitational politics and street violence are the only way they can make the government respond to their concerns about the unfairness of the pain that is inflicted on them. Urban inequality in particular makes mobilization for sectarian violence easier. The festering slums in the metropolitan cities of the poor countries absorb the poor migrants who are economic refugees from rural destitution. They provide the recruitment ground for the young toughs who serve the crime bosses and political leaders and the arena for the turf battles that the latter fight (and when the rival leaders belong to a different community, the fights take the form of communal riots). Without a massive program for vocational training and public works for the unemployed youth and for low-cost housing and improvement of amenities, the periodic eruptions will be difficult to stop. There is also the problem in the medium to long run that improvements of urban slums will attract more migration from the countryside, without further rural development and dispersal of industrial location.

As is discussed above, rumors, information cascades, and herd behavior play significant roles in urban communal riots, the actions of early leaders can influence the behavior of others, and information cascades are rather brittle. This suggests that the cascades may be sensitive to public information releases. Many people have been impressed, to give an example from a different arena, by the effectiveness of public releases of information on the hazards of smoking in altering herd behavior in smoking in some countries. If effectively transmitted in the early stages of a disturbance, public information on what actually happened, on how a disturbance started, on who tried to take advantage of it, and on instances of intercommunity cooperation in the face of tremendous odds can calm group anxieties and stop some of the rumors that fuel communal riots. The public information has to be released by an agency (say, a widely known, impartial, nongovernment organization of social workers) that is credible to all the communities involved. Government broadcasts by themselves are often not trusted because the ruling bureaucracy is identified by one community or the other as an accomplice.

Finally, what are the policy implications for the international community?[16] First of all, despite considerable odds against success, international public opinion can still be mobilized to support (and fund) nonvacillating and effective mediation (in peace making as well as peace keeping) by United Nations agencies in civil wars and to back up this support by a strong multinational rapid-deployment force and humanitarian aid early in the process. But the recent histories of Bosnia and Congo suggest that wrong and vacillating ways of providing support can be counterproductive. Half-measures and ambiguous commitments may sometimes be worse than no action.

Second, when the ruling government in a country has lost its legitimacy as an impartial mediator in intense conflicts among ethnic groups, the international community, particularly through various government and nongovernment organizations, can act as a third-party arbitrator in resolving disputes, in cutting through bargaining deadlocks, in underwriting commitments made by different groups and rendering them credible, in trying to ensure that promises are not reneged and elections are not rigged, in publicizing findings of impartial international enquiries into charges of abuse of human rights on the part of the state and the rebel groups, and in defusing inflammatory disinformation. Third-party application of rewards and penalties may push the contending groups toward the negotiating table, and a sustained process of enforcement can raise the cost of breaches of agreement (in the absence of which, for example, Jonas Savimbi in Angola defected from the Bicesse peace accords after a poor performance in the 1992 elections and resumed that country's civil war). In terms of penalties, sanctions by regional groups of countries (as, for example,

---

16. For a balanced discussion, see Lake and Rothchild (1996).

against Burundi and Liberia in 1996) may sometimes have more authority and legitimacy than those by the United Nations Security Council; financial sanctions targeted at personal assets of unscrupulous leaders may sometimes be more effective than broad-based sanctions against a whole population. In general, the countries concerned need all the help that they can get in restoring confidence in the institutions of the state that have some capacity to mediate effectively in internal conflicts.

Third, situations like Angola and Somalia (where the early stages of ethnic conflicts were proxy fights of superpowers) and Lebanon (where ethnic conflicts were proxy fights of powerful neighbors, Israel and Syria) have to be avoided early through multilateral efforts in future. In the last few years superpower competition has declined, but competition between major external parties for regional influence still complicates matters. If these external parties are perceived as partisan by the warring groups (as was the case, for example, with the French intervention in Rwanda in 1994 or the Ugandan intervention in eastern Congo more recently), international interventions may accentuate rather than resolve conflicts.

Fourth, the international community presumably may have more mechanisms at its disposal for preventing interstate wars than for preventing internal ethnic wars. The particular cases to watch for in this context are situations where an ethnic group is a dominant majority in one country but an oppressed minority in a neighboring country.

Fifth, international lending agencies have to be sensitive to the displacement effects of development projects, to the dismantling of the preexisting patronage-based social contract, and to the already emaciated programs of economic security for the poor, which they tend to push in their zeal to press ahead with market reforms and efficiency. Adjustment policies need to be suitably packaged with phased compensatory policies and temporary concessions to soften political resistance and build broad-based support.

Finally, ethnic hatred in some cases may be primordial, but it is acted on with particularly lethal effects with weapons provided by the armaments merchants of a handful of foreign countries. The Western countries are not nearly as active in stopping armaments sales as they are in their campaign to stop the international drug traffic (in fact, the two are linked: in some countries the ethnic rebels and even the government buy arms by selling drugs). Hardin (1995) cites a Somali's suggestion that the best thing foreigners could do in Somalia would be to buy back the assault rifles that they had given to rival gangs.

This chapter has emphasized the importance of some institutional failures rather than mere cultural and historical animosities behind the collapse of interethnic understandings and coordination. Both over-time comparisons (say, in Yugoslavia or India) and cross-country comparisons (say, between Malayasia on the one hand and Sri Lanka or Sudan on the other) suggest that the decline of mediating institutions (like the political party as a forum of transactional negotiations), the decline of the preexisting structures of credible commitment (in some African cases they were not firmly in place to start with), or the impact of built-in disincentives of the electoral and constitutional systems often trigger the disintegration of ethnic compromises. The rise in ethnic conflicts is not always associated with economic deterioration; sometimes quite the contrary is observed. The effects of market expansion are also ambiguous. In the context of various kinds of interethnic competition, ethnicity is more often a device to segment an expanding market, create rents, and channelize the flow to particular groups.[17] Ethnic bonding lowers the costs of collective action in appropriating the rent. As government has become more important in economic activities, more and more mobilized groups have used ethnicity for staking a claim in the process of rent-sharing; the subsequent privatization exercises have not escaped similar rentier pressures either. In our discussion of policy lessons we have tried to look for various ways, both political and economic, of constructing institutionalized incentives for conciliatory actions. There are obviously no easy solutions in this minefield of contemporary horrors.

---

17. Caselli and Coleman (2002) model how ethnic heterogeneity makes the winning coalition less susceptible to infiltration by members of the losing one. Conflict therefore is more likely when the characteristics that distinguish ethnicity are more difficult to change.

10   Collective Action and Cooperation

10.1

The literature on collective action in political science and economics is large, but the relationship between heterogeneity and inequality among the individual or group actors and collective action is still relatively underresearched. At the end of chapter 2, some general indications are given about why this is an important area in the discussion of institutional failures in developing countries. This chapter examines this relationship in more detail, first with examples that are drawn from the recent macroeconomic literature, particularly on fiscal crisis, in section 10.2, and then in sections 10.3 and 10.4 with a model that focuses on microeconomic issues that may arise in the matter of collective action in management of local environmental resources or in firms benefiting from a common provision of infrastructural services. We also discuss the commonality and difference in the two types of models considered in the two parts of this chapter. In the concluding section V we review the main issues of this chapter.

Nearly twenty years ago I published a book (Bardhan, 1984) in which I looked at the fiscal crisis of the Indian state as the result of an intricate collective-action problem (in an implicit analytical framework of a noncooperative Nash equilibrium) among its fragmented elite groups. These groups could not get their act together, for example, to generate the public savings that could be invested in correcting severe deficiencies in public infrastructure (from which all the groups could ultimately gain) and instead dissipated the surplus of the economy on short-run subsidies and unproductive expenditures out of the public-fisc common pool. In the last decade there has been some theoretical literature on the "common-pool problem" in fiscal policy in the context of fiscal stabilization in Latin America. This section and the next review this literature and connect it with our general theme of collective action. The general analytic setup for the type of common-pool problem considered here is an infinitely repeated game between a number of powerful interest groups that compete over a common pool of public saving. The two critical assumptions are (1) that each interest group is powerful to the extent that it is able to draw from the common pool of public saving without the consent of other groups and according to its own discretion (within some exogenously determined limits) and (2) that the costs of spending by any one group (such as the rate of interest on public debt or the inflation taxes generated by seignorage) are borne uniformly by all groups. The resulting situation lends itself to aggregate overspending: those with the power to control public spending compare its (private) marginal benefits against only a fraction of its (social) marginal costs.

In what contexts might special interests exert this degree of control over the allocation of public resources? Velasco (1998) mentions two contexts that may be of interest. First, when governments cannot credibly commit to implement efficient refinancing decisions with respect to state-supported firms, the resulting soft budget-constraint problem may place the managers of those firms in a position to have access to public funds with relative ease. Second, in countries in which state or provincial governments are strong in relation to the central government (Velasco mentions the examples of Argentina and Brazil, in particular), a number of mechanisms are available through which local governments might "pass on" their deficits so that they become the responsibility of federal authorities (and thus of taxpayers at large). Velasco describes three possible mechanisms:

• Borrowing from state development banks that in turn can rediscount their loans at the Central Bank (in effect, monetizing the subfederal deficits);

• Obtaining discretionary lump-sum transfers from the federal government, generally requested around election time and after large debts have been accumulated; and

• Accumulating arrears with suppliers and creditors, which (for legal or political reasons) eventually are cleared up by the federal authorities.

Finally, Velasco cites a number of cross-country empirical studies that have yielded results consistent with the hypothesis that decentralized control of fiscal policy erodes fiscal discipline—in particular, Von Hagen (1996), and Alesina, Hausmann, Hommes, and Stein (1996).

Some distinctions can be identified between the general analytic setup of the common-pool problems considered here and that of credible-commitment problems (discussed in chapter 4). One important distinction is that incentives to "defect" are in general one-sided in models of credible commitment and tend to be multilateral in models of common pool. To develop this point further, it is instructive to think of most problems of credible commitment as something resembling a sequential prisoner's-dilemma game in which one player must choose between "cooperation" or "defection" (or analogous concepts particular to a given context) before the other player makes his choice between the two options. A solution to this sequential prisoner's dilemma can be found in a credible commitment by the second-moving player to choose cooperation contingent on the first-moving player choosing the same. Such a commitment simplifies the payoff schedule facing the first-moving player (the one *to whom* a commitment has been made) to two—rather than four—possible payoff outcomes: (cooperate, cooperate) and (defect, defect). Under the assumption that mutual cooperation generates higher payoffs than mutual defection for everyone, a credible commitment by the second-moving player to cooperate is therefore sufficient to eliminate the first-moving player's incentives to defect. Cooperative norms in the context of credible commitment therefore hinge only on the second-moving player's incentives to defect—a unilateral incentive problem.

On the other hand, it may be useful to think of most problems of common pool as a *simultaneous* prisoner's-dilemma game, in which all players must choose at the same time between cooperation and defection. As in the standard prisoner's dilemma and in contrast to the sequential prisoner's dilemma that characterizes most models of credible commitment, a credible commitment by any given player to cooperate is insufficient in the context of the common-pool problem to eliminate the defection incentives of the other player(s). Due to the simultaneous nature of the game, a commitment by any given player to choose cooperation simplifies his opponents' payoff schedule to the two possible payoff outcomes (cooperate, cooperate) and (defect, cooperate) rather than the two outcomes (cooperate, cooperate) and (defect, defect), and so defection remains a dominant strategy for those to whom commitments have been made. In other words, each player must both receive and give a commitment if cooperation is to be achieved. Cooperative norms in the context of the common-pool problem must therefore take account of every player's incentives to defect—a multilateral incentive problem.

However, note that the multilateral incentive problem that characterizes the common-pool problem may be transformed into a credible commitment-type unilateral incentive problem through mechanisms that transfer the burden of commitment to an outside party, such as a moderator who promises to compensate individual decision makers for engaging in disciplined consumption (or, equivalently, threatens to punish them for appropriative behavior). For example, suppose that there are n claimants on a common pool and that the decentralized outcome yields a social surplus of D while the fully cooperative outcome yields a social surplus of C, $C > D$: cooperation might be sustained through a credible commitment by a third party to pay each individual decision maker C/n conditional on that individual choosing to cooperate. The role of behavior-contingent compensation by third parties in overcoming problems of common pool is examined by the literature on conditionality in foreign aid (surveyed by Drazen, 2000).

The models of common pool considered in this chapter share two common elements. The first is that discretionary appropriation of public funds by any given interest group yields short-term payoffs and long-term costs. In some cases, these costs arise purely out of the economy's production function, while in others, explicit punishment costs for norm violation are introduced through trigger strategies or other disciplinary mechanisms. The second shared element of the models is the assumption that the various interest groups competing over the common pool of public saving are essentially identical, to the extent that appropriation incentives are *symmetric* across groups in equilibrium (implying, in cases where cooperation is modeled explicitly, that either all or none of the groups' incentive compatibility constraints are satisfied in any given state of nature). This assumption stands in contrast with that in this chapter's working model (in the next section) on the relationship between inequality and cooperation, which examines the channels through which economic asymmetries among prospective collaborators (and the asymmetric payoffs, punishment costs, and incentive compatibility constraints they imply) affect the sustainability of cooperation.

Given the symmetric nature of agent behavior in the common-pool models considered in this section, a primary objective of the models is to identify the conditions under which sustainable consumption from the common pool can be achieved. In some cases, another objective is to identify mechanisms through which the economy may switch from one state (being on either a sustainable path or an unsustainable one) to the other as part of a dynamic process. The models differ in important ways in their predictions of when and where sustainable consumption is most likely to arise and, in particular, in their predictions of whether sustainable consumption is more likely to be achieved when assets to be appropriated are low (when the common pool is nearly depleted) or high (when the common pool is rich in resources). As Drazen (2000) observes, whether high or low levels of wealth better facilitate cooperation is determined primarily by model specification, including functional forms. However, let us make a quick observation about the two types of cases before moving on to the models in the next section. In cases where cooperation is more easily achieved at high levels of wealth, initial conditions matter, giving rise to the possibility of multiple equilibria: economies that start off with sufficiently high levels of wealth tend to be predisposed toward virtuous cycles of cooperation and wealth accumulation, whereas economies that start off poor tend to be doomed to uncooperative and growth-stifling equilibrium paths. In contrast, in cases where cooperation is more easily achieved at low levels of wealth, initial conditions tend to be irrelevant: regardless of starting position, economies tend to converge to a stable equilibrium path once common resources fall to a certain threshold level and cooperation is triggered.

10.2

The model of Mondino, Sturzenegger, and Tommasi (1998) provides an example in which sustainable consumption is triggered only after available resources have fallen to a sufficiently low level. Mondino and his coauthors are interested in explaining recurrent inflation-stabilization cycles, wherein economies that have experienced prolonged spans of mounting inflation respond with dramatic policy changes to right the economic ship, only to once again start down unsustainable policy trajectories and begin the process anew. In their model, agents at large are organized into two pressure groups of equal size. In each period of an infinitely repeated game, each pressure group may demand from the government a subsidy of fixed size S for its members. This assumption implies that the benefits of "grabbing" from the common pool are fixed and allows Mondino and his coauthors to focus on how the costs of grabbing evolve over time. Three additional assumptions complete the basic setup of the model: the government always accommodates every subsidy demand; it does so by printing money, which generates an inflation tax that must be borne by everyone holding the domestic currency; and to escape the inflation tax associated with seignorage, agents at large have the ability to transfer any portion of their wealth out of the domestic currency and into alternative assets that are shielded from domestic inflation but are otherwise comparatively inconvenient stores of wealth (the overall extent to which agents choose to hold their wealth in these alternative assets is what Mondino and his coauthors call the economy's degree of "financial adaptation").

The basic intuition behind the emergence of recurrent cycles of inflation followed by stabilization are now summarized. Suppose that the economy starts off in a position where monetization is high (implying that inflation must be low, since agents are willing to hold large amounts of the domestic currency). Note that since the stock of domestic currency in circulation composes the "tax base" for seignorage, a high degree of monetization implies that a given amount of seignorage may be financed by a relatively low inflation tax. Thus under current conditions (high monetization), interest groups are likely to find that the marginal benefits of seignorage-financed government spending exceed its marginal costs. But over time, as pork-barrel spending continues to characterize the equilibrium of the stage game, inflation starts to mount, and agents respond by steadily increasing their financial adaptation. This raises the costs of continued inflation, since financial adaptation is costly in and of itself (recall that agents prefer to store their wealth in the domestic currency, all else being equal) and continued seignorage in the face of increasing financial adaptation must be financed by an ever-decreasing tax base of domestic currency. Mondino and his coauthors assume that there is a nonconvexity in the cost schedule of financial adaptation, in that any agent who chooses to *completely* substitute out of the domestic currency must incur a substantial fixed cost $K > S$. This assumption ensures that the economy will eventually reach a threshold level of inflation after which the cost of continued inflation (and thus of further financial adaptation) exceeds the one-period benefit from receiving the government subsidy S. Once the economy reaches this threshold point, both pressure groups will find it optimal to accept a stabilization package (which is modeled simply as zero subsidies for that period) that brings the economy back to its low-inflation starting point. But since it is assumed that agents prefer, all else equal, to store their wealth in the domestic currency, stabilization brings us back to the initial high-monetization equilibrium, and the process begins anew.

The model of Mondino, Sturzenegger, and Tommasi is fully decentralized, so that a switch from unsustainable to sustainable consumption occurs if and only if it suits the private interests of individual decision makers. The model is specified in such a way that the benefits of grabbing from the common pool are fixed (the fixed subsidy S), whereas the costs of grabbing steadily increase over time so long as everyone continues to grab. As a result, grabbing ceases only after the common pool has been sufficiently depleted to bring the costs of additional grabbing above its fixed benefits. Velasco (1998, 1999) reaches a similar conclusion in a model that introduces explicit punishments for noncooperative behavior. As in the previous model, grabbing in the Velasco model exhibits increasing costs over time so long as everyone continues to grab. But in addition, the benefits that can be secured through grabbing also decrease over time with continued grabbing because discretionary grabbing reduces the income flow accruing to public assets and therefore reduces the pool of resources to be split among a given number of claimants.

The government in Velasco's model is composed of a number of powerful fiscal authorities, each representing a different interest group at large. These fiscal authorities are powerful in the sense that each may simply set the level of public spending to be devoted to his or her particular constituency, so long as aggregate spending in any one period does not violate a financial-solvency condition (which prevents government debt from growing without bound). Public spending by any one group benefits that group exclusively but must be financed with a common pool of public saving. In other words, the benefits of public spending are group-specific, while the costs are shared by all members of society. Given this setup, it is obvious that the economy will exhibit a tendency toward aggregate overspending, as each fiscal authority weighs the marginal benefit of spending against only a fraction of its social marginal cost. More specifically, each sees the cost of spending not as the rate of interest on public saving but as the rate of interest minus what the others will either choose to take out (if public saving is positive) or have to pay (if public saving is negative). In a dynamic setting, which is Velasco's focus, this means that the economy may accumulate debt even in contexts in which there is no social incentive to engage in intertemporal smoothing and that the practice of running deficits creates deadweight losses for the economy as a whole.

As is always the case in this type of setting, reputational mechanisms may help to enforce cooperative outcomes that leave everyone better off. Velasco formalizes the conditions under which cooperation between the fiscal authorities can be sustained as a trigger-strategy equilibrium, in which defection by any one fiscal authority is punished by a multilateral reversion to the uncooperative equilibrium. He shows that cooperation is sustainable only after public resources have been depleted beyond a threshold point. At low levels of public debt (or when resources to be appropriated are plentiful), the deadweight losses from additional debt accumulation are small in relation to the benefits of aggressive spending from a large asset stock, so it pays to deviate from the cooperative policy trajectory. As debt accumulates, the balance starts to shift: the deadweight losses from continued debt accumulation become more severe, and at the same time, the government's financial solvency condition becomes more restrictive, meaning that fewer funds are available to be appropriated through deviation. Only when the private payoff from stabilization eventually exceeds that of deviation does the cooperative equilibrium become sustainable under trigger strategies.

In contrast to Mondino, Sturzenegger, and Tommasi (1998) and Velasco (1998, 1999), Aizenman (1998) provides a model in which sustainable consumption is more likely to be achieved when the common pool is rich rather than depleted, raising the possibility of multiple equilibria. Aizenman models fiscal policy making in a union. The model is similar to the Velasco model, to the extent that public resources are up for grabs before a number of powerful fiscal authorities, but with two important added features. First, there now exists a central budget director that tries to coordinate the behavior of the numerous fiscal authorities; and second, the fiscal authorities now have personal motives to secure public spending, so that political representation is now subject to an agency problem. This is a rather complex model, and let us cut straight to its core result. The government consists of a budget director and a large number of governors, each of whom represents a province or state belonging to the union. At the start of each period, the budget director determines the government's *planned* level of aggregate expenditure for that period, of which each governor is granted an equal share. Each governor's discretion lies in whether she will comply with this spending limit or instead rely on public debt to finance additional spending. Governors who violate their assigned budgets face a risk of detection by the budget director ex post (that is, after the offending governors have secured whatever personal gains are associated with spending). Any governor who is caught violating her allotted budget is expelled from office. As a result, governors are less likely to engage in excess spending when the long-term benefits of remaining in office are perceived to be greater than the short-term benefits.

The public has preferences against debt accumulation and, like the budget director, can also punish fiscally undisciplined policymakers by removing them from office. The model's most critical assumption involves how this punishment is carried out. Specifically, Aizenman assumes that the public removes *all* governors from office in a single stroke when the public debt is perceived to have reached an inordinately high level.[1] Aizenman interprets this assumption to mean that the public uses the level of public debt as a basis for judging the competence of the existing administration as a whole. An alternative interpretation is that the public's tendency to levy wholesale rather than targeted punishments on incumbent policymakers reflects constraints that are imposed either by informational disadvantages or by the political process itself. The second interpretation may be preferred, since, in the absence of heterogeneity across prospective administrations, it is not clear why the public would choose to adopt this practice (which further externalizes the costs of "bad behavior" by individual policymakers) when it could secure better outcomes by being more discriminating in choosing whom to punish. In any case, the economy in the Aizenman model is likely to exhibit excessive public spending at precisely the worst possible times. Specifically, at times when the public debt is already substantial, each governor recognizes that her chances of remaining in office are slim regardless of whether she exercises fiscal discipline—because all governors are likely to be ousted by the public in the very near future in any case. This induces all governors to shift the focus of their intertemporal cost-benefit analysis toward the short run and thereby raises the comparative appeal of securing a short-run windfall through aggressive spending relative to sacrificing current consumption in an unlikely bid for job security. In other words, at high

---

1. This assumption is incorporated into the model as follows. Before the start of any given period, the *probability* that the incumbent administration (meaning all governors) will be allowed to remain in office is a decreasing function of the current level of public debt.

levels of public debt, each governor perceives that her days are limited and opts to go out in a final fiscal blaze of glory. Note that the budget director's goal to avert this type of race to the bottom may require him to set an otherwise inefficiently high target level for the public debt—because a high debt target increases the payoffs that accrue to governors in the cooperative equilibrium and thereby discourages deviation.

Finally, the model of Benhabib and Rustichini (1996) is similar in structure to the Velasco model and, like the Velasco model, also examines cooperative norms of sustainable consumption based on trigger strategies. In the Benhabib and Rustichini model, cooperation is in some cases more easily achieved at low levels of wealth and in other cases more easily achieved at high levels of wealth (whereas in the Velasco model, cooperation is possible only at low levels of wealth). Whether one or the other situation characterizes the economy is determined by the parameters of the model and, in particular, the curvature of the production function (where production is increasing in the stock of a common pool of capital) relative to the curvature of agents' utility functions (where utility is increasing in consumption of existing capital). When returns to consumption diminish at a high enough rate relative to the rate at which returns to capital diminish, cooperation is more likely achieved under "desirable" conditions, when wealth and consumption are both high. This happens because when the curvature of the utility function is pronounced in relation to the curvature of the production function, the marginal return to consumption is high relative to the marginal return to capital when both consumption and wealth are low (so that the benefit of appropriating additional consumption is high relative to the cost of future retaliation by other groups), while the marginal return to consumption is low relative to the marginal return to capital when both consumption and wealth are high (so that the benefit of appropriating additional consumption is low relative its punishment costs). Conversely and by symmetric logic, cooperation is more likely achieved under "duress" (when wealth and consumption are both low) when returns to capital diminish at a high rate relative to the rate at which returns to consumption diminish.

10.3

In this section, the focus is more on the micro context, and inequality rather than group heterogeneity is addressed. The model presented here aims to delineate some possible mechanisms through which economic inequality might determine the necessary features as well as overall sustainability of social norms of cooperation. The model stays neutral on the important but contested issue of the direct effects of inequality on aggregate economic outcomes and instead limits its focus to indirect effects that might operate via social norms. In particular, the model is specified in such a way that social welfare depends only on whether cooperation takes place. As a result, inequality affects social welfare if and only if it, affects the sustainability of social norms of cooperation.

The model considers distributional inequality with respect to a *non-transferable* resource, which we simply call private capital. Relatedly, it considers a setting in which cooperation promises to yield efficiency gains relative to the status quo not by promoting efficiency-enhancing redistributions of capital (from where its marginal return is already low to where it is still high) but instead by promoting the adoption of efficient technologies for producing *capital-complementing inputs*. Examples of such inputs could be R&D, irrigation, and infrastructural services. The need for cooperative norms arises in the model out of a common-pool problem in the production of the capital-complementing inputs. When agents combine their efforts to produce the inputs in an efficient manner, the fruits of their combined labor can be freely appropriated by any individual claimant. As a result, agents choose in decentralized equilibrium to adopt alternative production technologies that are economically inferior but free of the common-pool problem.

Like the models of a common pool that have been reviewed above from the fiscal-policy literature, the basic analytic setting is an infinitely repeated game, and the prospective social norm of cooperation is based on trigger strategies. At any given point in time, all agents are provided with the prospect of continued cooperation into the future so long as no one agent defects at the present. Unlike those models, which consider the effects of various state variables (such as the economy's aggregate wealth) on the sustainability of cooperation among *identical* agents, the primary focus here is on the implications of asymmetry across agents (caused by distributional inequality), and the primary state variable of interest describes the extent of this asymmetry. As one result, whereas the perceived desirability of cooperation relative to defection is symmetric across players in standard models of common pool (so that cooperation is enforceable through trigger strategies for either everyone or no one), incentives for cooperation tend to differ across players in our model.

In this model, incentives for cooperation tend to be stronger for wealthier agents (all else being equal), and there is always a threshold level of distributional inequality beyond which cooperation is enforceable for the richly endowed and unenforceable for the poorly endowed. This result is similar to that of common-pool models, in which cooperation is more easily sustained in times of plenty because wealth accumulation and incentives for maintaining cooperation are mutually reinforcing (Aizenman, 1998; Benhabib and Rustichini, 1996). However, at intermediate levels of distributional inequality, it is not always the richly endowed who are willing to cooperate and the poorly endowed who are not. This is due to another point of departure between our model and standard models of common pool: we assume that agents have access to asymmetric rather than symmetric *exit options*. And when the richly endowed have access to sufficiently attractive exit options (relative to those of the poorly endowed), the rich may fail to exercise discipline even though they stand to gain the most in absolute terms from cooperation. These differential exit options are particularly important in the context of management of environmental resources in the rural areas of developing countries. For example (as is illustrated in chapter 11), rich farmers with better urban connections or better access to alternative water supplies (say, from privately owned pumps) may be less interested in fostering cooperation on management of public irrigation systems. One may have a similar story on conservation of resources in a fishery with differential exit options for fishermen with different boat sizes.[2] For a general survey of the existing small literature on the role of inequality in collective action on the local commons, see Baland and Platteau (forthcoming).

Whether the rich or the poor face stronger incentives to defect can have important implications for whether cooperation can be salvaged in some instances with the aid of side payments. In particular, inequality acts to diminish the incentive effects of any given side payment on the richly endowed and to magnify its effects on the poorly endowed. As a result, cooperation aided by side payments tends to be more feasible when it is the poor and not the rich who must be compensated.

---

2. The model of Dayton-Johnson and Bardhan (2002) examines the effect of inequality in different boat sizes on conservation in a fishery with differential exit options for big boat-owning fishermen and with linear technology.

10.4*

The Model
Consider the following infinitely repeated game between two agents—one "rich" and "poor." Time proceeds in discrete periods, and the agents have a common discount factor of β.

Stage Game
The economy enters each new period with a total private-capital endowment of K, of which the rich agent controls share ρ and the poor agent controls share $1 - \rho$, where $\rho > 0.5$. Each agent's utility is increasing in his consumption of own-produced output Y_i and is decreasing in his effort level e_i:

$$U_i = Y_i - ce_i. \tag{10.1}$$

Production of output Y_i is assumed constant-returns-to-scale Cobb-Douglas with respect to private capital K_i and an unnamed complementary input labeled A_i:

$$Y_i = A_i^{\alpha} K_i^{(1-\alpha)}. \tag{10.2}$$

Property rights with respect to private capital are assumed to be fully secure. The complementary input A_i is produced by agent effort via one of two possible technologies and can be either private or public (in the nonexcludable sense), depending on the technology selected. Each agent has access to a unique "status-quo" technology, defined by one of the two equations

$$A_P = R_{LP}e_P \quad \text{(the poor agent's status quo technology)}$$
$$A_R = R_{LR}e_R \quad \text{(the rich agent's status quo technology),} \tag{10.3}$$

where $R_{LR} > R_{LP}$, so that the rich agent's status-quo production technology is superior[3] to that of the poor player. The agents may also

---

*This section introduces a formal model. Readers who are not interested in the technical details may skip this section.

3. The assumption that the rich agent's status-quo technology is superior to that of the poor agent is necessary for the existence of parameter values under which incentive compatibility is satisfied for the poor agent but not for the rich agent. If the two agents were to have access to the same status-quo technology (or if the poor agent was the one with access to the superior status-quo technology), then incentive compatibility for the rich agent would be satisfied whenever incentive compatibility for the poor agent is satisfied.

choose to employ a "cooperative" technology, which is defined by the equation

$$A_i + A_j = R_H(e_i + e_j), \tag{10.4}$$

where $R_H > R_{LR} > R_{LP}$. While the cooperative technology is therefore the most efficient option, its output (measured in units of the complementary input A) is subject to a pure common-pool problem—namely, each agent has the ability to grab all the fruits of cooperation, $R_H(e_i + e_j)$, for himself. In contrast, each agent is assured of securing the fruits of his own labor when using his status-quo technology. As a result, use of the cooperative technology for production of the complementary input A cannot be sustained in the absence of the appropriate enforcement mechanisms. Formally, the stage game can be represented as a prisoner's dilemma whose only Nash equilibrium involves mutual defection.

As is evident from table 10.1, we are making two simplifying assumptions. The first is that mutual defection yields payoffs that are equivalent to those obtained when each player simply chooses his status-quo technology (although all that matters is that mutual defection generates individual payoffs that are strictly greater than zero and strictly less than those from mutual cooperation). The second is that, in the fully cooperative outcome, the ratio of the players' payoffs is equal to the ratio of their contributions to the cooperative effort—namely, when both players cooperate, each player receives an amount of capital-complementing input equal to

Table 10.1
Payoff matrix (payoffs denoted in units of the production input A)

		Rich Agent	
		Cooperate	Defect
	Cooperate	$R_H e_R$	$R_H(e_R + e_P)$
		$R_H e_P$	0
Poor Agent		0	$R_{LR} e_R$
	Defect		
		$R_H(e_R + e_P)$	$R_{LP} e_P$

$$A_i = R_H e_i. \tag{10.5}$$

This assumption allows us to keep the algebra simple (in particular, by allowing us to restrict the issue of free-riding to instances where an agent chooses to defect from the cooperative norm) but also has two important implications. First, as we can soon verify by checking equation (10.8), it yields the social-surplus-maximizing distribution of the complementary input A, as the ratio A_i/A_j is equal to K_i/K_j in equilibrium.[4] Second, it implies that social welfare is independent of distributional inequality and depends only on whether cooperation takes place—that is, social welfare can take on only one of two possible values, one corresponding to the status-quo outcome and one corresponding to the decentralized outcome.

Stage-Game Payoffs

In the decentralized equilibrium, each agent chooses e_i to maximize equation (10.1), given equation (10.3). The solution to this optimization problem is

$$e_{i,statusquo} = K_i \left(\frac{\alpha R_{Li}^\alpha}{c} \right)^{1/(1-\alpha)}. \tag{10.6}$$

As is expected, each agent's optimal choice of effort is increasing in his holdings of private capital and decreasing in the cost of effort. Substituting equation (10.6) into equation (10.1) and recalling that each agent has a discount factor of β, the lifetime utility of each agent under the status quo can be written as

$$S_i = \frac{1}{1-\beta} \left(K_i \left(\frac{\alpha R_{Li}}{c} \right)^{\alpha/(1-\alpha)} (1 - \alpha) \right). \tag{10.7}$$

Let us now turn to stage-game payoffs under full cooperation. Since cooperation is assumed simply to allow each agent to secure a return to effort equal to R_H instead of R_{Li}—equation (10.5) versus equation (10.3)—each agent's effort choice under full cooperation is equal to

$$e_{i,cooperate} = K_i \left(\frac{\alpha R_H^\alpha}{c} \right)^{1/(1-\alpha)}, \tag{10.8}$$

and his lifetime utility under full cooperation can be expressed as

---

4. As can be easily verified, any equation of the form $S = A_1^z K_1^{1-z} + A_2^z K_2^{1-z}$, where the A_i's and K_i's must each sum to fixed quantities, is maximized when $A_1/A_2 = K_1/K_2$.

$$\mathbf{C}_i = \frac{1}{1-\beta} \left(K_i \left(\frac{\alpha R_H}{c} \right)^{\alpha/(1-\alpha)} (1 - \alpha) \right). \tag{10.9}$$

From equations (10.7) and (10.9), it is clear that the rich agent does better than the poor agent in both the status-quo and cooperative outcomes and, in addition, that the incremental payoff to cooperation relative to the status quo is higher for the rich agent than for the poor agent. Finally, the stage-game payoff from defecting when the other agent cooperates needs to be calculated. Since a defecting agent i appropriates the fruits of agent j's effort, the latter factors into his own effort choice. Given that agent j cooperates, agent i's optimal choice of effort is equal to

$$e_{i,defect} = K_i \left(\frac{\alpha R_H^\alpha}{c} \right)^{1/(1-\alpha)} - e_j, \tag{10.10}$$

revealing a free-rider effect for the defecting player i. Substituting equation (10.8) for e_j into equation (10.10) yields

$$e_{i,defect} = \text{Max} \left\{ (K_i - K_j) \left(\frac{\alpha R_H^\alpha}{c} \right)^{1/(1-\alpha)}, 0 \right\}. \tag{10.11}$$

We see from equation (10.11) that, when defecting, the poor agent chooses an effort level of zero, while the rich agent still chooses a strictly positive effort level (equal to his cooperative effort level minus the cooperative effort level of the poor agent). Substituting equation (10.11) into equation (10.1), we can calculate the stage-game payoffs from defection for the poor agent and the rich agent, respectively, as

$$D_{poor} = K \left(\frac{\alpha R_H}{c} \right)^{\alpha/(1-\alpha)} \rho^\alpha (1 - \rho)^{1-\alpha}, \tag{10.12}$$

and

$$D_{rich} = K \left(\frac{\alpha R_H}{c} \right)^{\alpha/(1-\alpha)} (\rho - \alpha(2\rho - 1)). \tag{10.13}$$

A quick glance at equations (10.12) and (10.13) reveals that both players' static payoffs from defection are a function of ρ, or the extent of inequality in the distribution of private capital. Consider equation (10.13) first. Depending on the parameter α, D_{rich} is either monotonically increasing or monotonically decreasing in inequality ρ. Specifically, D_{rich} is monotonically increasing in ρ if and only if

$$\alpha^{\alpha/(1-\alpha)} \geq 2\alpha^{1/(1-\alpha)},$$

or simply $\alpha \leq 0.5$. In other words, increasing inequality increases (decreases) the rich agent's static payoffs from defection when production relies more (less) heavily on private capital. Let us now consider equation (10.12). Intuitively, increasing inequality in the distribution of private capital exerts two competing effects on the one-time payoff that the poor agent can secure by defecting (D_{poor}). On one hand, increases in inequality increase the effort level of the rich agent in the cooperative equilibrium, meaning that the poor agent can grab more of the complementary input A by defecting. On the other hand, increases in inequality reduce the private-capital holdings of the poor agent, meaning that the poor agent has less use for any given amount of complementary input that he is able to secure for himself. From equation (10.12), we see that the first effect dominates for increases in inequality ρ up to $\rho = \alpha$ and that the second effect dominates when inequality rises beyond that level.

Therefore, whenever $\alpha \leq 0.5$ (so that production is more private-capital intensive), increases in inequality increase the defection payoffs of the rich agent and decrease the defection payoffs of the poor agent (since the defection payoffs for the poor agent are decreasing in inequality whenever $\rho > \alpha$, and $\rho > 0.5$ by definition). On the other hand, whenever $\alpha > 0.5$, the rich agent's defection payoffs are decreasing in inequality, while the relationship between the poor agent's defection payoffs and inequality is inverse U-shaped.

Social Norms

To identify the conditions under which trigger strategies can sustain cooperation in the infinitely repeated version of the stage game, a social norm of cooperation will be considered sustainable via trigger strategies if both players choose to cooperate with the understanding that defection at any time t will trigger a permanent reversion to the Nash equilibrium of the stage game. That is, cooperation is sustainable so long as no agent at any time t is willing to forsake the incremental returns to cooperation (relative to the status quo) from time $t+1$ onward in exchange for the one-time payoff from defection at time t. Formally, cooperation is sustainable if and only if

$$\mathrm{IC}_i: \quad \mathbf{C}_i \geq \mathrm{D}_i + \beta \mathbf{S}_i \tag{10.14}$$

for each agent i. The incentive compatibility constraints particular to this model are

$$\text{IC}_P: \quad \left(\frac{1}{1-\beta}\right)\left(1 - \beta\left(\frac{R_{LP}}{R_H}\right)^{\alpha/(1-\alpha)}\right) \geq \left(\frac{\rho}{1-\rho}\right)^{\alpha}\left(\frac{1}{1-\alpha}\right) \qquad (10.15)$$

and

$$\text{IC}_R: \quad \left(\frac{1}{1-\beta}\right)\left(1 - \beta\left(\frac{R_{LR}}{R_H}\right)^{\alpha/(1-\alpha)}\right) \geq \left(\frac{1-\rho}{\rho}\right)\left(\frac{\alpha}{1-\alpha}\right) + 1. \qquad (10.16)$$

As expected, the incentive compatibility constraints are identical when $\rho = 0.5$ and are both more likely to hold when the agents are more forward-looking (β is larger) and when the incremental return to co-operation relative to the status quo is larger (R_H is larger relative to the R_{Li}). We also see that increases in inequality ρ tend to make IC_P less likely to hold and IC_R more likely to hold. To understand intuitively why increasing inequality tends to make defection more attractive for the poor agent and less attractive for the rich agent, think of the returns to defection as the sum of two components: effort savings and pro-duction gains. Effort savings from defection fall with inequality for both the rich agent and the poor agent. Recall from equations (10.10) and (10.11) that a defecting rich agent always exerts an amount of effort equal to his cooperative-effort choice minus the poor agent's cooperative-effort choice, while a defecting poor agent always free-rides completely. Because greater inequality reduces the cooperative effort of the poor agent, a defecting rich agent has "more ground to make up," while a defecting poor agent has "less to retract." Thus effort savings are lower for both players when inequality is greater (effect 1). The relationship between inequality and production gains from defection is more complicated. On one hand, increasing inequal-ity means that the poor (rich) agent has less (more) private capital with which to complement whatever amount of the input A that he is able to appropriate from the opposing player by defecting (effect 2). On the other hand, because the rich agent exerts more effort than the poor player in the cooperative equilibrium, the poor agent has more of A to appropriate by defecting (effect 3). Finally, because the returns to A ex-hibit diminishing returns, the poor (rich) agent, who has less (more) of A in the cooperative equilibrium, has more (less) to gain from addi-tional stocks of A (effect 4). For the poor agent, effects 3 and 4 domi-nate effects 1 and 2; for the rich agent, effects 1, 3, and 4 dominate effect 2.

A quick glance at equations (10.15) and (10.16) reveals that there is always a level of inequality $\rho < 1$ beyond which it is impossible to maintain incentive compatibility for the poor agent (since the right-hand side of equation (10.15) goes to infinity as $\rho \to 1$), whereas there is always a level of inequality $\rho < 1$ beyond which incentive compatibility for the rich agent is certainly satisfied (since the right-hand side of equation (10.16) goes to zero as $\rho \to 1$). Finally, note that for intermediate levels of inequality, it is entirely possible for the poor agent's incentive-compatibility constraint to hold while that of the rich agent does not hold. Such situations are particularly likely to arise when the status-quo technology of the rich agent is sufficiently superior to the status-quo technology of the poor agent—that is, when the rich agent has an attractive "exit option."

Side Payments

When one of the two agents' incentive-compatibility constraint is violated by the terms of cooperation outlined above, cooperation might nevertheless be sustained with the aid of side payments: so long as one agent i's incentive-compatibility constraint is satisfied in the absence of side payments, the incorporation of a side payment from agent i to agent j into the terms of the social norm has the potential to sustain cooperation. Under this arrangement, the generic incentive compatibility constraint (equation (10.14)) becomes

$$\text{IC}_i: \quad \mathbf{C}_i + (\textit{transfer amount})/(1 - \beta) \geq \mathbf{D}_i + \beta \mathbf{S}_i. \tag{10.17}$$

We must now also take account of the two agents' individual-rationality constraints. Let T denote the amount that is transferred from the rich agent to the poor agent (where T can be negative), conditional on cooperation by both players. The individual-rationality constraints for the two agents are

$$\text{IR}_P: \quad (1 - \rho)K\left(\left(\frac{R_H}{c}\right)^{\alpha/(1-\alpha)} - \left(\frac{\alpha R_{LP}}{c}\right)^{\alpha/(1-\alpha)}\right)(1 - \alpha) + T \geq 0 \tag{10.18}$$

$$\text{IR}_R: \quad \rho K\left(\left(\frac{R_H}{c}\right)^{\alpha/(1-\alpha)} - \left(\frac{\alpha R_{LR}}{c}\right)^{\alpha/(1-\alpha)}\right)(1 - \alpha) - T \geq 0. \tag{10.19}$$

The incentive-compatibility constraints of the poor agent and the rich agent in the presence of side payments are, respectively,

$$\text{IC}_P: \quad \left(\frac{1}{1-\beta}\right)\left(1 - \beta\left(\frac{R_{LP}}{R_H}\right)^{\alpha/(1-\alpha)}\right) - \tau_P T$$

$$\geq \left(\frac{\rho}{1-\rho}\right)^{\alpha}\left(\frac{1}{1-\alpha}\right) \tag{10.20}$$

$$\text{IC}_R: \quad \left(\frac{1}{1-\beta}\right)\left(1 - \beta\left(\frac{R_{LR}}{R_H}\right)^{\alpha/(1-\alpha)}\right) - \tau_R T$$

$$\geq \left(\frac{1-p}{p}\right)\left(\frac{\alpha}{1-\alpha}\right) + 1, \tag{10.21}$$

where

$$\tau_P = \left(\frac{c}{\alpha R_H}\right)^{\alpha/(1-\alpha)}\left(\frac{1}{(1-p)K(1-\beta)}\right)\left(\frac{1}{1-\alpha}\right) \tag{10.22}$$

$$\tau_R = \left(\frac{c}{\alpha R_H}\right)^{\alpha/(1-\alpha)}\left(\frac{1}{pK(1-\beta)}\right)\left(\frac{1}{1-\alpha}\right). \tag{10.23}$$

Note that while the amount of the side payment T enters into the agents' individual-rationality constraints directly, it enters into their incentive-compatibility constraints with a multiplier τ_i, and the size of this multiplier is a function of inequality. In particular, as p increases, the "side-payment multiplier" in the poor agent's incentive-compatibility constraint (τ_P) becomes larger, while the side-payment multiplier in the rich agent's incentive-compatibility constraint (τ_R) becomes smaller.

Another way to describe this result is to say that, as inequality increases, the effect of any given transfer amount is magnified with respect to incentive-compatibility considerations for the poor agent and diminished with respect to incentive-compatibility constraints for the rich agent. This implies that, if cooperation requires a side payment *from the rich agent to the poor agent*, increases in inequality tend to make cooperation more attainable, all else equal. Intuitively, a very poor agent who chooses to defect in the absence of side payments might agree instead to cooperate for only a very small fee, since even a very small fee increases his payoffs from cooperation by a significant margin, in relative terms. At the same time, a very rich agent might be more than happy to offer this fee, since it is quite small in relation to the payoffs he can secure by convincing the poor agent to cooperate. On the other hand, and by similar logic, if cooperation requires a side payment from the *poor agent to the rich agent*, increases in inequality tend to make cooperation increasingly difficult to achieve, all else equal. Intuitively, a rich agent who demands a side payment in exchange for his cooperation is likely to ask too much of the poor agent, who is reluctant to sacrifice even a small share of his already meager prospective winnings from cooperation.

Explicit Punishments

Let us now abandon the possibility of side payments and suppose instead that each agent has the ability to help enforce the cooperative norm by setting aside resources to punish his opponent in the event that his opponent defects. In particular, suppose that by setting aside $f_i K$ units of capital at the beginning of the stage game, agent i can impose a one-time cost of $x f_i K$ on agent j in the event that agent j defects from the cooperative norm, where $x > 0$. Investments in punishment by either agent are unproductive in a strictly economic sense (they are "wasted" on the equilibrium path of cooperation) but may help to skew the incentive-compatibility considerations of his opponent in a way that favors cooperation and is mutually beneficial. Note that an agent will choose to invest in punishments only if he is otherwise (under the standard norm of cooperation) willing to cooperate while his opponent is not. Therefore, either only the rich agent invests in punishment, only the poor agent invests, or neither invests.

First consider the case where, in the absence of side payments, the rich agent is willing to cooperate and the poor agent is not. In this case, the individual-rationality constraints of the two agents are

$$\text{IR}_P: \quad R_H \geq R_{LP} \tag{10.24}$$

$$\text{IR}_R: \quad \rho \left(\left(\frac{R_H}{c} \right)^{\alpha/(1-\alpha)} - \left(\frac{R_{LR}}{c} \right)^{\alpha/(1-\alpha)} \right) \geq f_R \left(\frac{R_H}{c} \right)^{\alpha/(1-\alpha)}. \tag{10.25}$$

Note that the individual-rationality constraint of the poor agent is automatically satisfied (and unchanged from the baseline model), since punishments are never delivered on the equilibrium path of cooperation. The incentive-compatibility constraints of the poor and rich agents are, respectively,

$$\text{IC}_P: \quad \left(\frac{1}{1-\beta} \right) \left(1 - \beta \left(\frac{R_{LP}}{R_H} \right)^{\alpha/(1-\alpha)} \right)$$

$$\geq \left(\frac{\rho}{1-\rho} \right)^{\alpha} \left(\frac{1}{1-\alpha} \right) - \phi_P f_R \tag{10.26}$$

$$\text{IC}_R: \quad \left(\frac{1}{1-\beta} \right) \left(1 - \beta \left(\frac{R_{LR}}{R_H} \right)^{\alpha/(1-\alpha)} - \phi_R f_R \right)$$

$$\geq \left(\frac{1-\rho}{\rho} \right) \left(\frac{\alpha}{1-\alpha} \right) + 1, \tag{10.27}$$

where

$$\phi_P = \frac{1}{(1-\rho)} \left(\frac{x\left(\frac{c}{R_H}\right)^{\alpha/(1-\alpha)}}{\alpha^{\alpha/(1-\alpha)} - \alpha^{1/(1-\alpha)}} \right) \tag{10.28}$$

$$\phi_P = \frac{1}{\rho}. \tag{10.29}$$

We see from equation (10.25) that investments in punishment by the rich agent become more feasible with respect to individual-rationality considerations when inequality increases: increasing inequality increases the incremental payoff to cooperation relative to the status quo for the rich agent, so the rich agent potentially has more to divert toward investments in punishing the poor agent. In addition, we see from equations (10.26) through (10.29) that when inequality is more pronounced, the incentive effects of any given investment in punishment f_R by the rich agent are diminished for the rich agent and magnified for the poor agent. This implies that, all else being equal, threats of punishment levied by the rich agent against the poor agent are more likely to enforce cooperation by the poor agent when inequality is more pronounced.

In the opposite case, cooperation requires the poor agent to make investments in punishment. In this case, the individual-rationality constraints are

$$\text{IR}_P: \quad (1-\rho)\left(\left(\frac{R_H}{c}\right)^{\alpha/(1-\alpha)} - \left(\frac{R_{LP}}{c}\right)^{\alpha/(1-\alpha)} \right) \geq f_P \left(\frac{R_H}{c}\right)^{\alpha/(1-\alpha)} \tag{10.30}$$

$$\text{IR}_R: \quad R_H \geq R_{LR}, \tag{10.31}$$

while the incentive-compatibility constraints are

$$\text{IC}_P: \quad \left(\frac{1}{1-\beta}\right)\left(1 - \beta\left(\frac{R_{LP}}{R_H}\right)^{\alpha/(1-\alpha)} - \pi_P f_P \right)$$

$$\geq \left(\frac{\rho}{1-\rho}\right)^{\alpha}\left(\frac{1}{1-\alpha}\right) \tag{10.32}$$

$$\text{IC}_R: \quad \left(\frac{1}{1-\beta}\right)\left(1 - \beta\left(\frac{R_{LR}}{R_H}\right)^{\alpha/(1-\alpha)} \right)$$

$$\geq \left(\frac{1-\rho}{\rho}\right)\left(\frac{\alpha}{1-\alpha}\right) + 1 - \pi_R f_P, \tag{10.33}$$

where

$$\pi_P = \frac{1}{1-\rho} \tag{10.34}$$

$$\pi_R = \frac{1}{\rho} \left(\frac{x\left(\dfrac{c}{\alpha R_H}\right)^{\alpha/(1-\alpha)}}{1-\alpha} \right). \tag{10.35}$$

The situation here is in several important respects the opposite of the one just considered, in which the threat of punishment comes from the rich and is directed against the poor. From equation (10.30), investments in punishment by the poor agent become less feasible with respect to individual-rationality considerations when inequality increases: increasing inequality reduces the incremental payoff to cooperation relative to the status quo for the poor agent, so the poor agent has less to potentially divert toward investments in punishing the rich agent. In addition, we see from equations (10.32) through (10.35) that when inequality is more pronounced, the incentive effects of any given investment in punishment f_P by the poor agent are magnified for the poor agent and diminished for the rich agent. This implies that, all else equal, threats of punishment levied by the poor agent against the rich agent are less likely to enforce cooperation by the rich agent when inequality is more pronounced.

For the sake of keeping the model in this section tractable, a great deal of plausibility has been sacrificed. For example, the two-person (or two-group) setup is quite restrictive. For more general distributions (even just adding a third group called the "middle class"), "increasing inequality" can take many forms, even if only mean-preserving spreads are included. In Bardhan and Singh (2003) we generalize to the case of many persons. Similarly restrictive is the presumption that social welfare is independent of inequality and depends only on whether cooperation takes place or not (individual-rationality conditions ensure that cooperation, if chosen, will be Pareto superior to noncooperation, so that any concave aggregation of individual utilities will favor cooperation). One problem with the trigger strategies is that once the punishment phase is embarked on, there is no looking back. So if there are small shocks in the model, in the long run every game will collapse to the punishment path. Some existing literature suggests that some defection is tolerated because it could have been caused by an exogenous shock.

10.5

In this chapter we have discussed common pool problems in fiscal management when there are heterogeneous groups, and then related problems at the micro level for collective action when there is economic inequality. In the common-pool model of fiscal policy, the benefits of public spending on any one interest group are concentrated in that group, but the costs are uniformly distributed across all groups (for example, in the form of taxes or interest on public debt). The latter assumption can be interpreted to mean that all groups draw from a "common pool" of public resources. Each group therefore secures a large share of the total benefits from its particular brand of public spending while bearing a comparatively small share of the total costs. This sets the stage for a fiscal-policy version of the tragedy of the commons: each interest group pursues its fiscal agenda until the private benefits of doing so no longer exceed the private costs, at which time the private benefits have already fallen well below the social costs.

We began with a brief review of recent theoretical articles on fiscal management that operate within this common-pool framework. These articles are primarily interested in examining the feasibility of cooperative agreements between interest groups to overcome the fiscal common-pool problem. In the models, every interest group is better off when all groups adhere to a cooperative agreement than when none do. Yet when every other group cooperates, each group can secure a windfall gain by breaking its promise to adhere to the agreement—a classic prisoner's dilemma. The models differ sharply when it comes to predicting the conditions under which cooperation is sustainable. In some models, cooperation is sustainable only after fiscal conditions have become severely damaged, while in others, cooperation is sustainable only when fiscal conditions are still favorable.

The models considered from the existing literature in section 10.2 all assume that the relevant interest groups are economically identical, so that incentives for cooperation are symmetric across groups: either all groups are willing to cooperate, or none are. This assumption partly explains the existing literature's emphasis on aggregate fiscal conditions and their role in making cooperation more or less sustainable. After reviewing these models, we present a simple model in section 10.4 that considers an alternative setting in which economic differences create differential incentives for cooperation. In this model, distributional inequality across interest groups creates unequal returns to cooperation. All else being equal, the richly endowed stand to gain more from cooperation than the poorly endowed. At extreme levels of economic inequality, the rich are always eager to cooperate, while the poor refuse to do so. However, at intermediate levels of inequality, it may often be the poor who are willing to cooperate and the rich who are not. The model's results in this vein arise from the plausible assumption that the rich have access to more favorable exit options relative to those available to the poor.

The basic model is enriched by two mechanisms that might salvage cooperation when it is otherwise unsustainable—side payments from agents who are willing to cooperate to agents who are otherwise unwilling to cooperate and, relatedly, explicit punishments levied by the former against the latter (note that these mechanisms are sensible only in a setting of differential incentives for cooperation). Each of these two mechanisms may be useful for sustaining cooperation when the rich must induce the poor to cooperate, but they are likely to be much less effective when the poor must attempt to enforce discipline on the part of the rich.

11 Irrigation and Cooperation: An Empirical Study[1]

11.1

A controlled supply of water is crucial for much of the world's agriculture. This is particularly the case in many of the semiarid and uneven-rainfall areas of Asia. In 1853, when Karl Marx and Friedrich Engels first discussed, in correspondence, the problems of "Asiatic" societies, they immediately agreed on the particular importance of public irrigation in these societies (necessitated by what they called "climatic and territorial conditions") and of the particular social organizations that public irrigation requires.[2] Even though their emphasis on the idea of the centralized hydraulic state was somewhat misplaced, their valuable insights gave rise to a large anthropological literature on the relationship between irrigation and social and political organization.[3]

While a considerable amount of work has been done on studying the management of large canal systems and the structure and practices of the irrigation bureaucracy, economists have only recently started paying attention to issues of local community-level cooperation and other institutional arrangements that are key to substantially improving the

1. The data used in this chapter are taken from a survey designed with the help of Nirmal Sengupta at the Madras Institute of Development Studies, who supervised the data-collection process and has been very helpful at the data-analysis stage as well. The data analysis was conducted jointly with Laura Giuliano. Jeff Dayton-Johnson helped in the survey design. In the data-collection and -coding process we received invaluable assistance from R. Manimohan, A. Raman, and J. Jeyaranjan.
2. In this they were carrying forward a strand of European thinking on Asian history and society that was particularly fostered by Adam Smith and John Stuart Mill. For an account of the roots of Marx's thinking on this question in earlier European tradition as well as a critique of the ingredients of the concept of "Asiatic mode of production," see Anderson (1974).
3. For an early survey of this literature, see Hunt and Hunt (1976).

existing levels of utilization of irrigation potential. Community institutions can have various functions in different irrigation systems. For example, they pool efforts and resources in constructing and maintaining field channels at the local outlet level, regulate water allocation, and monitor violations. In cases of tank irrigation, these community institutions also pool efforts to desilt, weed, and stop encroachments on tank beds; repair, maintain, and control water allocation from public and community tubewells; control ground-water overexploitation with privately owned pumps in areas with fragile aquifers; and so on. Water reform—in the sense of building or promoting such community institutions of cooperation—is at least as important as land reform in rural development.[4]

But the history of local community-level cooperation in water management in South Asia is mixed.[5] Several examples of successful local community water management (although usually at a rather low organizational level) have been documented in different parts of the region, and some of them go many hundreds of years back in history and still survive. But in numerous cases of failure of cooperation, communities sometimes find themselves reduced to an anarchical scramble for water. Understanding the conditions that sustain and undermine local cooperation in situations of general social and economic interdependence is a goal of policy makers.

The usual game-theoretic models of cooperation among self-interested agents in repeated situations of strategic interdependence provide some useful insights. One such attempt at modeling collective action with a view to tracing the impact of wealth inequality is made in the second half of the preceding chapter. But in view of the admissibility of multiplicity of equilibria in these models, many of the comparative-static questions cannot be satisfactorily resolved without recourse to contextual data analysis. Besides, these models are often couched in a restrictive framework that is inadequate for capturing some of the salient issues of real-world cooperation (or lack of it). For a long time we will have to depend on arduous empirical work to give us clues about the building blocks to more satisfactory theoretical models and policy action. Much of the existing empirical literature on these issues is social-anthropological, without a great deal of quantifi-

---

4. I have elaborated on this theme in Bardhan (1984, ch. 16).
5. Apart from the well-known accounts in Ostrom (1990), Wade (1987), and Vaidyanathan (1985), see also Jayaraman (1981), Easter and Palanisami (1986), Sengupta (1991), and Vaidyanathan (1994).

cation, which makes deciphering the effect of a particular factor, controlling for other factors, difficult.

This chapter concentrates on a quantitative analysis of the physical, institutional, and socioeconomic determinants of cooperation in irrigation communities[6] on the basis of a large survey conducted in the South Indian state of Tamil Nadu. In section 11.2 we describe the variables and the data and our expected effects that the independent variables may have on cooperation, and in section 11.3 we report the actual results of the statistical analysis.

11.2

In all data were collected from 48 villages spread over 6 districts in Tamil Nadu, with a selected unit (called *ayacut*) of irrigation system in each village (either a tank or a branch of canal with roughly about 50 hectares size of command area). Half of the irrigation units belonged to canal systems, and the other half to more traditional tank systems. All the canal systems were under the general administration of the government (usually the Public Works Department, PWD). Within tank systems, half belonged to what are called "isolated or chain-tank" systems, and the other half to "system tanks" (where the tanks were, unlike in the former case, linked to larger irrigation units). Within each system the villages were randomly chosen. Within each village a stratified sample of ten farmers (stratified by land-size classes) was chosen. Most of the analysis here is done on the basis of data for the irrigation unit (the ayacut) as a whole; in some cases, data are derived from the individual farmers' responses. In general, on matters of cooperation, differences across villages were much more prominent than intravillage differences among the ten farmers.

First a few words on the description of the general functioning of the water users' organizations. The majority of the organizations surveyed are traditional and informal community organizations that have been in existence for some time (twenty-seven of the forty-eight surveyed are reported either as "traditional" or at least twenty years old). But only thirteen of these units have formal associations (and ten of these have formal associations not at the village or sluice levels but at

---

6. For a partially similar analysis of determinants of the adoption of distributive rules and of cooperative maintenance effort with data from fifty-four farmer-managed surface irrigation systems in central Mexico, see Dayton-Johnson (1998). We also compare some of our results with those of Lam (1998) for irrigation systems in Nepal.

the more aggregative zonal level). The organization in twelve of the (canal-based) irrigation units surveyed has been set up (relatively recently) and is run directly by the PWD. In another twelve canal-based irrigation units, although PWD is the overall official agency, the traditional village committee manages irrigation matters at the village level.

There is a great deal of variation among the organizations with respect to appointment of guards as monitors and enforcers, frequency of meeting, mobilization of collective labor, mobilization of funds, method of cost sharing, and involvement in nonirrigation activities.[7] Most of the users' organizations meet at least once every one to two years; only nine reported never meeting at all. The units run directly by the PWD reported meeting at most once a year (and often only every two years), while most others meet once or twice a year during the cropping season. Five of the units surveyed have organizations that reported having regular meetings at least ten times a year. One function of the water users' organization in many of the units surveyed is to mobilize community labor for the purpose of maintaining and repairing the field channels. Generally, it appears that community labor is most common in those organizations that are traditional or have existed for over forty years. While most of these units mobilize community labor both for regular maintenance and for emergency repairs, several units reported mobilizing community labor only in the event of emergency repairs. Community labor does not appear to be used systematically in any of those units where the PWD directly runs the organizations.

About three-quarters (thirty-seven in number) of the units surveyed have some formal system of fundraising. Of these, twenty-eight units have a system of dues, fines, or taxes. Such a system is most prevalent in those units that are canal-based. In the tank-based systems, an alternate system of fundraising is possible—the sale of collective resources such as fish and trees. Nineteen of the tank-based units have collective funds that are mobilized this way; ten of these units supplement the collective fund with a system of dues or tax collection. About half of the water users' organizations report participating in other, usually villagewide, activities, such as conducting the temple festival. This

---

7. Unfortunately, the data and descriptions regarding some of these organizational variables were not systematic or complete enough to allow reliable coding and inclusion in the subsequent regression analysis.

does not appear to be true of any of the organizations that are run by the PWD.

Since issues like cooperation and some of its determinants involve the quality of social and economic relations, much of the data are more qualitative (sometimes with yes-no answers) than quantitative, from which variables are constructed that therefore take only a limited range of values. A description of the dependent and independent variables, including their mean values with standard deviation and the range of variation, is given in table 11.1. Three alternative variables are used as indicators of cooperation[8] within the community on matters of irrigation: quality of maintenance of distributaries and field channels (DISTFDCH), absence of conflict in water allocation in the ayacut in the last five years (H20COOP), and extent of violations in water-allocation rules (VIOLH20). Table 11.1 shows a considerable amount of variations among the villages in the values of these variables.

Let us now describe and comment upon the explanatory variables that we have used. One obvious variable to consider is that relating to group size: NUMUSERS is the number of households[9] using the particular irrigation source (the number varies between 11 and 279, with a mean of 53). The common presumption in the literature on local commons is that cooperation works better in small groups. The early work of Olson (1965) suggests that collective action is easier to organize in small groups. In a game played by rotating irrigators (turn takers and turn waiters) with self-enforced rules (without formal guards), Weissing and Ostrom (1990) show in their theoretical model that in the equilibrium an increase in the number of irrigators is associated with an increase in the stealing of water, other things remaining the same.[10] In general, models of repeated games suggest that cooperative strategies are more likely to emerge and be sustained in smaller groups. In small irrigation communities, peer monitoring is easier, the "common-knowledge" assumption of models of strategic decisions is likely to be more valid, shared norms and patterns of reciprocity are more

---

8. These may not always be good indicators of cooperation among the farmers (this is discussed below).

9. An alternative variable, NUM_ACRE, is the number of households using the irrigation source per acre of the ayacut area. But usually this variable is less significant than NUMUSERS in regressions.

10. Of course, other things do not remain the same. As the data show (below), the existence of guards is positively (though not very significantly) correlated with NUMUSERS, and guards have a positive influence on cooperation.

Table 11.1
Dependent and Independent Variables

Variable Name	Number of Observations	Mean	Standard Deviation	Min.	Max.	Description of Variable
Alternate dependent variables:						
DISTFDCH	45	1.31	0.92	0	2	Index of quality of maintenance of distributaries and field channels
H2OCOOP	48	0.67	0.48	0	1	No conflict over water within village in the last five years*
VIOLH2O	48	0.52	0.50	0	1	Water-allocation rules frequently violated by at least one group*
Explanatory variables:						
NUMUSERS	48	52.67	54.29	11	279	Number of beneficiary households using this irrigation source
NUM_ACRE	48	0.36	0.02	0.06	1.07	Number of beneficiary households per acre of ayacut area
GINI	48	0.41	0.11	0	1	Gini coefficient of landholding of beneficiary households in the ayacut
CASTE75	48	0.69	0.47	0	1	At least 75% of sampled farmers are members of the same caste group*
AVGACCES	48	3.65	1.20	2	7	Number of months there is access to irrigation
TOPOGRPH	48	0.46	0.50	0	1	No equal access to water because of topographical nature of the ayacut*
LINED	48	1.96	0.82	1	3	If system is partially or fully lined
CANAL	48	0.50	0.51	0	1	If the ayacut is in a canal system*
PWDDECID	48	0.25	0.44	0	1	If PWD takes all decisions on water allocation*

TAILEND	48	0.75	0.44	0	1	If village is situated at tail end of the irrigation system*
PRIORAPP	48	0.44	0.50	0	1	No conflict with other villages over water*
LINKAGE	48	2.46	0.74	1	3	Index of connection with urban areas
MARKET	48	2.39	0.70	1	3	Measure of extent to which farmers are market oriented
OTHIRRIG	48	0.26	0.18	0	0.66	Estimated fraction of total irrigated land held by sampled farmers outside the ayacut
TRADLORG	48	0.56	0.50	0	1	Where irrigation organization has been there for 20 or more years*
GUARD	48	0.38	0.49	0	1	There exists at least one guard in the ayacut*
SHRPROP	48	0.19	0.39	0	1	Cost-sharing proportional to landholding*
LEGALRGT	48	0.33	0.48	0	1	When formal water rights exist, as opposed to customary rights*
WMARKET	48	0.44	0.50	0	1	If there is a market for well water*

* in the description of a variable indicates that the variable takes only two values, 0 and 1.

common, social sanctions may be easier to implement through reputation mechanisms and multiplex relationships, and even hydrologic needs of farmers may be relatively similar. On the other hand, there may be some positive economies of scale in larger groups, particularly in matters of pooling resources, appointing guards, lobbying with officials, and so on.

Another possibly important explanatory variable is heterogeneity, both social and economic. The only variable in our dataset that relates to social homogeneity or heterogeneity is CASTE75, which takes a value of 1 in villages where at least 75 percent of the sampled farmers are members of the same generic caste group (in most cases a "backward" caste group) in the village. By this crude measure, 69 percent of the ayacuts in the dataset are socially relatively homogeneous. In terms of economic heterogeneity, a variable called GINI measures the Gini coefficient of inequality of landholding of farmers in the ayacut area. The mean value of GINI in this dataset is 0.41.

Theoretically, the relationship between heterogeneity and successful collective action is rather complex.[11] On the one hand, there is the well-known suggestion of Olson (1965) that in a heterogeneous group a dominant member who enjoys a large part of the benefits of a collective resource is likely to see to its provision even if he has to pay all of the cost himself (with the small players free-riding on the contribution of the large player). On the other hand, the net benefits of coordination of each individual may be structured in such a way that in situations of marked heterogeneity or inequality some individuals (particularly those with better exit options) may not participate, and the resulting outcome may be more inefficient. In addition, the transaction and enforcement costs of cooperative arrangements may be high in situations of intravillage heterogeneity, conflicts, and inequality. Internalization of cooperative norms is more difficult under such circumstances; the degree of confidence or trust that individuals have in the likelihood that others will play their part in a cooperative agreement may be low. In anticipation that the relationship between inequality and cooperation may be nonlinear, a squared Gini coefficient (called GINISQU) has been introduced in the explanatory variables.[12]

---

11. For a theoretical analysis of some of the complexities, see Baland and Platteau (1997, 1998), Dayton-Johnson and Bardhan (2002), and chapter 10, sections 3 and 4, in this book.
12. For a theoretical analysis of a U-shaped relationship between wealth inequality and cooperation in the context of a two-player noncooperative model of conservation of a common-pool resource, see Dayton-Johnson and Bardhan (2002).

Another kind of factor that affects cooperation in water management is the physical condition of water availability. In conditions of extreme scarcity, arrangements of cooperation often break down. When irrigators have some significant access to water, they find it useful to co-operate in maintaining field channels and to obey allocation rules. In the dataset here, the villages with acute water scarcity in general have less cooperation, but (probably for historical reasons) the water-scarce villages are also more likely to have canal-based irrigation. So the effect of water scarcity is mixed up with that of possible bureaucratic ineffi-ciencies in release of canal water (more on this below). A variable AVGACCES indicates the number of months in a year that the farmers in the ayacut have access to water: it varies from two to seven months, with a mean of 3.7 (2.8 for the canal areas).[13] Two other variables relate to physical conditions: TOPOGRPH indicates where the topographical nature of the ayacut precludes equal access to water for all the farmers, and LINED indicates where the irrigation channel is lined.

For government involvement we have used two alternate variables —CANAL (to mark half the villages where it is a government admin-istered canal system), and the other is PWDDECID, i.e., where PWD makes all the decisions about water allocation and distribution. In the canal-area villages, there is not merely less water availability, but water is also more inequitably distributed: in nineteen out of twenty-four canal-area villages in the dataset (as opposed to two out of the twenty-four villages served by the tank systems), there is evi-dence of such inequity of water supply or access. In general, the water-release cycles may be more unreliable from the farmers' point of view when they are administered by PWD officials. Of course, there is potentially a major problem of endogeneity here: does the PWD get involved when irrigators' cooperation has failed?[14] After some back-ground checking, we have found that the villages where the PWD makes all the decisions are all located in the Coimbatore district and are precisely those where due to primarily physical reasons of long-term

---

13. It is well known in the irrigation literature that no single-dimensional variable can adequately capture the quality of water supply, which depends on many factors (like volume, timing, crop produced, and cultivation practice). As an alternative to the vari-able AVGACCES, we also tried a variable indicating whether water is "sufficient" for the paddy crop in the primary season, but this variable turned out to be less significant in the statistical analysis than AVGACCES.

14. Alternatively, the farmers may get involved in cooperation when the PWD fails to do its job, but this looks unlikely based on the details of the description of the irrigation units in the survey.

water scarcity, a large-scale interriver-basin water-transfer scheme (the Parambikulam Aliyar Project, PAP) had been undertaken by the government. The problem of endogeneity therefore may not be serious here.

A few variables relate to the locational context of the ayacut in question. The variable TAILEND refers to the cases where the village is situated at the tail end of the irrigation system, which, other things remaining the same, may unite the farmers of the village in their struggle to get more water away from the more favorably located villages. In the dataset, 75 percent of the villages are at the tail end of their respective systems. In general, only 44 percent of villages report that there is no conflict with other villages over water. As an alternative to TAILEND, the variable PRIORAPP indicates those villages where no water conflict is reported with other villages.

The locational context is also important in the matter of the exit options open to the villagers in conforming to cooperative arrangements. LINKAGE is a variable that is a proxy for the connection of the village to urban areas or transport and communication modes (like bus and telephone). The variable MARKET is a measure of the extent to which the farmers are oriented to selling their produce in the outside market. (Since how much a farmer sells his produce may be determined by his other characteristics—it may be endogenous—a predicted value of the MARKET variable is used in the regressions for determinants of cooperation.) A somewhat different kind of exit-option variable may be indicated by how much access an ayacut member has to water sources outside the ayacut.[15] The variable OTHIRRIG is the estimated fraction of the total irrigated land (of the sampled farmers in the ayacut) that is outside the ayacut. For all of these exit-option-like variables, the prior expectation is that they will have a negative effect on cooperation.[16]

The history of cooperation in a village may matter, as cooperation may be self-reinforcing, or "habit-forming," as Seabright (1997) explains in a theoretical model. A variable TRADLORG indicates villages that have had a water users' organization for twenty years or

15. Another variable was tried to indicate access of farmers to alternative, private sources of water within the village (like pumpsets and open wells). But in the dataset this variable is highly correlated with variables like CANAL. One possible reason may be that government canals increase the subsoil water for private wells.
16. Except in the case of MARKET, where the negative effect may be modified by the market opportunities for produce to raise the return to cooperation on water.

more. These villages are characterized by more use of community labor in maintenance works and emergencies, are more likely to hire guards (called *neerani* in much of this area) for monitoring and enforcement (indicated generally by the variable GUARD), and to use cost sharing proportional to land holding (indicated generally by variable SHRPROP). Since the use of guards and a cost-sharing regime may be endogenous, predicted values of these variables, PGUARD and PSHRPROP, are used in the cooperation regressions. Questions also were asked about the farmers' perception about the process of rule crafting. For example, the variable ELITERUL is used for villages where at least four out of ten sampled farmers believe that the water rules were crafted by the elite. (We also had a variable, FAIR, for villages where the rules are generally perceived as fair, but we dropped this variable as it almost coincides with cases of cooperative behavior).

11.3

The regression results are presented in table 11.2 (A, B, and C), table 11.3 (A and B), and table 11.4 (A and B). For some of the independent variables, the predicted values are estimated on the basis of first-stage regressions in table 11.5. We are primarily concerned with the signs of the regression coefficients.[17] Let us start with DISTFDCH, the index of quality of maintenance of distributaries and field channels, as the dependent variable. This index is uniformly lower in ayacuts with higher inequality in landholding: the coefficient for GINI is negative in all of the three alternative cases in table 11.2 and highly significant in two of the three cases. (A similar negative coefficient for GINI of land distribution has been observed by Dayton-Johnson, 1998, for farmer-managed irrigation systems in Mexico, and a negative coefficient has been observed for "variations of income among appropriators" in irrigation systems in Nepal by Lam, 1998). The coefficient is also lower, and significantly so, with ELITERUL—that is, for villages where rules are perceived to be crafted by the village elite.[18]

---

17. Since this is a logit analysis, the signs are to be appropriately interpreted as indicating directions of changes in the probability of the dependent variable taking on a particular value with changes in the values of an independent variable, even though in the statement of the results we sometimes do not spell it out fully.

18. From the data of the 480 sampled farmers it is clear that when an average farmer believes that the water rules have been crafted jointly (as opposed to by the elite or by the government), he is more likely to have positive comments about the water-allocation system and about rule compliance by other farmers.

Table 11.2
Ordered Logit Estimates, Dependent Variable: DISTFDCH

	A		B		C	
Variables	Coefficients	Level of Significance	Coefficients	Level of Significance	Coefficients	Level of Significance
NUMUSERS	-.0308	20%			-.0339*	10%
NUM_ACRE			3.5369	20%		
GINI	-31.1481*	5%	-12.0576	15%	-23.2620*	5%
AVGACCES	5.0160*	5%	3.3115*	5%	4.5637*	5%
LINED	-2.0352	15%	-6.2620*	5%		
PWDDECID	8.0913*	5%	10.8124*	5%	4.8454*	5%
TAILEND					1.5790	Insignificant
PRIORAPP			-6.0943*	5%	-2.2385	Insignificant
LINKAGE	-4.2195*	5%	-4.7874*	5%	-4.2900*	5%
OTHIRRIG	-4.8767	Insignificant	-4.7635	Insignificant		
PGUARD	9.0919*	5%	7.1193*	5%	10.3531*	5%
PSHRPROP	11.6709	15%			9.6847*	10%
ELITERUL	-8.8760*	5%	-6.6006*	5%	-7.9717*	5%
Number of observations	45		45		45	
Log likelihood	-15.4788		-14.6912		-16.5396	
Pseudo R-squared	0.5900		0.6109		0.5619	

Note: PGUARD and PSHRPROP are predicted values of the variables GUARD and SHRPROP, respectively.
* indicates significance at 10% level or below.

Table 11.3
Logit Estimates, Dependent Variable: H2OCOOP

Variables	A Coefficients	A Level of Significance	B Coefficients	B Level of Significance
NUMUSERS	−.0868	15%	−.0533*	5%
GINI	−106.6778*	5%	−77.4133*	5%
GINISQU	76.2725*	10%	59.8977*	10%
CASTE75	2.9169*	10%	2.1678	15%
AVGACCES	1.4893	20%		
LINKAGE	−3.2398	20%	−2.0861*	10%
PGUARD	22.4376	15%	15.3198*	10%
Number of observations	48		48	
Log likelihood	−10.3061		−11.7129	
Pseudo R-squared	0.6627		0.6166	

Note: GINISQU is the square of the value of the variable GINI.
* indicates coefficients that are significant at 10% level or below.

Table 11.4
Logit Estimates, Dependent Variable: VIOLH2O

Variables	A Coefficients	A Level of Significance	B Coefficients	B Level of Significance
NUMUSERS	.0350*	5%	.0289*	5%
GINI	25.3600	Insignificant		
GINISQU	−34.9862	Insignificant		
CASTE75	−.8536	Insignificant		
AVGACCES	−.8960	15%	−1.0435*	5%
TOPOGRPH	1.1632	Insignificant	1.1202	Insignificant
TAILEND			−.4413	Insignificant
LINKAGE	2.1425*	5%		
PMARKET			.499*	10%
OTHIRRIG	5.8283	15%	4.5255	15%
PGUARD	−7.5257*	5%	−3.4537*	5%
Number of observations	48		48	
Log likelihood	−15.7310		−20.0658	
Pseudo R-squared	0.5266		0.3961	

Note: GINISQU is the square of the value of the variable GINI; PGUARD and PMARKET are the predicted values of the variables GUARD and MARKET, respectively.
* indicates coefficients that are significant at the 10% level or below.

Table 11.5
First-Stage Logit Estimates

| Independent Variables | Dependent Variables | | | | | |
| | GUARD | | SHPROP | | MARKET | |
	Coefficients	Level of Significance	Coefficients	Level of Significance	Coefficients	Level of Significance
NUMUSERS	.0305	20%	.0265*	5%		
GINI	9.8339	15%	9.8831*	10%	−4.5713	15%
AVGACCES	−.8961	15%			.4339	Insignificant
CANAL	−4.2407*	5%	4.1930*	5%	2.8389*	5%
LINKAGE	1.5349*	10%				
TRADLORG	3.0781*	5%	2.6285*	5%		
LEGALRGT			2.0355*	10%		
WMARKET					2.0298*	5%
Number of Observations	48		48		48	
Log likelihood	−13.6321		−13.7212		−32.8864	
Pseudo R-squared	0.5707		0.4076		0.2917	

* indicates significance at 10% level or below.

As the preceding section suggests, the effect of number of users of the irrigation system can be ambiguous.[19] In the ordered logit estimates, the coefficient for NUMUSERS is negative but not significant in one case and significant at a 10 percent level in another. In another case, when the number of users per acre of the ayacut area is taken as an alternative, the coefficient is positive but not significant.[20]

AVGACCES, the number of months in a year that there is access to irrigation, is positively and significantly related to DISTFDCH in all three cases. The interpretation is that when there is access to an irrigation system over a longer period in the year, the return to investing effort in maintenance of field channels is higher (and may outweigh the increased maintenance costs that may follow from higher use).[21] The negative coefficient of LINED at first seems surprising[22] but probably means that when the channels are lined, they are more likely to be found occasionally in a "broken condition," compared to channels that are not lined at all. (In fact, of the fifteen units that are not lined at all, only two report the field channels to be in bad condition.)[23] An alternative explanation (suggested by Dayton-Johnson on the basis of his observations in Mexico) is that some poor villages are unable to properly take care of the modern water-control structures that tend to accompany lined canals, either because they cannot get replacement parts or because they do not know how to repair them (or both).

19. This is also empirically corroborated by Lam (1998).
20. In the corresponding OLS regressions neither NUMUSERS nor NUM_ACRE is at all significant.
21. There is reason to believe that the access to irrigation refers more to general accessibility to water sources and structures than to the flow of water through the field channels, so the reverse causation (better-maintained channels implying better access to irrigation water) is an unlikely explanation of the positive coefficient. In fact, in general in the canal areas AVGACCES is very low, and yet DISTFDCH is high.
22. Lam (1998, p. 180) finds a positive coefficient for his explanatory variable on lining but in a different context comments thus on the design of irrigation infrastructure constructed by the Department of Irrigation (DOI) in Nepal, which may be relevant here: "Although the unlined canal was prone to damage, it was easy to maintain. Whenever there was leakage, farmers could easily locate the leaks and seal the leaks with mud. Now that the DOI has lined the canals with bricks, farmers find it difficult to locate the leaks at all. Even if they can locate them, it is difficult to seal them. Farmers complain that there is little that they can do to keep the canal in good condition."
23. Following a suggestion from Gershon Feder, we ran a separate regression for the thirty units that are lined (partially or fully). The results are similar to those reported in table 11.2, except that the significance of some of the variables diminishes (partly because of the reduced number of observations).

Contrary to the general impression about the negative effect of government involvement, the coefficient for PWDDECID is positive and significant in all three cases. It is possible that when the PWD is actively involved in water allocation and in maintenance works above the outlet, returns to farmers' collective maintenance effort on channels below the outlet are higher. The detailed data show a picture that is a little more complex: of the twelve units where the PWD is actively involved, the field channels in half of the units are well maintained,[24] and those in the other half of the units are badly maintained. In the badly maintained units, farmers have more private sources of water (pumps and open wells) than farmers in the well-maintained units have (and the GINI coefficient of land distribution in the ayacut is considerably higher; as expected, inequality of landholding goes with more access to pumps and open wells).

The coefficient for TAILEND is positive but not significant. But the coefficient for PRIORAPP is negative, and in one case is highly significant. This suggests that water conflicts with other villages may be helping the farmers of the ayacut unite in cooperative maintenance effort.

The variable for urban connections, LINKAGE, has a highly significant negative coefficient in all the three alternate cases in table 11.2. This is consistent with expectations about the adverse effect of exit options on cooperative behavior (discussed in the preceding section). The variable OTHIRRIG, indicating access to alternative sources of irrigation outside the ayacut for the farmers, has an appropriately negative sign, but it is not significant.

The quality of maintenance is understandably highly positively correlated with the existence of a guard, whose enforcement of water-distribution rules increases the benefits of field-channel maintenance.[25] Since the appointment of a guard is itself dependent on some of the factors that enter into the determination of cooperative behavior, here only the predicted value, PGUARD, is used in this second-stage

---

24. In four of these six units it seems that the PWD, rather than a traditional village organization, looks after the field-channel maintenance as well (though the farmers make some cash contributions). This means that good maintenance may not always be simply interpreted as an indicator of cooperation among the farmers.

25. In some alternative regressions (not reported here), we have found that the interactive effect of PGUARD and NUMUSERS has a significant negative coefficient, indicating that the effectiveness of the guard system in encouraging cooperation decreases as the number of users increases.

regression.[26] In the first-stage logit analysis for GUARD (reported in table 11.5), the variables CANAL and TRADLORG are used as exogenous. In canal areas there is much less use of a guard, whereas in ayacuts with a traditional organization appointing a guard is common. Presumably, this is determined by historical-conventional factors. In fact, in areas where the government makes the decisions, the enforcement of rules is usually by government officials or police, not by guards.[27] The only other variable that is significant (at the 10 percent level) in the first-stage regression for GUARD is LINKAGE: it seems that better urban-linked villages use more guards. But table 11.2 suggests that, *controlling* for the positive effect on PGUARD, LINKAGE has a significant negative effect on maintenance of field channels.

In table 11.2 the positive (but not always significant) effect of the proportional cost-sharing rule on maintenance can be seen: cost sharing that is proportional to landholding may be perceived as more fair than, for example, cases where all farmers have to bear the same cost (even though the larger farmers get more of the benefit) or where there is no rule.[28] Since SHRPROP may itself be dependent on factors that enter into the determination of cooperative behavior, table 11.2 uses only the predicted value, PSHRPROP. The first-stage logit analysis for SHRPROP is reported in table 11.5. SHRPROP is positively and significantly related to the number of ayacut members, inequality of landholding among them, canal areas, ayacuts where the irrigation organization is old, and ayacuts where formal water rights is more prevalent.[29] Since GINI has a positive effect on SHRPROP (possibly indicating social pressure for a redistributive adjustment of the

---

26. A two-stage regression is somewhat problematic when the second stage is a nonlinear logit model. OLS can be used as a check to confirm the results, but with dependent variables that are grouped, with OLS the error terms cannot be assumed to be normally distributed. The assumption is even worse, and the results more biased, if OLS is used when the dependent variable takes on only 0–1 values, as in the case of H2OCOOP and VIOLH2O. In the case of DISTFDCH, we have used OLS as a check, and the results are largely confirmed (except for the variable NUMUSERS, as is noted in note 20).

27. In canal areas the water available to the ayacut also is from a flow (rather than from a storage reservoir, as in the case of tanks), and guarding against water theft may therefore be more serious in the case of canals than in the case of tanks. In any case, the TRADLORG variable is not statistically significant as a direct determinant in the cooperation regressions, and we therefore can legitimately use it as an instrumental variable.

28. Only about one in five villages has the proportional cost-sharing rule in the dataset.

29. In one-third of the villages in the dataset, formal water rights, as opposed to customary rights, exist. Again these are likely to be determined by historical-conventional factors, and we can therefore use this variable as a legitimate instrument.

cost-sharing rule to take account of wealth disparities) and PSHRPROP has a somewhat significant positive effect on DISTFDCH, the effect of inequality of land distribution on the quality of maintenance on field channels can be said to be twofold: the direct effect is negative, but the indirect effect, working through the cost-sharing rule, is positive.[30] Similarly, the effect of NUMUSERS is twofold: the direct effect is negative (though not always significant), but the indirect effect, working through the cost-sharing rule, is positive.

The dependent variable in table 11.3, H2OCOOP, is used where there has been no intravillage conflict over water over the previous five years. GINI is again significantly negative, but GINISQU is significantly positive, indicating the kind of U-shaped relationship between inequality and cooperative behavior discussed in the preceding section. The coefficient for CASTE75 is positive in both cases of table 11.3 and is significant in one, confirming that social homogeneity (in the form of 75 percent or more of the farmers belonging to the same caste group) is conducive to cooperation. The urban-connection variable, LINKAGE, is, as before, negative in its effect on cooperation, though significant in one of the two cases. Also as before, PGUARD has a positive effect, but it is significant in one of the two cases. The government-involvement variable, PWDDECID, did not turn out to be significant in this set of regressions. But looking at the detailed data, as in the case of the field-channel-maintenance regressions, in half of the twelve units where PWD takes all decisions, there was cooperation in water allocation, and in the other half there was conflict (and the former associated with more equality in land distribution and fewer private pumpsets and open wells than in the latter).[31]

In table 11.4 the dependent variable VIOLH2O is the opposite of cooperation; it indicates cases where water-allocation rules are frequently violated by at least one group. (Both for the ayacut as a whole and for the sampled farmers, the data definitely suggest that rule violations are more often made by the better-off farmers, presumably because they can get away with such violations more easily.)[32] Here the signs

---

30. In some alternative regressions (not reported here), we have found that the interactive effect of SHRPROP and GINI is positive in the DISTFDCH regression, suggesting that the higher the level of inequality, the more positive is the influence of proportional cost-sharing on the quality of maintenance.

31. Exactly the same pattern is observed in the other twelve canal-based units.

32. For example, in twenty-nine out of forty-eight villages rule violations are mainly by the rich farmers and other upper castes, as reported in the ayacut-level survey. Also at the level of the sampled farmers, the average farmer perception is that the rich (the top

of the coefficients for GINI, GINISQU, CASTE75, TAILEND, and OTHIRRIG are as expected from the earlier regressions, but they are not significant. NUMUSERS is positive and highly significant, indicating the difficulty of preserving cooperative behavior in large groups. AVGACCES, the duration of access to water, is negatively (and in one of the two cases highly significantly) related to violations, indicating that water scarcity encourages violations.

As before, the urban-connection variable, LINKAGE, has a negative impact on cooperation, and PGUARD has a positive effect. In one of the two regressions, PMARKET is used as an alternate outside-connection variable to LINKAGE. MARKET is a measure of the extent to which farmers are market-oriented (particularly in terms of sales of produce). Since this may be endogenously determined, PMARKET, the predicted value of MARKET, is used in the second-stage regression. The first-stage regression is reported in table 11.5. The only two variables that are significant (with a positive coefficient) in this first-stage regression are CANAL and WMARKET (indicating cases where there is a market for well water in the village),[33] the two variables chosen as instruments. From the second-stage regression it can be seen that like LINKAGE, PMARKET increases the probability of violation of water-allocation rules.

TOPOGRPH (the case where the topographical nature of the ayacut precludes equal access to water), TAILEND, and OTHIRRIG have coefficients of expected signs, but they are generally not significant.

From the list of independent variables, PWDDECID and ELITERUL had to be dropped because in both cases their values perfectly predicted the value of the dependent variable. This means in *all* the villages where PWD decides on water allocation and distribution, frequent rule violations are reported:[34] this may be because the rules are typically rigid and insensitive to local needs, farmers are less normatively committed, officials are bribed to look the other way, and so on. Lam (1998) reports from his study of irrigation systems in Nepal that in nearly half of the government-agency-managed systems the extent of rule breaking is medium or high, whereas the corresponding

---

four out of the ten sampled landholding farmers in the village) comply with rules significantly less than the poor (the bottom four out of the ten sampled farmers), particularly in water allocation and financial cost sharing.

33. About 44 percent of the villages in our dataset have a market for well water.

34. We also have evidence in our dataset that the farmers contribute to the village collective fund much less when the government is involved, presumably because the government is then assumed to be the financier of last resort.

percentage of rule breaking in farmer-managed systems is only about 12 percent. In contrast, in the villages where the village elite, rather than a government department, crafts the rules, there is no violation of rules reported. Since (as is noted above) the better-off are usually the more frequent violators of rules, they tend not to violate rules crafted by themselves.

In all of the twelve PWD-run units, there are rotational water-allocation rules by which farmers are allotted a certain number of hours of water access per acre or are allowed access to water only in alternate weeks. In *all* of these twelve units, these rotational rules are frequently violated, and particularly the rich farmers appropriate more water than is their due. And yet in half of these units (particularly where the inequality in land distribution among the farmers is low), field channels are well maintained, and there was no incidence of water conflicts within the village in the last five years. This means that inflexible rules of the government (enforced by corruptible agents) are frequently violated without necessarily damaging intravillage cooperation, suggesting again that when rules do not enjoy the backing of community norms, rule obedience is not necessarily an indicator of cooperation among farmers.

Summing up the seven regressions in tables 11.2, 11.3, and 11.4, in this dataset cooperative behavior in an irrigation community is by and large significantly related (negatively) to inequality of landholding and to urban or market connections and (positively) to duration of access to water, monitoring by guards, and in some cases social homogeneity, small group size, proportional cost-sharing rule, and collective adversarial relation with other villages over water. PWD involvement in water allocation and maintenance can have a positive effect on field-channel maintenance (if farmers do not have much access to their own private sources of water like pumpsets and open wells); but such involvement in this dataset is in water-scarce areas, and too much water scarcity may not be conducive to cooperation. Government involvement also encourages violations of specific inflexible rules by farmers and means fewer cases of ayacut communities appointing their own monitoring guards, which adversely affects cooperation. When the rules are crafted by the village elite, members of the elite violate the water-allocation rules less; otherwise, those in the elite are the most frequent violators of rules. Sometimes when inflexible rules are made and enforced by the government, their violations are not necessarily inconsistent with cooperative behavior among farmers themselves.

When an average farmer believes that the water rules have been crafted jointly (as opposed to by the elite or by the government), he is more likely to have positive comments about the water-allocation system and about rule compliance by other farmers.

Although this chapter is primarily meant to examine the factors underlying farmers' cooperation or lack of it, it offers several policy lessons. Decision-making and rule-crafting authority needs to be devolved to the local farmers (who do not cooperate as well when insensitive external rules are imposed on them). Also, land reform—apart from its direct incentive effects on farm productivity—can get poor farmers more actively involved in local self-governing institutions. Finally, the disruptive effects that the expansion of market linkages and of elite access to private sources of water can have on traditional community arrangements must not be minimized.

12 Global Rules, Markets, and the Poor

12.1

In the earlier chapters of this book I have largely confined myself to institutions in the domestic economy. In this final chapter I pay some attention to the implications of global institutional rules and market processes for the lives of the world's poor, and the importance of domestic institutions in this context. A raging issue in academic and public debates (which have spilled over into the streets in noisy demonstrations in recent years) concerns the impact of these global rules and processes on the well-being of the poor. Of course, as is common in contentious public debates, different people mean different things by globalization; some interpret it to mean the global reach of new technologies (particularly in information and communications) and capital movements, some refer to outsourcing by domestic companies in rich countries, and others protest against the tentacles of corporate capitalism or U.S. hegemony. As I see it, a large part of the opposition to globalization relates to three different issues:

• The fragility of valued local and indigenous cultures as they face the onslaught of global mass production and cultural homogenization (through global brand-name products, movies, music, fast foods, soft drinks, the Internet, and so on);

• The devastation caused to fragile economies by billions of dollars of volatile short-term capital as it stampedes around the globe in herdlike movements; and

• The damage caused to the jobs, wages, and incomes of poor people by the dislocations and competition of international trade and foreign investment and by the weakening of the state's ability to compensate for this damage and in general to alleviate poverty.

These three issues are interrelated. For example, the elimination of ethnic handicrafts by imports of manufactures may be seen as both an economic loss and a cultural loss. When short-term speculative capital rushes out of a developing country, it inevitably affects negatively the country's medium to long-term investment climate as well. But these three issues are conceptually separable. In this chapter, I mainly discuss the third issue: I interpret globalization to mean openness to foreign trade and *long-term* capital flows and try to understand the possible difficulties that poverty-alleviation policies in poor countries may face from such international economic integration. For this understanding we need first to look at the processes by which globalization may affect the conditions of the poor and then analyzes the ways in which the policies meant to relieve those conditions are limited by global constraints. In general, I believe that globalization can cause many hardships for the poor, but it also opens up opportunities that some countries can utilize and others do not, depending largely on their domestic political and economic institutions. The net outcome is often complex and almost always context-dependent, belying the glib pronouncements for or against globalization made in the opposing camps. I also emphasize the scope that institutions of international coordination have among the involved parties and for public-private partnerships to resolve many controversial policy issues.

For the record, let me say that on the other two important issues (the fragility of local cultures and economies afflicted by capital flights), which are not covered in the rest of this chapter, I generally favor some modest restrictions on the full fury of globalization. There are valid arguments for cultural protection[1] that even an economist can make: (1) preservation of cultural diversity on the same lines as that for biodiversity and "option value" in environmental economics; (2) intertemporal irreversibility and externality in production in the form of "forgetting by not doing" in production of local varieties, on lines similar to the more familiar case of "learning by doing"; (3) endogenous preferences, when what we choose depends on the range of varieties available and also when these preferences may be molded by giant international firms selling some standardized products but with large advertisement budgets. On the issue of the fragility of local economies

---

1. For an attempt to formalize these arguments in terms of theoretical models, see Aubert, Bardhan, and Dayton-Johnson (2003).

to capital flights, much of the financial crises in developing countries in recent years was initially caused by overexposure to foreign-currency-denominated short-term debts. It is now recognized that these are particularly crisis-prone financial instruments. In most cases there was too little discipline in borrowing before the crises and too much discipline afterward. Many international economists (even those who otherwise support free trade) now believe that some form of control is needed over short-term capital flows, particularly if domestic financial institutions and banking standards are weak, but they differ on the specific forms that such control should take and on the assessment of the effects of the rise in the cost of capital this may entail. I also think that it is imperative for the international community to work toward the creation and supervision of some international hedging and insurance institutions against the impact of capital-flow volatility.

I am also leaving out globalization in the form of international labor flows or more emigration of workers from poor to rich countries. If significant numbers of unskilled workers were allowed entry into rich countries even in limited and regulated doses, a large dent could have been made in world poverty, many times what can possibly be brought about by other forms of international integration,[2] but few people (even among those who are concerned about the world's poor) seem prepared to entertain this idea.

12.2

One common cliché that appears often in the literature as well as in the streets is that globalization is making the rich richer and the poor poorer. While relative inequality may be increasing in many countries[3] (on account of a whole host of factors, including globalization), my focus in this chapter is on the conditions of those trapped in absolute poverty (measured by some bare minimum standard) in low-income countries. It is not at all clear that the poor are getting poorer everywhere, when the large strides in international economic integration

---

2. Walmsley and Winters (2002) have estimated that the global gains that would accrue from allowing even temporary entry of both skilled and unskilled labor services equivalent to 3 percent of workforce in OECD countries would amount to about one and a half times the total gains that would accrue from merchandise trade liberalization.

3. Whether world income distribution as a whole is getting more unequal is moot, as hundreds of millions of poor people in large countries like China, India, and Indonesia have improved their living standards in recent years.

that have taken place in recent decades are taken into account.[4] A quarter of a century ago, most of the world's poorest people were concentrated in East, Southeast, and South Asia, sub-Saharan Africa, and Central America. Since then, poverty (the percentage of people below some poverty line) has substantially declined in large parts of China, Indonesia, and South Asia, and significant improvements have been made in other social indicators (like literacy or longevity)[5] in most low-income countries, while poverty has remained stubbornly high in sub-Saharan Africa. But correlation does not imply causation: just as a large decline in poverty in China along with globalization does not necessarily mean a causal relation between them, the same may be the case for the nondecline in Africa. Much of the persistence or even deterioration in poverty in Africa may have little to do with globalization and more to do with the unstable or failed political regimes, wars, and civil conflicts that have afflicted several of those countries. If anything, such political instability reduced the extent of globalization in these countries, as it scared off many foreign investors and traders. Similarly, proglobalizers point to the fact that wages and (possibly) living standards are often better for the poor in coastal cities in China than for the poor in the remote areas in western China who are cut off from the international economy or for the poor who live on the Mexican border with the United States, where the *maquiladora* are located, than for the poor in the interior provinces. But the causal mechanisms at work must be identified before anybody will accept them as persuasive.

The causal processes through which international economic integration can affect poverty involve primarily the poor in their capacity as workers and as recipients of public services. Let us first take the case of poor workers. They are mainly either self-employed or wage earners. The self-employed work as farmers on tiny farms, as artisans, and as petty entrepreneurs in small shops and firms. The major constraints

---

4. For example, Chen and Ravallion (2001) estimate that the proportion of the total population of the developing countries living in households with consumption expenditure per capita less than about $1 per day in 1998 (at 1993 purchasing-power parity) was 23 percent (25 percent if one were to exclude China), compared to 28 percent in 1987. The total number of poor people measured this way was about the same between the two years, about 1.2 billion. (Note that the end year 1998 partly includes the impact of the Asian financial crisis.) Bourguignon and Morrisson (2002) suggest a much larger decline in poverty over the last thirty years or so. These estimates are subject to many caveats about measuring poverty in terms of one common dollar standard of poverty for many different countries.
5. Longevity in the southern African countries afflicted by the AIDS pandemic has, however, begun to decline.

they usually face are in credit, marketing, insurance, infrastructure (like roads, power, ports, and irrigation), and government regulations (involving venal inspectors, insecure land rights, and so on). These often require substantive domestic policy changes, and foreign traders and investors are not directly to blame (in fact, they may sometimes help to relieve some of the bottlenecks in infrastructure, services, and in essential parts, components, and equipment). If these changes are not made and the self-employed poor remain constrained, then it is difficult for them to withstand competition from large agribusiness or firms (foreign or domestic).

Less constrained small farms or firms are sometimes more productive than their larger counterparts and are also sometimes more successful in export markets. Small producers (for example, coffee producers of Uganda, rice growers in Vietnam, and garment producers in Bangladesh or Cambodia) are often heavily involved in exports. But in exports the major hurdle they face is often due to not more globalization but *less*. Developed-country protectionism and subsidization of farm and food products and simple manufactures (like textiles and clothing) severely restrict their export prospects for poor countries.[6] According to estimates of the World Bank, the total losses incurred by exporters of textiles and garments on account of these trade barriers amount to more than $30 billion, and the loss to poor countries from agricultural tariffs and subsidies in rich countries is estimated to be about $20 billion. I wish the antiglobal protesters of rich countries turned their energies toward the vested interests in their own countries that prolong this protectionism[7] and cripple the efforts of the poor of the world to climb out of their poverty. Pro-poor opponents of the North American Free Trade Agreement (NAFTA) point out how competition from U.S. agribusiness is destroying the livelihoods of small farmers in Mexico, but they are not equally vocal about the huge farm subsidies in the United States (substantially larger now under the U.S. Farm Act of 2002) that are partly responsible for this. U.S. wheat export prices are estimated to be 46 percent below cost of production, U.S. corn export prices are at 20 percent below cost, and so on.[8] The average

---

6. This is not to minimize the trade barriers imposed by developing countries on imports of other developing countries.

7. For example, 90 percent of farm support in the United States goes to the largest 25 percent of farms; much of it is therefore part of corporate welfare.

8. See, for example, the recent Oxfam Report, *Rigged Rules and Double Standards: Trade, Globalization, and the Fight against Poverty* (2002).

cow in the European Union gets a government subsidy per year that is nearly twice the per-capita income of India.

Another increasingly important barrier to trade many small farmers of developing countries face in world markets is that rich countries now shut out many of these imports under a whole host of safety and sanitary regulations (sometimes imposed under pressure from lobbyists of import-competing farms in those countries). These regulations actually increase the need for involving rich-country transnational companies in marketing poor-country products. These companies can deal with the regulatory and lobbying machinery in rich countries far better than the small producers of poor countries can, and at the same time they can provide to consumers credible guarantees of quality and safety. Of course, these companies will charge hefty fees for this marketing service (usually much larger than the total production cost), but the small farmers will usually be better off with them rather than without.

Similarly, small producers of manufactures or services in developing countries may find it very difficult, costly, and time-consuming to establish brand name and reputation in quality and timely delivery—which are crucial in marketing, particularly in international markets (much more important than comparative costs of production, which traditional trade theory emphasizes). This is where multinational marketing chains with global brand names, mediating between domestic suppliers and foreign buyers, can be very helpful for a long time, and the high marketing margin they charge may sometimes be worth paying. At the same time, coordinated attempts on the part of developing countries, with technical assistance from international organizations, to build international quality-certification institutions for their products should be a high priority.

At the lower end of the value chain, more than fifty developing countries depend on three or fewer primary commodities for more than half of their export. Exports of such products are often a curse as well as a blessing for these countries, as their prices fluctuate wildly and the economy is too dependent on them. As a result of the recent elimination of the erstwhile inefficiently run marketing boards and dismantling of wasteful stabilization schemes (and to the extent this has not been replaced by private monopolies), farmers in many African countries now receive a higher fraction of a more volatile (and in some cases, lower) world market price. International commodity agreements among these countries to control their supply in the world market have not worked well in the past. To reduce their economic vulnerability, they probably do not have many alternatives beyond attempting to diversify in production and skill-formation, to move up the supply chain toward activities with more value addition for the same commodity, and to arrange at an international level institutions of insurance for farmers in poor countries.

Turning to poor wage earners, the theoretical literature on how international trade affects the absolute level of the real wage of unskilled workers is extremely small relative to the literature on wage inequality (which, though an important issue, is not my concern here). There are at least seven types of theoretical mechanisms through which this effect may be significant in developing countries and the net effect.

• When applied to a simple two-country (rich-poor) two-factor (capital-labor) world, the traditional Stolper-Samuelson mechanism suggests that workers in the poor country (which presumably has abundant supplies of unskilled labor) have a comparative advantage in products that are intensive in unskilled labor and therefore should benefit from trade liberalization. This advantage is complicated by the fact that developing countries (say, Brazil, Mexico, or Turkey) may import labor-intensive products from even poorer countries (say, China, Indonesia, or Bangladesh), so that trade liberalization even in terms of this mechanism may lead to lower wages in the former set of developing countries (Wood, 1997).

• If some factors of production are intersectorally immobile, and some goods are nontraded, the real wage of an unskilled worker in a poor country may not go up with trade liberalization even in an otherwise standard model of trade theory. Consider a three-good model in a hypothetical African country: one nontradable good (say, a subsistence food crop) is grown largely by women who for various social and economic reasons cannot move to other sectors; another good (say, an exportable tree crop) is produced largely by men in a capital-intensive way (maybe simply because tree crops lock up capital for a long period); and the third good is an importable (say, processed food) that is somewhat substitutable in consumption for the subsistence food. In this three-sector model it is not difficult to show that the real wage of women may go down when the importable processed food is made cheaper by trade liberalization (under the condition that the elasticity of substitution in consumption of the two foods is sufficiently high).

• Consider a two-period model where labor on a long-term contract is trained in the first period and this training bears fruit in the second period, when these long-contract workers are more productive than untrained short-contract casual laborers. If opening the economy increases the competition and the probability of going out of business, then employers may go more for short-contract, less productive, and lower-wage laborers, bringing down the average wage. By a similar reasoning a firm may have less incentive in an open economy to invest in developing a reputation for fairness in wage payments.

• On the other hand, increased foreign competition may lead to the exit of old inefficient firms, the entry of new more efficient firms, or a better allocation of resources within existing firms. This may lead to a rise in average wages in industries that attain such productivity gains.[9]

• If firms that face more foreign competition and pressure to reduce costs outsource activities to smaller firms or household enterprises in the informal sector,[10] the average wage (of those formerly employed in the formal sector) may go down, but this need not impoverish workers in general if the poorer informal workers get more employment this way.

• If technical changes in rich countries are biased against the services of unskilled labor (for which there is plenty of evidence) and if globalization means that the impact of rich countries reaches remote corners of the world, then the employment and wages of unskilled workers in poor countries will go down (as has been reportedly the case, for example, with global tenders to construction companies like Bechtel or Mitsui that use labor-saving technology rendering many construction workers unemployed in India).

• As foreign competition (or even the threat of it) lowers profit margins, the old rent-sharing arrangements between employers and unionized workers come under pressure. Rents decline both for capital and labor, but labor may have to take a larger cut if, as has been

---

9. The positive link between trade liberalization and productivity has been found in Chile, Colombia, Ivory Coast, Brazil, India, and South Korea. One of the most careful micro studies on this question is by Pavcnik (2002), who finds that massive trade liberalization in Chile in the late 1970s and early 1980s led to growth of productivity at the plant level at the average rate to 3 to 10 percent. For the other country studies, see the references in Pavnick (2002).

10. Attanasio, Goldberg, and Pavcnik (2002) find some evidence that the increase in the size of the informal sector in Colombia toward the end of the 1990s is related to increased foreign competition.

argued, the increase in the (perceived) elasticity of demand in the product market (a small increase in price leads to a larger fall in demand due to the competition of foreign products) leads to an increase in the elasticity of demand for labor (a small wage increase leads to a sharper fall in employment), lowering its bargaining power and generally weakening unions.[11] This may lead to lower wages and, sometimes more important, increased risk of unemployment. Scheve and Slaughter (2002) show how globalization of production through multinational enterprises in particular and related trade can make labor demand more elastic (through increased product-market competition and substitution of foreign factors of production, including intermediate inputs for domestic factors) and thereby raise economic insecurity for workers.

12.3

The micro empirical evidence on the effect of foreign trade and investment on the wages of unskilled labor in developing countries is rather limited (I am ignoring the usual, flawed, cross-country regressions). The usual citations are on correlations and do not include a careful empirical analysis of the causal process. For example, the critics of NAFTA will readily point to the decline in real wages of unskilled workers in Mexico in the few years immediately after NAFTA came into operation, overlooking the fact that much of the decline may be due to the peso crisis that engulfed Mexico in this period, which had little to do with the opening of trade with North America. The effects of trade reform on wages need to be disentangled from those flowing from macroeconomic policy changes or other ongoing deregulatory reforms and technological changes.

On the whole, the labor-market effect of trade liberalization in developing countries on the basis of the few microeconometric studies

---

11. See Currie and Harrison (1997), Rodrik (1997), Leamer (1998), and Reddy (2001). The theoretical relation between product market-demand elasticity and the elasticity of derived demand for labor is somewhat more complex than usual in the case of imperfect competition. The empirical evidence in developing countries on the trade-induced changes in the elasticity of demand for labor is rather scanty. Krishna, Mitra, and Chinoy (2001) do not find much support for a positive effect of trade on labor-demand elasticity on the basis of plant-level data in Turkey. Fajnzylber, Maloney, and Ribeiro (2001)—on the basis of plant-level data and taking both incumbent and exiting or entering firms into account—find in Chile and Colombia very ambiguous effects of trade liberalization on wage elasticities.

is rather mixed and quantitatively small. Analyzing a set of twenty-five trade-liberalization episodes in developing countries, using internationally comparable sectoral labor data, Seddon and Wacziarg (2002) conclude that trade liberalization has far smaller effects on intersectoral reallocation (even at the three-digit level within manufacturing) than is conventionally presumed. It is more likely that much of the structural change is intrasectoral and that some of the potential changes are neutralized by policies like exchange-rate depreciation, labor regulations, and sector-specific subsidies. The micro studies of effects of trade reform in Mexico and Morocco by Revenga (1997), Feliciano (2001), and Currie and Harrison (1997) attribute the small effect on employment to labor regulations or to the firms that adjust to trade reform by reducing their formerly protected profit margins, by raising productivity, and not by laying off workers. But even when the net effect on employment is relatively small, there may be a considerable amount job reallocation and dislocation, as Levinsohn (1999) finds, using firm-level data in Chile. Daveri, Manasse, and Serra (2003), on the basis of a sample of firms in six manufacturing sectors in India in 1997 to 1999, confirm that employees of foreign-exposed, particularly exporting, firms face more wage and employment variability but at the same time enjoy a higher probability of being trained and promoted than in firms not exposed to foreign competition. Comparing factories owned by multinational firms with domestic factories of the same size and efficiency in Indonesia, Bernard and Sjoholm (2003) find that the probability of closure was 20 percent higher for the former over a fifteen-year period.

Goldberg and Pavcnik (2001), on the basis of panel data from the Colombian National Household Survey from 1985 to 1994, look at the effect of trade policy on industry wage premiums—that is, the part of wages that cannot be explained by worker or firm characteristics. They find that the two most protected sectors in Colombia were (1) textiles and apparel and (2) wood and wood-product manufacturing. These are relatively unskilled labor-intensive sectors, and with industry-fixed effects, trade protection is found to increase industry wage premiums. This is consistent with traditional trade theory, particularly because such protection of labor-intensive industries in developing countries may be against imports from even more labor-abundant countries, as we have noted in our first theoretical mechanism above.

Even when poor unskilled workers lose from trade liberalization in such contexts, it may be possible to combine a policy of trade liberalization with a domestic policy of compensating the losers at low cost.

Harrison, Rutherford, and Tarr (2003) have used a computable general-equilibrium model for Turkey to show with a numerical exercise that a direct income subsidy to the losers of trade reform, financed by a value-added tax, is quite cost effective. The main problem, of course, is that of credible commitment on the part of the ruling politicians that losers will be compensated. Recent history in many countries is full of reneged promises on the part of governments to help displaced workers. This is a particularly important matter in poor countries where there is little effective social protection available from the state. Rich countries have better social safety nets and some programs in place to help displaced workers to adjust (like the federal adjustment-assistance program in the United States). International organizations that preach the benefits of free trade should take responsibility for funding and facilitating such adjustment-assistance programs in poor countries that can help workers in coping with job losses and getting retrained and redeployed. There should be more income-support programs (like the Trabajar program in Argentina) and programs to train and help the unemployed in finding new jobs (like the Probecat in Mexico).

Until issues of general economic security for poor workers in developing countries are satisfactorily resolved, globalization is bound to raise anxiety and hostility among workers who are worried about their job security. If mass politics in a country is organized, as it usually is, so that the nation-state is the primary political forum for demanding and getting redistribution and insurance (rendered more important by the economics of international specialization), then to the extent that the nation-state is weakened by forces of international economic integration, it requires alternative ways of organizing those functions, either by internationalizing them through supranational welfare institutions or by decentralizing them downward to local bodies and community organizations. The problem with supranational institutions is that political solidarities are difficult to organize at the international level and global federalism is only a distant dream of some internationalists. The problem with local organizations is that the rich often either secede from the local welfare state (bringing down its support structure) or capture and undermine it (as is discussed in chapter 6). In any case, local bodies are less well equipped to serve social-insurance functions when local risks are covariate. Much depends on a society's institutions of conflict management and coordination. It is not a coincidence that countries that have a better record in building these institutions have coped better with the dislocations brought about by international trade: the major example is the case of Scandinavian countries, where in spite of a strong tradition of an organized labor movement and worker solidarity over many decades of the last century, the unions there in general have been in favor of an open economy.

Let us now briefly turn to the case of the poor as recipients of public services. In low-income developing countries, the poor (particularly those who are in the preponderant informal sector) do not receive much effective social protection from the state (which makes them particularly vulnerable when job displacements are brought about by international competition), but the public sector is usually involved in basic services like education and health and public-works programs. Cuts in public budgets on these basic services are often attributed to globalization, as the budget cuts to reduce fiscal deficits often come as part of a package of macroeconomic stabilization prescribed by international agencies like the International Monetary Fund (IMF). I agree with a common characterization that some of the conditions that the IMF imposes on crisis-affected countries are analogous to medieval ways of trying to cure a patient by bloodletting. But the fiscal deficits in these poor countries are often brought about in the first place by domestic profligacy in matters of subsidies to the rich, salaries for the bloated public sector, or military extravaganza. Faced with mounting fiscal deficits, governments often find it politically easiest to cut public expenditures for the voiceless poor, primarily because of the domestic political clout of the rich (who are disinclined to share in the necessary fiscal austerity) and it is always convenient to blame an external agency for a problem that is essentially domestic in origin.

The low quality and quantity of public services like education and health in poor countries are not caused only by just their relatively low share of the public budget. Much of the limited money allocated in the budget does not reach the poor because of top-heavy administrative obstacles and bureaucratic and political corruption. Again, this is a domestic institutional failure and is not largely an external problem. The major effort required here is to strengthen the domestic institutions of accountability.

12.4

Let us now take up the general issue of possible loss of national policy options relevant for the poor brought about by a developing country's participation in international trade and investment and in the framework of global institutions and rules that govern them. First of all, I agree with the antiglobal protesters that many of the international organizations that define the rules of the international economic order are accountable more to the corporate and financial community of rich countries than to the poor and that the decision-making processes in these organizations need to be much more transparent and responsive to the lives of the people that their decisions crucially affect.[12] At the same time, the protesters in rich countries often speak in the name of the world's poor but support policies that sometimes may actually harm them (more on this below).

On the issue of a government's fiscal options in a global economy, many people are of the opinion that the scope for taxing capital to raise revenue is severely limited by the threat of capital flight in the long run, as well as the problem of short-term speculative capital flows. (In fact, capital itself does not have to flee the country; quite often accounting practices, through strategic bookkeeping adjustments, allow the base for capital taxes to migrate even when capital itself does not.) While this limitation can be serious, it should not be exaggerated. Most countries collect only a small part of their revenues from capital taxation, even in relatively closed economies. In any case, there are strong arguments for funding redistributive policies through progressive consumption taxes (say, VATs) rather than taxes on capital or labor. There also is a need for tax coordination across countries, and some evidence suggests that capital taxation is declining and also converging across countries. But again, this should not be overstated. Even in the highly integrated European Union, corporate tax rates have substantially converged—not to zero, as some people anticipated, but to about 35

---

12. The protesters' demand for the abolition of the World Trade Organization (WTO) is misplaced, however. When a developing country faces the United States in bilateral trade negotiations (rather than a multilateral organization like the WTO), the United States is likely to be more dominant and arbitrary than the WTO (which in its arbitration decisions has sometimes ruled against the U.S. position). Moreover, in the WTO each member country has one vote (the convention is to reach decisions by "consensus," as the protracted delay caused by one developing country in the agreement among ministers in the WTO meeting at Doha in December 2001 showed), whereas in the Bretton Woods institutions (the IMF and the World Bank) voting is dollar-weighted. But the rich countries (and their large corporate lobbies) undoubtedly exercise a dominant effect on the agenda setting and decision making of the WTO, as with the Bretton Woods institutions. At the Doha meeting there were some welcome signs of a slow opening of the process to the developing countries. But serious efforts are needed to strengthen the technical negotiation capacities of poor countries in international trade forums where they face the well-equipped and well-funded teams of lawyers and negotiators representing rich countries.

percent. In general, between two equilibria—one with high taxes and a high public-goods provision and the other with low taxes and low public goods—capital need not choose the latter over the former.

Serious obstacles to redistributive policies are often domestic. At the micro level of firms, farms, neighborhoods, and local communities, there is scope for a great deal of efficiency-enhancing egalitarian measures that can help the poor and are not blocked primarily by the forces of globalization. Various asset-redistribution and poverty-alleviation policies (like land reform, expansion of education, training and health facilities for the poor, making available guaranteed public works programs as a last resort for the unemployed, organising cooperative and peer-monitored credit and marketing for small firms and farms, facilitating formation of local community organizations to manage the local environmental resources) can improve productive efficiency, expand opportunities for the poor, and yet be within the range of capability of domestic institutions of the community and the polity. The main hindrance in devoting substantial fiscal and organizational resources to these projects is the considerable opposition from domestic vested interests—landlords, corrupt or inept politicians and bureaucrats, and the currently subsidized rich. Closing the economy does not reduce the power of these vested interests. If anything, the forces of competition unleashed by international integration may reduce their monopoly power.

More empirical work needs to be done in poor countries on this question of comparative market structure with or without an open economy. On the one hand, an open economy is likely to be more "contestable" (with even monopoly sellers facing more threats of potential entry) than an economy where domestic sellers are sheltered from foreign competition. On the other hand, the giant transnational companies with deep pockets can afford to resort to predatory pricing vis-à-vis smaller domestic sellers, particularly in industries where economies of scale and other entry barriers are important. One can only note that globalization may actually increase the competition among different transnationals in international markets. In general, it is not clear whether domestic consumers (and workers) always prefer domestic monopolists to foreign ones. Some may prefer to be exploited by Citibank rather than by the local loan shark.

It is true that the monopoly marketing chains, like those we have referred to earlier, eat up a large part of the gains from trade that form the staple of international economics textbooks. Just to cite one example, even today, long after the infamous days of the reign of the United Fruit Company, in Ecuador the local producer gets only $2 or $3 for each 43-pound box of bananas that is sold by the marketing chains in the United States or Europe for about $25. But the important question here is the counterfactual. The trade economists state that the alternative scenario of no trade is worse for the poor banana grower. Activist-protesters who suggest that the monopolist transnational marketing company should keep lower margins therefore should agitate more for antitrust action, not antitrade action. Otherwise their protests often end up merely strengthening the hands of protectionists of rich countries. Faced with this outcome, the producers in poor countries have to ask themselves essentially the trade economists' counterfactual: yes, we know the world is unfair, but can we do any better by closing down our economy? But this also means there should be energetic international attempts to certify codes against international restrictive business practices and to establish, as the 2002 Oxfam Report on *Rigged Rules and Double Standards* (referred to earlier) recommends, an antitrust investigation agency, possibly under WTO auspices.

Trade economists usually do not consider the possible impact of international operations on the domestic political equilibrium. Large transnational companies that work through the rich-country governments and with threats of financial withdrawal can sometimes shift the political equilibrium, particularly in small countries and weak states, although the crass manipulations and "gunboat diplomacy" of the past are getting somewhat more difficult than before. Others suggest that in countries with some established political and bureaucratic structures, if the internationally exposed sector becomes better-off, it may undermine older alliances that may have retarded economic progress. We need more systematic empirical studies of how opening the economy may change the nature of politics in a developing country, controlling for other factors. There is some evidence (Diaz-Cayers, Magaloni, and Weingast, 2000) that in Mexico the post-NAFTA exposure to international trade helped in bringing about the erosion of support for the long-dominant and corrupt ruling party, the Partido Revolucionairo Institucional (PRI). The mechanisms that are involved in forging the political coalitions and institutions that may ultimately help the poor are likely to vary from one country to another.

While the transnational companies may have deeper pockets and larger political clout than the poor unskilled laborers of a country have, there is very little evidence that the latter get lower wages and fewer jobs in the presence of those companies, compared to what they get in their absence, other things remaining the same (see, for example, Aitken, Harrison, and Lipsey, 1996; Harrison and Scorse, 2003). Contrary to the impression created by the campaign in affluent countries against "sweatshops" run by transnational companies in poor countries, the poor are often banging at the gates of these sweatshops for a chance to enter, since their current alternatives—inferior occupations, work conditions, or unemployment—are much worse.

Here again there is a clash of counterfactuals between the two sides of the debate. The protesters say (at least implicitly) that the wage paid by, say, Nike, may be higher than the wage in the vast hinterland from which streams of poor workers come, but it is lower than what it would be if Nike's (monopolist, on dominant-employer) profits were lower. The trade economists say that if there were no Nike, the wage would revert to the low hinterland wage, and some of them also implicitly deny the existence of the (local) monopsony and so presume that the implementation of a minimum ("fair") wage will push some workers to the hinterland. Clearly, there is a need here for good empirical projects to investigate the nature of the labor markets that face international firms like Nike in poor countries.[13] In the absence of solid empirical evidence, the applicability of the standard argument for minimum wage (given by progressive labor economists and sociologists in the context of a monopsonist employer) to the current problem must be questioned. The monopsony power of Nike would imply that if Nike tries to hire more workers from the hinterland, it will drive up the marginal cost of labor against itself. If instead there is an almost "unlimited" supply of hinterland labor "banging at the gates," then the marginal and average cost of hiring labor for Nike should not be very different, and so the usual argument that a minimum wage will not reduce employment under monopsony should not apply here.

Similarly, those who complain about the exploitation of young women in the garment factories of transnational companies do not often appreciate the relative improvement in the conditions and status

---

13. The very few solid empirical studies in developing countries have conflicting results. Alatas and Cameron (2003) uses the large geographic variations in the significant rise in (real) minimum wages in the 1990s to identify the employment effect of minimum wages at the firm level in the Indonesian clothing, textile, footwear, and leather sector. They find that the employment effect is negligible for large firms, foreign or domestic. A contrary finding, also using firm-level data, is Bell (1997), who finds a significant negative employment effect of minimum wages in Colombia. The latter is confirmed by Maloney and Mendez (2003) on the basis of a rotating panel dataset in Colombia.

of these women (say, in the garment industry in Bangladesh or Mauritius) compared to the alternatives otherwise available to them. This is not an argument against efforts to improve their work conditions (and certainly not in favor of the totally indefensible cases of forced labor or hazardous or unsafe work conditions),[14] but the reality of the severely limited opportunities faced by the poor and the unintended consequences of trying to restrict rich-country imports of "sweatshop" products must be looked at in terms of the harm it causes to displaced poor workers.[15]

A similar argument applies to the case of child labor. Simply banning imports of products that have been made with child labor is likely to send the children not to schools but to much inferior occupations in the usually much larger nontraded sector.[16] In India, for example, an estimated 95 percent of child workers are in the nontraded sector anyway. In Vietnam a quarter of all children work in agriculture. From 1993 to 1997 the government gradually relaxed its rice export quota, which led rice producers to get a better price. Using the Vietnam Living Standards Survey data for a panel of four thousand households in this period, Edmonds and Pavcnik (2001) estimate that this better price received for rice can account for almost half of the decline in child labor that took place in this period. Here is a case where increased earning opportunities from participation in the international market with a product that is intensive in child labor led to the decline of child labor.

---

14. Conceptually, unsafe and hazardous work conditions and forced labor should be distinguished from low-wage jobs. Under capitalism, workers who are willing to sell themselves as serfs are not permitted to do so, and unsafe work conditions that can cause bodily injury are strictly regulated. That is the reason that safe work conditions are part of the ILO core labor standards that have been ratified by most countries. But the case for stopping workers from accepting low-wage jobs is much weaker.

15. To be fair to the antisweatshop campaigns, some, though not all, of the organizations involved do worry about these unintended consequences. Through the efforts of these campaigns some of the gross abuses of worker rights have come to international attention. The important issue is how to address the abuses without hurting the intended beneficiaries.

16. In 1993 Senator Tom Harkins in the U.S. Congress brought a bill to ban imports of products manufactured using child labor. The bill was not passed, but almost immediately after the introduction of the bill the garment industry in Bangladesh dismissed an estimated fifty thousand children it formerly employed. UNICEF (1997) and others investigated what had happened to these children. It was found (with the concerted effort of some education NGOs) that about ten thousand children did go back to school, but the rest went to much inferior occupations, including stone breaking and child prostitution. Later an agreement between the manufacturers in Bangladesh and UNICEF and ILO tried to provide better opportunities for some of the children.

A policy of trade sanctions against Vietnamese rice, with the apparent good intention of reducing child labor in its production, could have the opposite effect.

Clearly, taking mainly a legal or regulatory approach (like simply banning child labor or boycotting their produce) to achieve an otherwise laudable social goal is the wrong way to go about it.[17] Unintended consequences abound, and the solutions are often more complex than the simplistic remedies proposed by some activists. Mexico's widely noted Programa de Educación, Salud y Alimentación (PROGRESA) pays a subsidy to the mother conditional on her children's school attendance and has made a significant dent on child labor. The program (now under a different name) has expanded substantially in Mexico, and NAFTA or global integration has not come in the way. There are now similar programs in other countries (like Bolsa Escola in Brazil). Coordinated action among the different parties is essential. A good example is the Partners' Agreement to Eliminate Child Labor in the Soccer Ball Industry in Pakistan in the mid-1990s. The transnational sporting goods companies (involved in production in the city of Sialkot in Pakistan of a large fraction of the world supply of soccer balls), the Pakistan Chamber of Commerce, International Labor Organization (ILO), and some NGOs reached an agreement to eliminate child labor in that industry, provide scholarships to the displaced children, arrange the school facilities needed, and monitor the agreement (IPEC, 1999). Such coordination programs—if they can involve all the different parties involved (including the small producers)—rather than trade boycotts or exogenously imposed "codes of conduct" are likely to be much more effective and equitable.

12.5

Environmentalists argue that trade liberalization damages the poor by encouraging overexploitation of the fragile environmental resources (forestry, fishery, surface and ground-water irrigation, grazing lands)

---

17. A popular movement to deter child labor in developing countries is consumer product labeling (like *Rugmark* certification for hand-knotted carpets in India) by which rich-country consumers can express their preference in the market for products which do not use production conditions (like use of child labor) distasteful to them and may be prepared to pay a premium for this. But as Brown (2003) shows, even in the most optimistic case where consumers are willing to pay the full additional cost of hiring only adult labor, and there are no lapses in monitoring or certification, this may not be enough to reduce the labor-force participation of children.

on which the daily livelihoods of particularly the rural poor crucially depend. Here also the answers are complex, and mere trade restriction is not the solution. The environmental effects of trade liberalization on the rural economy depend on the crop pattern and the methods of production. Take, for example, an African rural economy where the exportable product is a capital-intensive tree crop (like coffee or cocoa), the import substitute is a land-intensive crop (like maize), and there is a labor-intensive subsistence (nontraded) crop (like roots and tubers). The economy may have a comparative advantage in tree crops. In this case an increase in import substitution leads to an expansion of cultivated land under the land-intensive crop as well as a shortening of the fallow period, leading to depletion of natural vegetation and biomass. Trade liberalization in this context, through encouraging the production of the less land-intensive tree crop, can significantly improve the natural biomass, as has been shown by Lopez (2000) for Côte d'Ivoire in the latter part of the 1980s, using data from the Living Standards Survey and some remote sensing data from satellite images.

One reason that land-intensive crops may lead to overuse of land and depletion of natural vegetation (or that expansion of the agricultural frontier in general leads to deforestation) is the lack of well-defined property rights or the lack of their enforcement in public or communal land. In such cases the private cost of expanding production is less than the social cost, and environmental resources are overused and degraded. If the country exports such resource-intensive products, foreign trade may make this misallocation worse. International trade theorists point out that trade restriction is not the first-best policy in this situation; correcting the property rights regime is. But the latter involves large changes in the legal, regulatory, or community institutional framework that take a long time to implement, and given the threshold effects and irreversibilities in environmental degradation (a forest regeneration requires a minimum stock, for example), the country may not afford to wait. In that case some program of (time-bound) trade restriction coupled with serious attempts at the overhaul of the domestic institutional framework may be necessary. In other cases domestic-policy changes can be implemented much more quickly, and restricting trade is unnecessary and undesirable. For example, administered underpricing of precious environmental resources (irrigation water in India, energy in Russia, timber concessions in Indonesia) is a major cause of resource depletion, and correcting it should not take much time. Domestic vested interests, not globalization, are responsible for the prolongation of such socially damaging policies.

In the case of some resource-intensive exports, it is difficult for a country by itself to adopt environmental regulations if its international competitors, which have the ability to undercut it in international markets, do not adopt those regulations at the same time. Here again there is an obvious need for coordination in the environmental regulation policies of the countries concerned. Given the low elasticity of demand for many resource-intensive primary export commodities from developing countries in the world market, such coordinated policies might raise prices and the terms of trade but need not lead to a decline in export revenue.

A charge that is commonly made against multinational companies is that they flock to developing-country "pollution havens" to take advantage of lax environmental standards. In one of the few careful empirical studies of the question, Eskeland and Harrison (2003) examine the pattern of foreign investment in Mexico, Venezuela, Morocco, and Côte d'Ivoire. They find no evidence that foreign investment in these countries is related to pollution-abatement costs in rich countries. They also find that within a given industry foreign plants are significantly more energy-efficient and use cleaner types of energy compared to their local peers.

Finally, I largely agree with many who protest against the fairness of the current state of trade-related intellectual property rights (TRIPs). TRIPs were brought within the WTO purview under considerable U.S. pressure, and developing countries reluctantly went along in exchange for the promise (partly and sometimes covertly defaulted on) of substantial reductions in trade protections on textiles and farm products by rich countries. A World Bank study estimates that the TRIPs arrangement will raise the revenue of six rich countries by about $40 billion. One can imagine the increased burden, for example, on private households and public-health programs in poor countries as the protected drug prices rise under TRIPs. For many products the cited justification for patents (keeping incentives alive for new research) does not warrant rapacious monopoly pricing for a prolonged period (the patent life in the rest of the world was raised under TRIPS to the U.S. standard of twenty years).[18] Even when the original patent runs out,

---

18. For a theoretical model showing that a harmonization of patent policies across rich and poor countries is likely to benefit rich countries at the expense of poor countries, see Grossman and Lai (2002).

the transnational company holding the patent often has various ways of effectively extending it (by slightly changing the composition of ingredients in the product), bribing or intimidating the potential producers of the generic substitute, and keeping many customers hooked on the original brand through high-pressure advertisements. In some cases the patent holder privately appropriates the benefits of publicly funded research. In other cases private companies in rich countries patent plant genetic and other resources that are collected from poor countries and whose uses have been part of the common-knowledge pool of communities for centuries. Many scientific researchers also recognize that existing patents often act as obstacles to further research that tries to build on earlier findings (in developing countries this includes adapting new technology to their special conditions). This issue relates to the question of optimal patent *breadth*—or how broadly the protection of existing innovations ought to extend to related innovations in the future.

The problem of international patents for life-saving drugs in poor countries recently caught public attention in connection with controversies about the prices of antiretroviral drugs for AIDS patients in Africa. In that case transnational pharmaceutical companies threatened action (until they relented under international public pressure) against poor countries, even when the latter were only trying to adopt measures (like "compulsory licensing" and "parallel imports") that are deemed legitimate in national public-health emergencies under current interpretations of the WTO rules.

The major problem in corporate drug research is that only a tiny fraction of what companies spend on finding new diet pills or anti-wrinkle creams is spent on drugs or vaccines against the major killer diseases of the world, like malaria or tuberculosis. Even public research budgets, like the budgets of the National Institutes for Health in the United States, allocate less than 1 percent to tropical diseases. Since these diseases kill millions of people (many of them children) mainly in countries with low purchasing power, the transnational pharmaceutical companies are less interested. There are now the beginnings of some international attempts to make credible arrangements on the part of international organizations—like WHO and the World Bank, in collaboration with NGOs like Médecins sans Frontières, private foundations (like the Gates Foundation), and donor agencies and local governments—have made credible commitments to purchase vaccines to be developed by transnational companies against some of the killer diseases. This is another major example of how international coordination and public-private partnerships can be vital in resolving complex, international global-public-good problems like vaccine research. For other diseases (like diabetes or cancer) that kill large numbers of people in both rich and poor countries, the incentive argument for enforcing patents in poor countries is weak, since the market in rich countries is large enough (provided resale can be limited) to motivate the transnational drug companies to carry out research.[19]

Important incentive issues over the design and interpretation of program rules for vaccine-purchase commitments are discussed in detail in Kremer (2001). Depending on the legal language or on the details specified in the contract, commitments could be made more or less binding. The options range from simply announcing a vague intention to purchase vaccines to drafting a detailed contract specifying eligibility requirements and pricing rules to cover all conceivable contingencies. In general, there is the familiar tradeoff between flexibility and commitment from the perspective of the program sponsor. On one hand, detailed commitments may be necessary to raise the expected revenue of vaccine developers to a point that is sufficient for incentives to investment. On the other hand, various unforeseen contingencies can lead the sponsor to regret the letter of the contract. Given the highly unpredictable nature of scientific research, a particular hazard may be that detailed contracts are likely to include rules or requirements that, in hindsight, are responsible for steering the course of research away from the most desirable path. For example, suppose that the sponsor commits to purchase any malaria vaccine that meets a set of eligibility requirements X. If at some point during research, scientists discover two potential vaccines, only one of which is expected to satisfy all of the conditions in X, they will be likely to shift their efforts toward development of that program-eligible vaccine without further consideration of its effectiveness or social value in relation to the alternative. The larger the set of conditions X, the more likely such distortions are to occur.

The interpretation of any given set of rules governing a vaccine-purchase commitment emerges as an issue once vaccines have been

---

19. Lanjouw (2002) has suggested a small change in the administration of patent laws in rich countries that forces pharmaceutical companies to choose between patent protection in rich countries and protection in a designated list of poor countries. The companies can give up protection in those poor countries for drugs against global diseases since the larger market is in rich countries, but still preserve the vast majority of patent incentives.

developed and tested. Disputes that emerge between the program sponsor and the vaccine supplier over the precise application of pricing and eligibility rules to the developed vaccine can be settled only by third-party adjudicators, whose discretion constitutes another source of commitment failure. If adjudicators are tempted to side with the program sponsor whenever disputes arise, pharmaceutical executives will be reluctant to begin investment in the first place. The review of credible commitment issues in chapter 4 is pertinent in this context. For example, one way for the program sponsor to allay vaccine suppliers' fears of unfair dispute settlement would be to delegate adjudication responsibilities to independent third parties that are insulated from political pressures. Such schemes could be especially effective if they are designed in a way to incorporate reputational considerations. In this vein, Kremer (2001) discusses the possibility of either setting up policy institutions that are responsible for overseeing long-term relationships between vaccine developers and developing countries or otherwise extending the scale or scope of the program to ensure repeated interactions. One possibility would be to establish a program that covers a large number of different diseases that primarily affect developing countries. Since developing treatments for the diseases would take time and proceed in discrete steps, the programs' administrators would have an incentive to build a reputation for fair play. Kremer discusses a number of other strategies for enhancing the credibility of purchase commitments, including establishing a minimum purchase price and making the rules for determining eligibility and pricing as transparent as possible.

Given the complications that arise out of the uncertainty surrounding the sponsor's commitments to follow through on payment agreements, one possible alternative is to set up programs to pay for vaccine research. Such "push" programs differ from the "pull" programs that have been considered above by paying for research inputs rather than rewarding research outputs, roughly speaking. In a context of collaborative research, or wherever researchers can be made more productive if they are made aware of the working results of other researchers, push programs could have the important additional virtue of providing incentives for information sharing. The desire to obtain additional push funding in the future creates an incentive for researchers to demonstrate positive returns from past or existing funding, and this can often be accomplished only through publication in journals or other activities that make information public. In contrast, researchers who expect to be rewarded if and only if they are the first to the finish line with an innovation (as with pull programs) have an incentive to keep their progress secret. Kremer therefore argues that push programs may be especially effective at the early stages of research, when the returns to collaboration are likely to be greatest. However, push programs suffer from two major drawbacks that can make pull programs more desirable at later stages of research. The first is the moral-hazard problem created by upfront funding. Once researchers have secured funding, they may be tempted to pursue activities other than those most desired by the sponsor. The second problem with push programs is that they can attract demand for funding from all researchers and research institutions that feel they have some hope of meeting eligibility requirements, regardless of whether they have the capabilities—or the intentions—to invest the funds toward outcomes ultimately desired by the sponsor. For example, a pharmaceutical firm might attempt to secure public funds to finance research that appears pertinent to diseases that concern the sponsor but that is actually directed toward more financially lucrative treatments of other diseases or disorders. In contrast, pull programs that reward investment that is contingent on the outcomes desired by the sponsor induce researchers to self-select projects that are most likely to serve that end.

12.6

In general while globalization in the sense of opening an economy to trade and long-term capital flows can constrain some policy options and wipe out some existing jobs and entrepreneurial opportunities for the poor and for small enterprises, in the medium to long run it need not make the poor much worse off if appropriate domestic policies and institutions are in place and appropriate coordination among the involved parties can be organized. If the institutional prerequisites can be managed, globalization opens the door for some new opportunities even for the poor. But domestic institutional reform is not easy, and it requires political leadership, popular participation, and administrative capacity, which are often lacking in poor countries. One can only say that if we keep focusing on agitating against transnational companies and international organizations like the WTO, attention often gets deflected from the domestic institutional vested interests, and the day of politically challenging them gets postponed. In fact, in some cases opening the economy may unleash forces for such a challenge.

As in the debates several decades ago on "dependency" theories, there is often a tendency to attribute many of the problems of under-development to the inexorable forces of the international economic and political order, ignoring the sway of the domestic vested interests. In many countries poverty alleviation—in the form of expansion of credit and marketing facilities, land reform, public-works programs for the unemployed, or provision of education and health—need not be blocked by the forces of globalization. This requires a restructuring of existing budget priorities and a better and more accountable political and administrative framework, but the obstacles to these are often largely domestic (particularly in countries where some coherent governance structures are in place). In other words, for these countries, globalization is often not the main cause of their problems, contrary to the claim of critics of globalization, just as globalization is often not the main solution for these problems, contrary to the claims of some enthusiastic free-traders.

All this does not absolve the responsibility of international organizations and entities to help the poor of the world—by working to reduce rich-country protections on goods produced by the poor, by taking energetic antitrust actions to challenge the monopoly power of international (producing and trading) companies based in rich countries, by facilitating international partnerships in research and development of products (for example, drugs, vaccines, and crops) that are suitable for the poor, by organizing substantial (and effectively governed) financial and technology transfers, by providing international adjustment assistance for displaced workers, and by helping poor countries to build (legal and technical) capacity in international negotiations and quality-certification organizations. Globalization should not be allowed to be used—either by its critics or by its proponents—as an excuse for inaction on domestic and international fronts in relieving the poverty that oppresses billions of the world's people.

References

Acemoglu, D. 2002. "Why Not a Political Coase Theorem? Social Conflict, Commitment and Politics." NBER Working Paper No. 9377.

Acemoglu, D. 2003. "The Form of Property Rights: Oligarchic vs. Democratic Societies." NBER Working Paper No. 10037.

Acemoglu, D., S. Johnson, and J. A. Robinson. 2001. "The Colonial Origins of Comparative Development: An Empirical Investigation." *American Economic Review*, 91(5), 1369–1401.

Acemoglu, D., S. Johnson, and J. A. Robinson. 2002. "Reversal of Fortune: Geography and Institutions in the Making of the Modern World Income Distribution." *Quarterly Journal of Economics*, 117(4), 1231–1294.

Acemoglu, D., and J. Robinson. 2000. "Political Losers as a Barrier to Economic Development." *American Economic Review*, 90, 126–130.

Acemoglu, D., and J. Robinson. 2001. "Inefficient Redistribution." *American Political Science Review*, 95(3), 649–661.

Acemoglu, D., and J. A. Robinson. 2002. "Economic Backwardness in Political Perspective." NBER Working Paper No. 8831.

Acemoglu, D., and T. Verdier. 2000. "The Choice between Market Failures and Corruption." *American Economic Review*, 90(1), 194–211.

Adams, G. 1981. *The Politics of Defence Contracting: The Iron Triangle*. New Brunswick: Transaction Books.

Ades, A., and R. Di Tella. 1997. "National Champions and Corruption: Some Unpleasant Interventionist Arithmetic." *Economic Journal*, 107, 1023–1042.

Ades, A., and R. Di Tella. 1999. "Rents, Competition and Corruption." *American Economic Review*, 89(4), 982–993.

Aghion, P., and P. Bolton. 1987. "Contracts as a Barrier to Entry." *American Economic Review*, 77, 388–401.

Aghion, P., and J. Tirole. 1997. "Formal and Real Authority in Organizations." *Journal of Political Economy*, 105, 1–29.

Aitken, B., A. Harrison, and R. Lipsey. 1996. "Wages and Foreign Ownership: A Comparative Study of Mexico, Venezuela, and the United States." *Journal of International Economics*, 40(3/4), 345–371.

Aizenman, J., A. 1998. "Fiscal Discipline in a Union." In F. Sturzenneger and M. Tommasi, eds., *The Political Economy of Reform.* Cambridge, MA: MIT Press.

Akerlof, G. A. 1984. *An Economic Theorist's Book of Tales.* Cambridge: Cambridge University Press.

Alam, M. S. 1995. "A Theory of Limits on Corruption and Some Applications." *Kyklos*, 48, 419–435.

Alatas, V., and L. Cameron. 2003. "The Impact of Minimum Wages on Employment in a Low Income Country: An Evaluation Using the Difference-in Differences Approach." Unpublished, Melbourne.

Alchian, A., and H. Demsetz. 1972. "Production, Information Costs and Economic Organization." *American Economic Review*, 62, 777–795.

Alderman, H. 1998. "Social Assistance in Albania: Decentralization and Targeted Transfers." LSMS Working Paper No. 134, World Bank, Washington, DC.

Alesina, A., and A. Drazen. 1991. "Why Are Stabilizations Delayed?" *American Economic Review*, 81(5), 1170–1188.

Alesina, A., R. Hausmann, R. Hommes, and E. Stein. 1996. "Budget Institutions and Fiscal Performance in Latin America." NBER Working Paper No. 5586.

Alesina, A., E. Spolaore, and R. Wacziarg. 2000. "Economic Integration and Political Disintegration." *American Economic Review*, 90, 1276–1296.

Anderson, P. 1974. *Lineages of the Absolutist State.* London: New Left Books.

Anderson, B. 1983. *Imagined Communities: Reflections on the Origin and Spread of Nationalism.* London: Verso.

Andvig, J. C. 1991. "The Economics of Corruption: A Survey." *Studi Economici*, 43, 57–94.

Andvig, J. C., and K. O. Moene. 1990. "How Corruption May Corrupt." *Journal of Economic Behaviour and Organisation*, 13, 63–76.

Aoki, M. 2001. *Towards a Comparative Institutional Analysis.* Cambridge, MA: MIT Press.

Aoki, M., K. Murdock, and M. Okuno-Fujiwara. 1997. "Beyond the East Asian Miracle: Introducing the Market Enhancing View." In M. Aoki, H. Kim, and Okuno-Fujiwara, M., eds. *The Role of Government in East Asian Economic Development: Comparative Institutional Analysis.* Oxford: Oxford University Press.

Armendariz de Aghion, B. 1999. "Development Banking." *Journal of Development Economics*, 58, 83–100.

Attanasio, O., P. K. Goldberg, and N. Pavcnik. 2002. "Trade Reforms and Wage Inequality in Colombia." Unpublished.

Aubert, C., P. Bardhan, and J. Dayton-Johnson. 2003. "Artfilms, Handicrafts, and Other Cultural Goods." Unpublished.

Azfar, O., S. Kähkönen, and P. Meagher. 2002. "Conditions for Effective Decentralized Governance: A Synthesis of Research Findings." IRIS Center Working Paper, University of Maryland, College Park.

Bagehot, W. 1992. "The English Constitution: The Cabinet." In A. Lijphart, ed., *Parliamentary versus Presidential Government*. Oxford: Oxford University Press.

Bailey, F. G. 1971. *Gifts and Poison: The Politics of Reputation*. New York: Schocken Books.

Baland, J. M., and J. P. Platteau. 1997. "Wealth Inequality and Efficiency in the Commons: The Unregulated Case." *Oxford Economic Papers*, 49(4), 451–482.

Baland, J. M., and J. P. Platteau. 1998. "Wealth Inequality and Efficiency in the Commons: The Regulated Case." *Oxford Economic Papers*, 50(1), 1–22.

Baland, J.-M., and J.-P. Platteau. Forthcoming. "Collective Action and the Commons: The Role of Inequality." In J.-M. Baland, P. Bardhan, and S. Bowles, eds., *Inequality, Collective Action and Environmental Sustainability*.

Baland, J.-M., and J. A. Robinson. 2003. "Land and Power." Centre for Economic Policy Research.

Banerjee, A. 1997. "A Theory of Misgovernance." *Quarterly Journal of Economics*, 112, 1289–1332.

Banerjee, A., and L. Iyer. 2002. "History, Institutions and Economic Performance: The Legacy of Colonial Land Tenure Systems in India." Unpublished, MIT.

Banfield, E. C. 1958. *The Moral Basis of A Backward Society*. Chicago: Free Press.

Bardhan, P. 1984. *Land, Labour and Rural Poverty*. New York: Columbia University Press.

Bardhan, P. 1984. *The Political Economy of Development in India*. New Delhi: Oxford University Press.

Bardhan, P. 1987. "The Dominant Proprietary Classes and India's Democracy." In A. Kohli, ed., *India's Democracy: An Analysis of Changing State-Society Relations*. Princeton: Princeton University Press.

Bardhan, P. 1989a. "Alternative Approaches to the Theory of Institutions in Economic Development." In P. Bardhan, ed., *The Economic Theory of Agrarian Institutions*. Oxford: Clarendon Press.

Bardhan, P. 1989b. "The New Institutional Economics and Development Theory: A Brief Critical Assessment." *World Development*, September, 1389–1395.

Bardhan, P. 1990. "Introduction to a Symposium on the State and Economic Development." *Journal of Economic Perspectives*, 4, 3–7.

Bardhan, P., and D. Mookherjee. 1999. "Relative Capture at Local and National Levels: An Essay in the Political Economy of Decentralization." CIDER Working Paper, University of California, Berkeley.

Bardhan, P., and D. Mookherjee. 2000a. "Corruption and Decentralization of Infrastructure Delivery in Developing Countries." Working Paper, University of California, Berkeley. *Economic Journal*.

Bardhan, P., and D. Mookherjee. 2000b. "Capture and Governance at Local and National Levels." *American Economic Review*, 90(2), 135–139.

Bardhan, P., and D. Mookherjee. Forthcoming. "Decentralizing Anti-Poverty Program Delivery in Developing Countries." *Journal of Public Economics*.

Bardhan, P., and N. Singh. 2003. "Inequality, Coalitions, and Collective Action." Unpublished.

Bardhan, P., and C. Udry. 1999. *Development Microeconomics*. Oxford: Oxford University Press.

Baron, D. 1994. "Electoral Competition with Informed and Uninformed Voters." *American Political Science Review*, 88, 33–47.

Barro, R., and D. Gordon. 1983. "Rules, Discretion, and Reputation in a Model of Monetary Policy." *Journal of Monetary Economics*, 12(1), 101–121.

Barry, B. 1989. *Democracy, Power and Justice: Essays in Political Theory*. Oxford: Clarendon Press.

Bartlett, R. 1989. *Economics and Power: An Inquiry into Human Relations and Markets*. Cambridge: Cambridge University Press.

Basu, K. 1986. "One Kind of Power." *Oxford Economic Papers*, 38, 259–282.

Basu, K. 2000. *Prelude to Political Economy: A Study of the Social and Political Foundations of Economics*. Oxford: Oxford University Press.

Bates, R. 1973. *Ethnicity in Contemporary Africa*. Syracuse, NY: Syracuse University.

Bayly, C. A. 1983. *Rulers, Townsmen and Bazaar: North Indian Society in the Age of British Expansion 1770–1870*. Cambridge: Cambridge University Press.

Beck, P. J., and M. W. Maher. 1986. "A Comparison of Bribery and Bidding in Thin Markets." *Economics Letters*, 20, 1–5.

Bell, L. 1997. "The Impact of Minimum Wages in Mexico and Colombia." *Journal of Labor Economics*, 15(3), S102–S135.

Benabou, R. 1994. "Education, Income Distribution, and Growth: The Local Connection." NBER Working Paper No. 4798, Cambridge, MA.

Benhabib, J., and A. Rustichini. 1996. "Social Conflict and Growth." *Journal of Economic Growth*, 1, 125–142.

Bernard, A., and F. Sjoholm. 2003. "Foreign Owners and Plant Survival." National Bureau of Economic Research Working Paper No. 10039.

Besley, T., and A. Case. 1995. "Incumbent Behavior: Vote-Seeking, Tax-Setting and Yardstick Competition." *American Economic Review*, 85(1), 25–45.

Besley, T., and S. Coate. 1998. "Sources of Inefficiency in a Representative Democracy: A Dynamic Analysis." *American Economic Review*, 88(1), 139–156.

Besley, T., and S. Coate. 2000. "Centralized versus Decentralized Provision of Local Public Goods: A Political Economy Analysis." Unpublished, London School of Economics.

Besley, T., and J. McLaren. 1993. "Taxes and Bribery: The Role of Wage Incentives." *Economic Journal*, 103, 119–141.

Bhavnani, R., and D. Backer. 2000. "Localized Ethnic Conflict and Genocide: Accounting for Differences in Rwanda and Burundi." *Journal of Conflict Resolution*, 44, 283–306.

Bikhchandani, S., D. Hirshleifer, and I. Welch. 1992. "A Theory of Fads, Fashion, Custom, and Cultural Change as Informational Cascades." *Journal of Political Economy*, 100, 992–1026.

Binswanger, H. P., K. Deininger, and G. Feder. 1995. "Power, Distortions, Revolt and Reform in Agricultural Land Relations." In J. R. Behrman and T. N. Srinivasan, eds., *Handbook of Development Economics*. Amsterdam: Elsevier.

Bird, R. M. 1995. "Decentralizing Infrastructure: For Good or for Ill?" In Estache (1995).

Blanchard, O., and A. Shleifer. 2000. "Federalism with and without Political Centralization: China versus Russia." NBER Working Paper No. 7616, Cambridge, MA.

Bliss, C., and R. Di Tella. 1997. "Does Competition Kill Corruption?" 105, 1001–1023.

Block, R. 1993. "Killers." *New York Review of Books*, 40(19), 9–10.

Bockstette, V., A. Chanda, and L. Putterman. 2002. "States and Markets: The Advantage of an Early Start." *Journal of Economic Growth*, 7, 347–369.

Bordieu, P. 1971. *Outline of a Theory of Practice*. Cambridge: Cambridge University Press.

Bourguignon, F., and C. Morrisson. 2002. "Inequality among World Citizens: 1820–1992." *American Economic Review*, 92(4), 727–744.

Bowles, S. 2003. *Economic Institutions and Behavior*. New York: Oxford University Press.

Bowles, S., and H. Gintis. 1992. "Power and Wealth in a Competitive Capitalist Economy." *Philosophy and Public Affairs*, 21(4), 324–353.

Boycko, M., A. Shleifer, and R. Vishny. 1995. *Privatizing Russia*. Cambridge, MA: MIT Press.

Brenner, R. 1976. "Agrarian Class Structure and Economic Development in Pre-industrial Europe." *Past and Present*, 70(1), 30–70.

Brown, D. K. 2003. "Consumer Product Labels and Foreign Child Labor." Unpublished, Tufts University, Medford, MA.

Buchanan, J. 1987. "The Constitution of Economic Policy." *American Economic Review*, 77(3), 243–250.

Busch, L. A., and A. Muthoo. 2002. "Power and Inefficient Institutions." Discussion Paper, University of Essex.

Cadot, O. 1987. "Corruption as a Gamble." *Journal of Public Economics*, 33, 223–244.

Campos, E., and H. L. Root. 1996. *The Key to the East Asian Miracle: Making Shared Growth Credible*. Washington, DC: Brookings Institution.

Carruthers, B. G. 1990. "Politics, Popery, and Property: A Comment on North and Weingast." *Journal of Economic History*, 50(3), 693–698.

Caselli, F., and W. J. Coleman. 2002. "On the Theory of Ethnic Conflict." Unpublished paper, Harvard University.

Chattopadhyay, R., and E. Duflo. 2001. "Women as Policy Makers: Evidence from a India-Wide Randomized Policy Experiment." Unpublished, MIT, Cambridge, MA.

Chen, S., and M. Ravallion. 2001. "How Did the World's Poorest Fare in the 1990's?" *Review of Income and Wealth*, 47(3), 283–300.

Clark, G. 1995. "The Political Foundations of Modern Economic Growth: England, 1540–1800." *Journal of Interdisciplinary History*, 26(2), 563–588.

Coady, D. 2001. "An Evaluation of the Distributional Power of Progresa's Cash Transfers in Mexico." International Food Policy Research Institute Working Paper, Washington, DC.

Coase, R. 1937. "The Nature of the Firm." *Economica*, 4, 386–405.

Coate, S., and G. Loury. 1993. "Will Affirmative Action Policies Eliminate Negative Stereotypes?" *American Economic Review*, 83, 1220–1240.

Collier, P., and A. Hoeffler. 2003. "Greed and Grievance in Civil War." Unpublished, Oxford University.

Conning, J., and M. Kevane. 2001. "Community Based Targeting Mechanisms for Social Safety Nets." World Bank, Washington, DC.

Crook, R., and J. Manor. 1991. "Enhancing Participation and Institutional Performance: Democratic Decentralization in South Asia and West Africa." Report to Overseas Development Administration, UK.

Crook, R., and J. Manor. 1998. *Democracy and Decentralization in South Asia and West Africa.* Cambridge: Cambridge University Press.

Currie, J., and A. Harrison. 1997. "Sharing the Costs: The Impact of Trade Reform on Capital and Labor in Morocco." *Journal of Labor Economics*, 15(3), S44–S71.

Dahl, R. 1957. "The Concept of Power." *Behavioral Science*, 2, 201–215.

Da Rin, M., and T. Hellman. 1996. "Banks as Catalysts for Industrialization." Unpublished, Stanford University.

Das, M. K. 2000. "Kerala's Decentralized Planning." *Economic and Political Weekly*, 35, 4300–4303.

Das-Gupta, A., and D. Mookherjee. 1998. *Incentives and Institutional Reform in Tax Enforcement: An Analysis of Developing Country Experience.* New Delhi: Oxford University Press.

Daveri, F., P. Manasse, and D. Serra. 2003. "The Twin Effects of Globalization." Luca d'Agliano Foundation, Turin.

Dayton-Johnson, J. 1998. "Rules and Cooperation on the Local Commons: Theory with Evidence from Mexico." Ph.D. dissertation, University of California, Berkeley.

Dayton-Johnson, J., and P. Bardhan. 2002. "Inequality and Conservation on the Local Commons: A Theoretical Exercise." *Economic Journal*, 112, 577–602.

de Figueiredo, R., and B. Weingast. 1997. "Self-Enforcing Federalism." Unpublished paper, Stanford University.

de Figueiredo, R., and B. Weingast. 1999. "The Rationality of Fear: Political Opportunism and Ethnic Conflict." In Walter and Snyder (1999).

Delli Carpini, M., and S. Keeter. 1996. *What Americans Know about Politics and Why It Matters.* New Haven: Yale University Press.

Demsetz, H. 1972. "When Does the Rule of Liability Matter?" *Journal of Legal Studies*, 1, 13–28.

Dewatripont, M. 1988. "Commitment through Renegotiation-proof Contracts with Third Parties." *Review of Economic Studies*, 55, 377–389.

Dewatripont, M., and E. Maskin. 1995. "Credit and Efficiency in Centralized and Decentralized Economies." *Review of Economic Studies*, 62(4), 541–555.

Diaz-Cayers, A., B. Magaloni, and B. R. Weingast. 2000. "Democratization and the Economy in Mexico: Equilibrium (PRI) Hegemony and Its Demise." Unpublished, Stanford University and UCLA.

Dion, D. 1997. "Competition and Ethnic Conflict: Artifactual?" *Journal of Conflict Resolution*, 41, 638–648.

Di Tella, R., and E. Schargrodsky. 2003. "The Role of Wages and Auditing during a Crackdown on Corruption in the City of Buenos Aires." *Journal of Law and Economics*, 46, 269–292.

Dixit, A. 1996. *The Making of Economic Policy: A Transaction Cost Politics Perspective*, Cambridge, MA: MIT Press.

Dixit, A. 2001. "Some Lessons from Transaction-Cost Politics for Less Developed Countries." Unpublished paper, Princeton University.

Dixit, A. K., and J. Londregan. 1995. "Redistributive Politics and Economic Efficiency." *American Political Science Review*, 89(4), 856–866.

Djankov, S., E. L. Glaeser, R. La Porta, F. López-de-Silanes, and A. Shleifer. 2003. "The New Comparative Economics." NBER Working Paper No. 9608.

Dow, G. 1987. "The Function of Authority in Transaction Cost Economics." *Journal of Economic Behavior and Organization*, 8, 13–38.

Drazen, A. 2000. *Political Economy in Macroeconomics*. Princeton: Princeton University Press.

Drèze, J., and M. Saran. 1995. "Primary Education and Economic Development in China and India: Overview and Two Case Studies." In K. Basu et al., eds., *Choice, Welfare and Development: A Festchrift in Honor of Amartya K. Sen*. Oxford: Clarendon Press.

Durlauf, S. 1996. "A Theory of Persistent Income Inequality." *Journal of Economic Growth*, 1, 75–93.

Easter, K. W., and K. Palanisami. 1986. "Tank Irrigation in India and Thailand: An Example of Common Property Resource Management." Staff Paper, Department of Agricultural and Applied Economics, University of Minnesota.

Edmonds, E., and N. Pavcnik. 2001. "Does Globalization Increase Child Labor? Evidence from Vietnam." Unpublished, Dartmouth College.

Eichengreen, B. 2002. "Capitalizing on Globalization." *Asian Development Review*, 19(1), 17–69.

Elster, J. 1989. *The Cement of Society: A Study of Social Order*. New York: Cambridge University Press.

Elster, J. 1994. "The Impact of Constitutions on Economic Performance." *Proceedings of the World Bank Annual Conference on Development Economics*. Washington, DC: World Bank.

Elster, J. 1999. "Accountability in Athenian Politics." In Przeworski, Stokes, and Manin (1999).

Engerman, S. L., and K. L. Sokoloff. 2002. "Factor Endowments, Inequality, and Paths of Development among New World Economies." NBER Working Paper, October.

Engineer, A. A. 1989. *Communalism and Communal Violence in India: An Analytical Approach to Hindu-Muslim Conflict.* Delhi: Ajanta Publications.

Englebert, P. 2000. *State Legitimacy and Development in Africa.* Boulder: Rienner.

Eskeland, G., and A. Harrison. 2003. "Moving to Greener Pastures? Multinationals and the Pollution Haven Hypothesis." *Journal of Development Economics,* 70(1), 1–24.

Estache, A., ed. 1995. *Decentralizing Infrastructure: Advantages and Limitations.* World Bank Discussion Paper No. 290, Washington, DC.

Evans, P. 1995. *Embedded Autonomy.* Princeton: Princeton University Press.

Faguet, J.-P. 2001. "Does Decentralization Increase Government Responsiveness to Local Needs? Decentralization and Public Investment in Bolivia." Centre for Economic Performance Working Paper, London School of Economics.

Fajnzylber, P., W. F. Maloney, and E. Ribeiro. 2001. "Labor Demand and Trade Reform in Latin America." Unpublished, World Bank, Washington, DC.

Fearon, J., and D. Laitin. 1996. "Explaining Interethnic Cooperation." *American Political Science Review,* 90, 715–735.

Fearon, J., and D. Laitin. 2000. "Violence and the Social Construction of Ethnic Identity." *International Organization,* 54(4), 845–877.

Feliciano, Z. M. 2001. "Workers and Trade Liberalization: The Impact of Trade Reforms in Mexico on Wages and Employment." *Industrial and Labor Relations Review,* 55(1), 95–115.

Ferejohn, J. 1999. "Accountability and Authority: Toward a Theory of Political Accountability." In Przeworski, Stokes, and Manin (1999).

Fernandez, R., and D. Rodrik. 1991. "Resistance to Reform: Status Quo Bias in the Presence of Individual-Specific Uncertainty." *American Economic Review,* 81(5), 1146–1155.

Foster, A. D., and M. R. Rosenzweig. 2001. "Democratization, Decentralization and the Distribution of Local Public Goods in a Poor Rural Economy." Unpublished, University of Pennsylvania, Philadelphia.

Frankel, F. R., Z. Hasan, R. Bhargava, and B. Arora. 2000. *Transforming India: Social and Political Dynamics of Democracy.* New Delhi: Oxford University Press.

Galasso, E., and M. Ravallion. 2001. "Decentralized Targeting of an Anti-Poverty Program." Development Research Group Working Paper, World Bank, Washington, DC.

Gambetta, D. 1988. "Mafia: The Price of Distrust." In D. Gambetta, ed., *Trust Making and Breaking Cooperative Relations.* Oxford: Basil Blackwell.

Geddes, B. 1994. *Politician's Dilemma: Building State Capacity in Latin America.* Berkeley: University of California Press.

Genicot, G. 2002. "Bonded Labor and Serfdom: A Paradox of Voluntary Choice." *Journal of Development Economics,* 67, 101–127.

Gerschenkron, A. 1962. *Economic Backwardness in Historical Perspective.* Cambridge, MA: Harvard University Press.

Goldberg, P., and N. Pavcnik. 2001. "Trade Protection and Wages: Evidence from Colombian Trade Reform." Unpublished.

Gordon, P. J. 1994. "Welfare of the Poor Given a Corrupt Non-Market System." Unpublished, University of West Indies, Jamaica.

Greif, A. 1992. "Institutions and International Trade: Lessons from the Commercial Revolution." *American Economic Review*, 82(2), 128–133.

Greif, A. 1997. "Microtheory and Recent Developments in the Study of Economic Institutions through Economic History." In D. M. Kreps and K. F. Wallis, eds., *Advances in Economic Theory* (vol. 2). Cambridge: Cambridge University Press.

Greif, A. 1997. "Microtheory and Recent Developments in the Study of Economic Institutions through Economic History." In D. M. Kreps and K. F. Wallis, eds., *Advances in Economic Theory* (vol. 2). New York: Cambridge University Press.

Greif, A., P. Milgrom, and B. Weingast. 1994. "Coordination, Commitment, and Enforcement: The Case of the Merchant Guild." *Journal of Political Economy*, 102(3), 745–776.

Grossman, G., and E. Helpman. 1996. "Electoral Competition and Special Interest Politics." *Review of Economic Studies*, 63, 265–286.

Grossman, H. I., and M. Kim. 2001. "Predation, Efficiency, and Inequality." Working Paper, Brown University.

Grossman, G., and E. Lai. 2002. "International Protection of Intellectual Property." Unpublished.

Guinnane, T. W. 1994. "A Failed Institutional Transplant: Raiffeisen's Credit Cooperatives in Ireland, 1894–1914." *Explorations in Economic History*, 31(1), 38–61.

Guriev, S. 2003. "Red Tape and Corruption." CEPR Discussion Paper DP3972.

Hamilton, A. 1961/1787. *"Federalist 70."* In A. Hamilton, J. Madison, and J. Jay, *The Federalist*, ed. B. F. Wright, Cambridge, MA: Harvard University Press.

Hanson, R. L., and J. T. Hartman. 1994. "Do Welfare Magnets Attract?" Institute for Research on Poverty, University Wisconsin, Madison.

Hardin, R. 1995. *One for All: The Logic of Group Conflict*. Princeton: Princeton University Press.

Harrison, A., and J. Scorse. 2003. "The Impact of Globalization on Compliance with Labor Standards: A Plant-Level Study." Unpublished, University of California, Berkeley.

Harrison, G. W., T. F. Rutherford, and D. G. Tarr. 2003. "Trade Liberalization, Poverty and Efficient Equity." *Journal of Development Economics*, 71, 97–128.

Harsanyi, J. 1976. "Measurement of Social Power, Opportunity Costs and the Theory of Two-Person Bargaining Games." In J. Harsanyi, *Essays on Ethics, Social Behaviour and Scientific Explanation*. Dordrecht: Reidel.

Hart, O., and J. Moore. 1990. "Property Rights and the Nature of the Firm." *Journal of Political Economy*, 98, 1119–1158.

Hasan, Z. 2000. "Representation and Redistribution: The New Lower Caste Politics of North India." In F. R. Frankel et al. (2000).

Hatlebakk, M. 2002. "A New and Robust Subgame Perfect Equilibrium in a Model of Triadic Power Relations." *Journal of Development Economics*, 68, 225–232.

Heller, P. 2000. "Degrees of Democracy: Some Comparative Lessons from India." *World Politics*, 52, 484–519.

Hellman, J. S., G. Jones, D. Kaufmann, and M. Schankerman. 2000. "Measuring Governance, Corruption, and State Capture." Policy Research Working Paper, World Bank, Washington, DC.

Herbst, J. I. 2000. *States and Power in Africa: Comparative Lessons in Authority and Control.* Princeton: Princeton University Press.

Hillman, A. L., and E. Katz. 1987. "Hierarchical Structure and the Social Costs of Bribes and Transfers." *Journal of Public Economics*, 34, 129–142.

Hirschman, A. 1977. *The Passions and the Interests: Political Arguments for Capitalism before Its Triumph.* Princeton: Princeton University Press.

Hirshleifer, J. 1991. "The Paradox of Power." *Economics and Politics*, 3, 177–200.

Hobbes, T. 1651/1904. *The Leviathan.* ed. A. R. Waller. Cambridge: Cambridge University Press.

Hobsbawm, E., and T. Ranger, eds. 1983. *The Invention of Tradition.* Cambridge: Cambridge University Press.

Holmstrom, B., and J. Roberts. 1998. "The Boundaries of the Firm Revisited." *Journal of Economic Perspectives*, 12, 73–94.

Horowitz, D. 1985. *Ethnic Groups in Conflict.* Berkeley: University of California Press.

Horowitz, D. 1989. "Incentives and Behavior in the Ethnic Politics of Sri Lanka and Malaysia." Working Paper in Asian-PacificStudies, Duke University.

Horowitz, D. 1998. "Structure and Strategy in Ethnic Conflict: A Few Steps Toward Synthesis." In B. Pleskovic and J. E. Stiglitz, eds., *Annual World Bank Conference on Development Economics.* Washington, DC: World Bank.

Hunt, R., and E. Hunt. 1976. "Canal Irrigation and Local Social Organization." *Current Anthropology*, 17, 389–411.

Huntington, S. P. 1968. *Political Order in Changing Societies.* New Haven: Yale University Press.

Ignatieff, M. 1993. "The Balkan Tragedy." *New York Review of Books*, 40(9), 3–5.

International Program on the Elimination of Child Labor (IPEC). 1999. *IPEC Action against Child Labor: Achievements, Lessons Learned, and Indications for the Future.* Geneva: ILO.

Isham, J., D. Narayan, and L. Pritchett. 1995. "Does Participation Improve Performance? Establishing Causality with Subjective Data." *World Bank Economic Review*, 9(2), 175–200.

Jain, S., and S. W. Mukand. 2003. "Redistribution Promises and the Adoption of Economic Reform." *American Economic Review*, 93(1), 256–264.

Jayaraman, T. K. 1981. "Farmers' Organizations in Surface Irrigation Projects: Two Empirical Studies from Gujarat." *Economic and Political Weekly*, 16(39), A89–A98.

Jones, B. 1999. "Military Intervention in Rwanda's Two Wars: Partisanship and Indifference." In Walter and Snyder (1999).

Kakar, S. 1996. *The Colors of Violence*. Chicago: University of Chicago Press.

Kalai, E., and M. Smorodinsky. 1975. "Other Solutions to Nash's Bargaining Problem." *Econometrica*, 43, 513–518.

Kangle, R. P. 1972. *The Kautiliya Arthasastra* (pt. 2). Bombay: University of Bombay.

Kaufmann, D., A. Kraay, and P. Zoido-Lobatón. 2002. "Governance Matters II: Updated Indicators for 2000/01." World Bank Policy Research Deaprtment Working Paper No. 2772, Washington, DC.

Kaviraj, S. 1995. "Democracy and Development in India." In A. K. Bagchi (ed.), *Democracy and Development*, New York, St. Martin's Press.

Keefer, P., and S. Knack. 1995. "Polarization, Property Rights, and the Links between Inequality and Growth." Working Paper, American University, Washington, DC.

Keynes, J. M. 1936. *The General Theory of Employment, Interest and Money*. London: Macmillan.

Khanna, T., and Y. Yafeh. 2000. "Business Groups and Risk Sharing around the World." Harvard Business School Working Paper No. 01-041.

King, E., and B. Ozler. 1998. "What's Decentralization Got to Do with Learning? The Case of Nicaragua's School Autonomy Reform." Development Research Group Working Paper, World Bank, Washington, DC.

Klitgaard, R. 1988. *Controlling Corruption*. Berkeley: University of California Press.

Knight, J. 1992. *Institutions and Social Conflict*. New York: Cambridge University Press.

Kohli, A. 1990. *Democracy and Discontent: India's Growing Crisis of Governability*. Cambridge: Cambridge University Press.

Kranton, R. E., and A. V. Swamy. 1999. "The Hazards of Piecemeal Reform: British Civil Courts and the Credit Market in Colonial India." *Journal of Development Economics*, 58(1), 1–24.

Kremer, M. 2001. "Creating Markets for New Vaccines." In A. B. Jaffe, J. Lerner and S. Stern (eds.). *Innovation Policy and the Economy* (35–118). Cambridge, MA: MIT Press.

Krishna, P., D. Mitra, and S. Chinoy. 2001. "Trade Liberalization and Labor-Demand Elasticities: Evidence from Turkey." *Journal of International Economics*, 55, 391–409.

Krueger, A. O. 1974. "The Political Economy of the Rent-Seeking Society." *American Economic Review*, 64, 291–303.

Kuran, T. 1987. "Preference Falsification, Policy Continuity and Collective Conservatism." *Economic Journal*, 97, 642–665.

Kuran, T. 1995. "From Melting Pot to Salad Bowl: A Theory of Ethnic Dissimilation." Working Paper, University of Southern California.

Laffont, J.-J., and M. Meleu. 2001. "Separation of Powers and Development." *Journal of Development Economics*, 64(1), 1–24.

Laffont, J.-J., and T. N. Guessan. 1999. "Competition and Corruption in an Agency Relationship." *Journal of Development Economics*, 60(2), 271–296.

Lake, D. A., and D. Rothchild. 1996. "Containing Fear: The Origins and Management of Ethnic Conflict." *International Security*, 21, 41–75.

Lam, W. F. 1998. *Governing Irrigation Systems in Nepal: Institutions, Infrastructure, and Collective Action.* Oakland, CA: ICS Press.

Lamoreaux, N. R., and J. L. Rosenthal. 2001. "Organizational Choice and Economic Development: A Comparison of France and the United States during the Mid-Nineteenth Century." Unpublished, UCLA.

Lanjouw, J. O. 2002. "A New Global Patent Regime for Diseases: U.S. and International Legal Issues." *Harvard Journal of Law and Technology*, 16(1), 85–124.

La Porta, R., F. López-de-Silanes, A. Shleifer, and R. Vishny. 1998. "The Quality of Government." *Journal of Law Economics and Organization*, 15, 222–279.

La Porta, R., F. López-de-Silanes, and G. Zamarripa. 2003. "Related Lending." *Quarterly Journal of Economics*, 118(1), 231–268.

Leamer, E. E. 1998. "In Search of Stolper-Samuelson Linkages between International Trade and Lower Wages." In S. M. Collins, ed., *Imports, Exports, and the American Worker.* Washington, DC: Brookings Institution Press.

Leff, N. H. 1964. "Economic Development through Bureaucratic Corruption." *American Behavioral Scientist*, 8, 8–14.

Levinsohn, J. 1999. "Employment Responses to International Liberalization in Chile." *Journal of International Economics*, 47(2), 321–344.

Li, J. S. 2003. "Relation-Based versus Rule-Based Governance: An Explanation of the East Asian Miracle and Asian Crisis." *Review of International Economics*, 11(4), 651–673.

Liebermann, Y., and M. Syrquin. 1983. "On the Use and Abuse of Rights." *Journal of Economic Behavior and Organization*, 4, 25–40.

Lien, D. H. D. 1986. "A Note on Competitive Bribery Games." *Economics Letters*, 22, 337–341.

Lijphart, A. 1977. *Democracies in Plural Societies: A Comparative Exploration.* New Haven: Yale University Press.

Lin, Y. 2003. "Industrial Structure, Technical Change, and the Role of Government in Development of the Electronics and Information Industry in Taipei, China." Economics and Research Department Working Paper, Asian Development Bank, Manila.

Lohmann, S. 1992. "Optimal Commitment in Monetary Policy: Credibility versus Flexibility." *American Economic Review*, 82(1), 273–286.

Lohmann, S. 1998. "Reputational versus Institutional Solutions to the Time-Consistency Problem in Monetary Policy." In S. Eijffinger and H. Huizinga, eds., *Positive Political Economy: Theory and Evidence.* Cambridge: Cambridge University Press.

Lopez, R. 2000. "Trade Reform and Environmental Externalities in General Equilibrium: Analysis for an Archetype Poor Tropical Country." *Environment and Development Economics* 4(4), 337–404.

Lui, F. T. 1985. "An Equilibrium Queuing Model of Bribery." *Journal of Political Economy*, 93, 760–781.

Lukes, S. 1977. *Essays in Social Theory*. New York: Columbia University Press.

Lundberg, M., and L., Squire. 1999. "Growth and Inequality: Extracting the Lessons for Policymakers." Working Paper, World Bank, Washington DC.

Machiavelli, N. 1513/1961. *The Prince*, ed. G. Bull. London: Penguin Books.

Madison, J. 1961/1787. "*Federalist 10*." In A. Hamilton, J. Madison, and J. Jay, *The Federalist*, ed. B. F. Wright, Cambridge, MA: Harvard University Press.

Mailath, G. J., and A. Postlewaite. 1990. "Asymmetric Information Bargaining Problems with Many Agents." *Review of Economic Studies*, 57(3), 351–368.

Maloney, W. F., and J. N. Mendez. 2003. "Measuring the Impact of Minimum Wages: Evidence from Latin America." NBER Working Paper No. 9800, Cambridge, MA.

Mani, A., and S. W. Mukand. 2000. "Democracy and the Politics of Visibility." Working Paper, Vanderbilt University.

Manin, B., A. Przeworski, and S. Stokes. 1999a. "Elections and Representation." In Przeworski, Stokes, and Manin (1999).

Manin, B., A. Przeworski, and S. Stokes. 1999b. "Introduction." In Przeworski, Stokes, and Manin (1999).

Mann, M. 1986. *The Sources of Social Power*. Vol. 1, *A History of Power from the Beginning to A.D. 1760*. Cambridge: Cambridge University Press.

Mauro, P. 1995. "Corruption and Growth." *Quarterly Journal of Economics*, 109, 681–712.

Mauro, P. 1995. "Corruption and Growth." *Quarterly Journal of Economics*, 110, 681–712.

Mauro, P. 1996. "The Effects of Corruption on Growth, Investment, and Government Expenditure." In K. A. Elliott, ed., *Corruption in the World Economy*. Washington, DC: Institute for International Economics.

McEvedy, C., and R. Jones. 1978. *Atlas of World Population*. London: Penguin and Allan Lane.

McMillan, J., and C. Woodruff. 1999. "Interfirm Relationships and Informal Credit in Vietnam." *Quarterly Journal of Economics*, 114(4), 1285–1320.

Menger, C. 1963. *Problems of Economics and Sociology*. Translated by F. J. Nock. Urbana: University of Illinois Press. Originally published in 1883.

Menkhoff, L., and C. Suwanaporn. 2003. "The Rationale of Bank Lending in Pre-Crisis Thailand." ZEF Discussion Paper No. 66, Bonn.

Miguel, E., and M. K. Gugerty. 2002. "Ethnic Diversity, Social Sanctions, and Public Goods in Kenya." Unpublished, Berkeley, CA.

Milgrom, P., D. C. North, and B. Weingast. 1990. "The Role of Institutions in the Revival of Trade: The Medieval Law Merchant, Private Judges, and the Champagne Fairs." *Economics and Politics*, 2(1), 1–23.

Mitra, S. K., and V. B. Singh. 1990. *Democracy and Social Change in India: A Cross-Sectional Analysis of the National Electorate.* New Delhi: Sage.

Mondino, G., F. Sturzenegger, and M. Tommasi. 1998. "Recurrent High Inflation and Stabilization: A Dynamic Game." In F. Sturzenneger and M. Tommasi, eds., *The Political Economy of Reform.* Cambridge, MA: MIT Press.

Mookherjee, D., and I. P. L. Png. 1995. "Corruptible Law Enforcers: How Should They Be Compensated?" *Economic Journal,* 105, 145–159.

Morris, C. T., and I. Adelman. 1989. "Nineteenth-Century Development Experience and Lessons for Today." *World Development,* 17(9), 1417–1432.

Morriss, P. 1987. *Power: A Philosophical Analysis.* Manchester: Manchester University Press.

Murphy, K., A. Shleifer, and R. Vishny. 1989. "Industrialization and the Big Push." *Journal of Political Economy,* 97(5), 1003–1026.

Murphy, K., A. Shleifer, and R. Vishny. 1993. "Why Is Rent-Seeking So Costly to Growth?" *American Economic Review,* 83, 409–414.

Muthoo, A. 1999. *Bargaining Theory with Applications.* Cambridge: Cambridge University Press.

Myrdal, G. 1968. *Asian Drama* (vol. 2). New York: Random House.

Naipaul, V. S. 1997. *India Today,* 22, 36–39.

Naqvi, N., and F. Wemhoner. 1995. "Power, Coercion and the Games Landlords Play." *Journal of Development Economics,* 47, 191–205.

North, D. C. 1981. *Structure and Change in Economic History.* New York: Norton.

North, D. C. 1990. *Institutions, Institutional Change and Economic Performance.* New York: Cambridge University Press.

North, D. C., and B. Weingast. 1989. "Constitutions and Commitment: Evolution of Institutions Governing Public Choice." *Journal of Economic History,* 49(4), 803–832.

Nugent, J. B., and J. Robinson. 1998. "Are Endowments Fate? On the Political Economy of Comparative Institutional Development." Department of Economics, USC.

Oates, W. 1972. *Fiscal Federalism.* New York: Harcourt Brace Jovanovich.

Oldenburg, P. 1987. "Middlemen in Third-World Corruption." *World Politics,* 39, 508–535.

Olson, M. 1965. *The Logic of Collective Action: Public Goods and the Theory of Groups.* Cambridge, MA: Harvard University Press.

Olson, M. 1993. "Dictatorship, Democracy, and Development." *American Political Science Review,* 87, 567–576.

Ostrom, E. 1990. *Governing the Commons: The Evolution of Institutions for Collective Action.* Cambridge: Cambridge University Press.

Ouchi, W. G. 1980. "Markets, Bureaucracies, and Clans." *Administrative Science Quarterly,* 25(1), 129–141.

Pack, H. 2003. Review of S. L. Parente and E. C. Prescott, *Barriers to Riches*. *Journal of Development Economics*, 70(1), 243–247.

Pandey, G. 1990. *The Construction of Communalism in Colonial North India*. New Delhi: Oxford University Press.

Parente, S. L., and E. C. Prescott. 2000. *Barriers to Riches*. Cambridge, MA: MIT Press.

Parker, P. M. 1997. *National Cultures of the World: A Statistical Reference*. Westport, CT: Greenwood Press.

Pavcnik, N. 2002. "Trade Liberalization, Exit and Productivity Improvements: Evidence from Chilean Plants." *Review of Economic Studies* 69(1), 245–276.

Persson, T., G. Roland, and G. Tabellini. 1997. "Separation of Powers and Political Accountability." *Quarterly Journal of Economics*, 112(4), 1163–1202.

Powell, R. 1999. *In the Shadow of Power: States and Strategies in International Politics*. Princeton: Princeton University Press.

PROBE. 1999. *Public Report on Basic Education for India*. New Delhi: Oxford University Press.

Przeworski, A. 2004. "Geography vs. Institutions Revisited: Were Fortunes Reversed?" Unpublished, New York University, New York.

Przeworski, A., M. Alvarez, J. A. Cheibub, and F. Limongi. 2000. *Democracy and Development: Political Institutions and Material Well-Being in the World, 1950–1990*. Cambridge: Cambridge University Press.

Przeworski, A., and F. Limongi. 1993. "Political Regimes and Economic Growth." *Journal of Economic Perspectives*, 7, 51–69.

Przeworski, A., S. Stokes, and B. Manin, eds. 1999. *Democracy, Accountability, and Representation*. Cambridge: Cambridge University Press.

Putnam, R. 1993. *Making Democracy Work: Civic Traditions in Modern Italy*. Princeton: Princeton University Press.

Qian, Y., and G. Roland. 1998. "Federalism and the Soft Budget Constraint." *American Economic Review*, 88(5), 1143–1162.

Qian, Y., and B. Weingast. 1997. "Federalism as a Commitment to Preserving Market Incentives." *Journal of Economic Perspectives*, 11(4), 83–92.

Rajan, R. R., and L. Zingales. 1999. "The Tyranny of the Inefficient: An Enquiry into the Adverse Consequences of Power Struggles." Working Paper, Graduate School of Business, University of Chicago.

Rasmusen, E., and M. Ramseyer. 1994. "Cheap Bribes and the Corruption Ban: A Coordination Game among Rational Legislators." *Public Choice*, 78, 305–327.

Redding, S. G. 1990. *The Spirit of Chinese Capitalism*. New York: de Gruyter.

Reddy, S. 2001. "Liberalization, Distribution and Political Economy." Unpublished, Barnard College, New York.

Reinikka, R., and J. Svensson. 2001. "Explaining Leakage of Public Funds." Development Research Group Working Paper, World Bank, Washington, DC.

Revenga, A. 1997. "Employment and Wage Effects of Trade Liberalization: The Case of Mexican Manufacturing." *Journal of Labor Economics*, 15(3), S20–S43.

Robinson, J. A. 1998. "Theories 'Bad' Policy." *Journal of Policy Reform*, 3, 1–46.

Rodden, J., and S. Rose-Ackerman. 1997. "Does Federalism Preserve Markets?" *Virginia Law Review*, 83(7), 1521–1572.

Rodrik, D. 1992. "Political Economy and Development Policy." *European Economic Review*, 36, 529–536.

Rodrik, D. 1997. *Has Globalization Gone Too Far?* Washington, DC: Institute of International Economics.

Rodrik, D. 1998. "Where Did All the Growth Go? External Shocks, Social Conflicts, and Growth Collapses." NBER Working Paper No. 6350, Cambridge, MA.

Rodrik, D., A. Subramanian, and F. Trebbi. 2002. "Institutions Rule: The Primacy of Institutions over Geography and Integration in Economic Development." Unpublished, Harvard University.

Roemer, J. 1982. *A General Theory of Exploitation and Class*. Cambridge, MA: Harvard University Press.

Rogoff, K. 1985. "The Optimal Degree of Commitment to an Intermediate Monetary Target." *Quarterly Journal of Economics*, 100(4), 1169–1190.

Romer, P. 1994. "New Goods, Old Theory, and the Welfare Costs of Trade Restrictions." *Journal of Development Economics*, 43, 5–38.

Root, H. 1994. *The Foundation of Privilege: Institutional Innovation and Social Choices in Old Regime France and England*. Berkeley: UC Press.

Rose-Ackerman, S. 1978. *Corruption: A Study in Political Economy*. New York: Academic Press.

Rose-Ackerman, S. 1994. "Reducing Bribery in the Public Sector." In D. V. Trang, ed., *Corruption and Democracy*. Budapest: Institute for Constitutional and Legislative Policy.

Rose-Ackerman, S. 1996. "When Is Corruption Harmful?" Washington, DC: World Bank.

Rosenstein-Rodan, P. 1943. "Problems of Industrialization of Eastern and Southeastern Europe." *Economic Journal*, 53, 202–211.

Rosenstone, S., and J. Hansen. 1993. *Mobilization, Participation and Democracy in America*. New York: Macmillan.

Rosenthal, H., and E. Berglöf. 2003. "The Political Origin of Finance: The Case of Federal Bankruptcy Law in the United States." Weatherhead Center Conference Paper, Harvard University.

Rubinstein, A. 1987. "Perfect Equilibrium in a Bargaining Model." In K. Binmore and P. Dasgputa, eds., *The Economics of Bargaining*. Oxford: Basil Blackwell.

Rudner, D. W. 1994. *Caste and Capitalism in Colonial India: The Nattukottai Chettiars*. Berkeley: University of California Press.

Sah, R. K. 1991. "Fallibility in Human Organizations and Political Systems." *Journal of Economic Perspectives*, 5, 67–88.

Sah, R. 1999. "Persistence and Pervasiveness of Bureaucratic Corruption and Cheating by Citizens in LDC's." Unpublished, University of Chicago.

Santos, B. D. S. 1998. "Participatory Budgeting in Porto Alegre: Toward A Redistributive Democracy." *Politics and Society*, 26(4), 461–510.

Schelling, T. 1960. *The Strategy of Conflict*. Cambridge, MA: Harvard University Press.

Scheve, K. F., and M. J. Slaughter. 2002. "Economic Insecurity and Globalization of Production." National Bureau of Economic Research. Working Paper No. 9339.

Scott, J. C. 1985. *Weapons of the Weak: Everyday Forms of Peasant Resistance*. New Haven: Yale University Press.

Seabright, P. 1996. "Accountability and Decentralization in Government: An Incomplete Contracts Model." *European Economic Review*, 40(1), 61–89.

Seabright, P. 1997. "Is Cooperation Habit-Forming?" In P. Dasgupta and K. G. Maler, eds., *The Environment and Emerging Development Issues*. Oxford: Clarendon Press.

Seddon, J., and R. Wacziarg. 2002. "Trade Liberalization and Intersectoral Labor Movements." Unpublished, Stanford University.

Sen, A. K. 1983. "Development: Which Way Now?" *Economic Journal*, 93, 745–762.

Sen, A. 1984. *Resources, Values and Development*. Oxford: Basil Blackwell.

Sen, A. K. 1999. *Development as Freedom*. New York: Knopf.

Sengupta, N. 1991. *Managing Common Property: Irrigation in India and the Philippines*. New Delhi: Sage.

Shapiro, C., and J. E. Stiglitz. 1984. "Equilibrium Unemployment as a Worker Discipline Device." *American Economic Review*, 74, 433–444.

Shapley, L. S., and M. Shubik. 1954. "A Method of Evaluating the Distribution of Power in a Committee System." *American Political Science Review*, 48, 787–792.

Shirk, S. 1993. *The Political Logic of Economic Reform in China*. Berkeley: University of California Press.

Shleifer, S., and R. Vishny. 1993. "Corruption." *Quarterly Journal of Economics*, 108, 599–617.

Simon, H. A. 1957. *Models of Man: Social and Rational*. New York: Wiley.

Singh, N., and D. Wright. 1995. "Political Institutions, Identity and Conflict in Developing Countries." Working Paper, University of California, Santa Cruz.

Skaperdas, S. 1992. "Cooperation, Conflict, and Power in the Absence of Property Rights." *American Economic Review*, 82, 720–739.

Stepan, A. 1999. "Federalism and Democracy." *Journal of Democracy*, 10(4), 19–33.

Stiglitz, J. E. 1989. "Rational Peasants, Efficient Institutions, and a Theory of Rural Organization." In Bardhan (1989a).

Sutton, J. 1986. "Non-cooperative Bargaining Theory: An Introduction." *Review of Economic Studies*, 53, 709–724.

Svensson, J. 2003. "Who Must Pay Bribes and How Much? Evidence from a Cross Section of Firms." *Quarterly Journal of Economics*, 118(1), 207–230.

Taylor, M. 1982. *Community, Anarchy and Liberty*. Cambridge: Cambridge University Press.

Taylor, C. L., and M. C. Hudson. 1972. *World Handbook of Political and Social Indicators*. Ann Arbor, MI: ICSPR.

Theobald, R. 1990. *Corruption, Development and Underdevelopment*. Durham: Duke University Press.

Tiebout, C. M. 1956. "A Pure Theory of Local Expenditures." *Journal of Political Economy*, 64(5), 416–424.

Tirole, J. 1996. "A Theory of Collective Reputations." *Review of Economic Studies*, 63, 1–22.

Tommasi, M., and F. Weinschelbaum. 1999. "A Principal-Agent Building Block for the Study of Decentralization and Integration." University of San Andres, Argentina.

Treisman, D. 1999. "Political Decentralization and Economic Reform: A Game-Theoretic Analysis." *American Journal of Political Science*, 43(2), 488–517.

Tullock, G. 1980. "Rent-Seeking as a Negative-Sum Game." In J. Buchanan, R. Tollison, and G. Tullock, eds., *Towards a Theory of the Rent-Seeking Society*. College Station: Texas A&M University Press.

Tullock, G. 1980. "Efficient Rent-Seeking." In J. M. Buchanan, R. D. Tollison, and G. Tullock, *eds., Toward a Theory of the Rent-Seeking Society*. College Station: Texas A&M Press.

Tullock, G. 1990. "The Costs of Special Privilege." In J. Alt and K. Shepsle, eds., *Perspectives on Positive Political Economy*. Cambridge: Cambridge University Press.

UNICEF. 1997. *The State of the World's Children 1997*. London: Oxford University Press.

Vaidyanathan, A. 1985. "Water Control Institutions and Agriculture: A Comparative Perspective." *Indian Economic Review*, 20(1), 25–83.

Vaidyanathan, A. 1994. "Transferring Irrigation Management to Farmers." *Economic and Political Weekly*, 29(47), 2965–2967.

Van Rijckeghem, C., and B. Weder. 2001. "Bureaucratic Corruption and the Rate of Temptation: Do Wages in the Civil Service Affect Corruption, and by How Much?" *Journal of Development Economics*, 65, 307–332.

Varshney, A. 2002. *Ethnic Conflict and Civic Life: Hindus and Muslims in India*. New Haven: Yale University Press.

Velasco, A. 1998. "The Common Property Approach to the Political Economy of Fiscal Policy." In F. Sturzenneger and M. Tommasi, eds., *The Political Economy of Reform*. Cambridge, MA: MIT Press.

Velasco, A. 1999. "A Model of Fiscal Deficits and Delayed Fiscal Reforms." In J. Poterba and J. von Hagen, eds., *Fiscal Institutions and Fiscal Performance*. Chicago: University of Chicago Press.

Von Hagen, J. 1996. "Budgeting Procedures and Fiscal Performance in the European Communities." Economic Papers No. 96, Commission of European Communities.

Wade, R. 1985. "The Market for Public Office: Why the Indian State Is Not Better at Development." *World Development*, 13, 467–497.

Wade, R. 1987. *Village Republics: Economic Conditions for Collective Action in South India.* Cambridge: Cambridge University Press.

Wade, R. 1990. *Governing the Market: Economic Theory and the Role of the Government in East Asian Industrialization.* Princeton: Princeton University Press.

Wade, R. 1997. "How Infrastructure Agencies Motivate Staff: Canal Irrigation in India and the Republic of Korea." In A. Mody, ed., *Infrastructure Strategies in East Asia.* Washington DC: World Bank.

Waller, C. J., T. Verdier, and R. Gardner. 1999. "Corruption: Top Down or Bottom Up?" Unpublished.

Walmsley, T., and A. Winters. 2002. "Relaxing Restrictions on the Temporary Movement of Natural Persons: A Simulation Analysis." GTAP Resource Center Paper No. 949, Purdue University.

Walter, B., and J. Snyder, eds. 1999. *Civil Wars, Insecurity, and Intervention.* New York: Columbia University Press.

Weingast, B. R. 1994. "Constructing Trust: The Political and Economic Roots of Ethnic and Regional Conflict." Unpublished, Stanford University.

Weingast, B. 1995. "The Economic Role of Political Institutions: Market-Preserving Federalism and Economic Development." *Journal of Law, Economics, and Organization*, 11(1), 1–31.

Weingast, B. 1998. "American Democratic Stability and the Civil War: Institutions, Commitment, and Political Behavior." In R. Bates et al., eds., *Analytic Narratives.* Princeton: Princeton University Press.

Weissing, F., and E. Ostrom. 1990. "Irrigation Institutions and the Games Irrigators Play: Rule Enforcement without Guards." In R. Selten, ed., *Game Equilibrium Models.* Berlin: Springer-Verlag.

Wildasin, D. E. 1997. "Externalities and Bailouts: Hard and Soft Budget Constraints in Inter-Governmental Fiscal Relations." Vanderbilt University, Nashville.

Williamson, O. 1985. *The Economic Institutions of Capitalism.* New York: Free Press.

Wood, A. 1997. "Openness and Wage Inequality in Developing Countries: The Latin American Challenge to East Asian Conventional Wisdom." *World Bank Economic Review* 11(1), 33–57.

Woodward, S. 1999. "Bosnia and Herzegovina: How Not to End Civil War." In Walter and Snyder (1999).

World Bank. 1999. *Beyond the Center: Decentralizing the State.* Washington, DC: World Bank.

World Bank. 2000. *Entering the Twenty-first Century.* Washington, DC: World Bank.

Wraith, R., and E. Simkins. 1963. *Corruption in Developing Countries.* London: Allen and Unwin.

Yadav, Y. 2000. "Understanding the Second Democratic Upsurge: Trends of Bahujan Participation in Electoral Politics in the 1990's." In Frankel et al. (2000).

Yang, M. M. 1989. "The Gift Economy and State Power in China." *Comparative Study of Society and History*, 31, 25–54.

Young, H. P. 1998. *Individual Strategy and Social Structure: An Evolutionary Theory of Institutions*. Princeton: Princeton University Press.

Zhuravskaya, E. V. 2000. "Incentives to Provide Local Public Goods: Fiscal Federalism, Russian Style." *Journal of Public Economics*, 76(3), 337–368.

Author Index

Subject Index